The Subject

In the annals of twentieth century American business one man has occupied a unique position by virtue of his extraordinary accomplishments, his princely generosity, and his self-effacing modesty. Through a combination of brilliant direction and far-seeing vision he guided the development and promotion of his company's best-known product from a position as a popular national beverage to that of the world's pre-eminent thirst-quencher. His name is Robert Winship Woodruff and his domain is The Coca-Cola Company.

Now nearly 93 years old and theoretically retired, Mr. Woodruff continues to be the single most important influence in the company which he actively directed for so many years. Increasingly in his old age he has stunned both the business world and the groves of academe by bestowing vast sums of money upon his *alma mater,* Emory University, and other institutions. Similar largesse has transformed the face of his home town of Atlanta and enriched its cultural institutions.

For decades Robert Woodruff insisted that his philanthropies be handled anonymously, but in recent years he has gradually permitted his name to be identified with his benevolences. He has been hailed by *Fortune, Holiday, Time* and other publications as a modern Croesus who delights in distributing the millions which he seemed to amass almost as a by-product of his shrewdness in the world of business.

While Mr. Woodruff has been known in the areas of business, education and civic betterment, the man behind the image has been screened from public view. Now a close friend and favorite hunting companion lifts the veil and reveals the private Robert Woodruff, the man whose warmth and good humor have delighted a devoted circle of friends from the high to the lowly. This is his story, told with candor, keen insight, and understanding.

The Author

Charles Elliott is both a noted writer and a sportsman who has hunted and fished in every state of the union and in much of South America. His long career in field and stream began following his graduation from the University of Georgia and has included stints as director of State Parks, commissioner of Natural Resources, and as Southeast Regional forester and Eastern director of public relations for the National Park Service.

For many years Charles Elliott's by-line has been familiar to readers of *Outdoor Life, The Atlanta Journal and Constitution,* and other publications. When not in the field shooting or away casting in lakes and rivers, he can usually be found at home in Covington, Georgia. There, in a book and trophy-lined study, he sits at his typewriter and turns out the books and articles which have an ever-widening following. He is married and has one son.

"Mr. Anonymous"

ROBERT W. WOODRUFF

of Coca-Cola.

ROBERT WINSHIP WOODRUFF

"Mr. Anonymous"

ROBERT W. WOODRUFF

of *Coca-Cola*

by

Charles Elliott

Cherokee Publishing Company

ATLANTA

1982

Copyright © 1982

Charles Elliott

Library of Congress Catalog Card Number: 82-611 59
International Standard Book Number: # 0-87797-087-4

Copies of *"Mr. Anonymous." Robert W. Woodruff of Coca-Cola* may be obtained through leading booksellers or by ordering direct from Cherokee Publishing Company's sales office: P.O. Box 1081, Covington, Georgia 30209. Send check or money order for $14.95 per copy plus $1.10 postage and, for Georgia residents, sales and local option taxes as applicable.

PRINTED IN THE UNITED STATES OF AMERICA

Acknowledgements

*O*ne *of my regrets is that I came along a bit late to grow up with Robert W. Woodruff so that I might have had an opportunity to share with him many of the experiences of his early years. The stories written here of those years have come from various sources, such as friends close to him during the first half of his life, some from historians who had cause to research the activities of this man during that period, and from a rather complete set of records compiled and kept by his secretary.*

Mr. Woodruff himself has been the most vital source of information. Many details of both his business and personal ventures remain etched in his memory. Sometimes a specific date or a name eludes him, but often these may be verified from the records.

During that half of his life that I have known Mr. Woodruff, I have spent many delightful hours with him, riding over his Wyoming ranch, or hunting on his Georgia farm, or sitting with a pipe beside an open fire, as he recalled vivid details of his fascinating span.

During these years he told to me—and sometimes repeated—stories not recorded in the voluminous collection of clippings, special correspondence and pictures that he calls his "scrapbooks." These accounts from him we accepted at face value, give or take a few pinches of poetic license, and pass them on in the same spirit they were given, especially where they help bring out some obscure facet of his personality.

Once I expressed to Mr. Woodruff that anyone who would attempt to write a story of his life must be slightly "off the rocker." His years have been so full, with so many threads of activity running through his hours and his days, that trying to put

them down in orderly fashion and yet, through all these complexities, maintain a single, simple thread of story, is a well nigh impossible chore.

Fiction is one thing; fact is something entirely different.

More persons than its humble author are involved in this biography. There are the friends and acquaintances who gave of their time to talk about Mr. Woodruff—though I seemed to get the continuing impression that they enjoyed recounting those incidents and experiences in which they were in one way or another involved with him. Most of those are mentioned by name throughout the book.

There are a few to whom I'd like to express special thanks for their assistance. These include such authors as E. J. Kahn, Jr. and Harold Martin, from whom I borrowed certain biographical facts; Hunter Bell, who spent long days digging out historical lore about The Coca-Cola Company, Mr. Woodruff and those associated with both; Mrs. Martha Ellis, his niece, who is familiar with and helped with many of the details of his stories; Mrs. Virginia Schneider, for her glowing account of "Miss" Nell; James E. Carson, who helped me evaluate certain phases of the original manuscript; Mrs. Lucille Huffman, his secretary of fifty years, for her always cheerful help in digging through the old files to locate elusive data; J. W. Jones, whose knowledge of places, events and dates helps to make this an accurate account, and for the many hours he devoted as a consultant and in the precise job of editing; to Boisfeuillet Jones, who has worked with him in many of his philanthropies; and to Mr. Woodruff himself for his patience and help in recalling so many colorful, humorous and dramatic moments of his life.

Contents

Illustrations

MR. AND MRS. ERNEST WOODRUFF
Parents of Robert Winship Woodruff

ROBERT WINSHIP

GEORGE W. WOODRUFF

GRANDFATHERS OF ROBERT WINSHIP WOODRUFF

"Mr. Anonymous"

ROBERT W. WOODRUFF

of Coca-Cola.

Those Who Came Before

No one knows when begins the molding of the die that creates any individual. It might have started an eternity of eternities ago. All evidence is that it took a long time a-building.

Whether he comes willingly or unwillingly into the world, a baby does not reach up and pull his intellect, instincts and personality out of nowhere. He is born not only of flesh and blood, but of the genes of generations that culminate in him, and upon which he builds to become the adult he eventually will be.

His immediate ancestors are the bearers of those genes, which have been passed down through the ages to each individual in a special formula that helps determine the physical looks, character and capacity of that person.

Were it possible to return along his ancestral lines and meet those responsible for his existence, one might be amazed at how like some of his ancestors a person is in thought and deed. For it is from those who came before him that he inherits the tendencies toward such traits as honesty, ambition and vision, or the antitheses of these.

Rare indeed it is to find a man with only one complete and never-changing personality. So far as we know, there has been only One in two thousand years. Most of us have two sides, or even more, to our characters. We may be blessed with all the basic virtues and in spite of these have periods of harshness to balance the gentle things we do. We may be patient and considerate with one problem, then stirred to anger at another equally as trivial. These traits help to make up the human side of our natures.

One person often says of another, "he gets his sweet disposition from his mother," or "he's as mean and tight-fisted as his old man was." This may be entirely true, but the genes are just as likely to come from much farther back along the ancestral line.

To help evaluate his driving force, his restless spirit, his spiritual approach to life, his deep concern for others, his toughness when necessary—to understand the man himself—go back for several generations for a brief look at those people whose genes culminated in Robert Winship Woodruff.

The records show that behind him are centuries of endeavor, of imagination, of vision, of positive action—all of which seem to have climaxed in what many have called a giant of this century.

When following the fabulous background of Robert Woodruff's ancestors on both sides of the family, one is impressed that the strides made by the various individuals, the accomplishments, the attitude they had toward life, were no more than a building process toward his business and humanitarian ideals. When you examine the records and hear the stories left by these people, you can almost picture this ancestor or that one as Mr. R. W. Woodruff himself.

As with most Anglo-Saxon names, Woodruff (it had several spellings, as Woodrove, Woodrough, Woodrow, Woodroue, Woodrof and possibly others) seems to have originated from an occupation. The Wood-Reeve was a minor English official; a type of forest warden or wood-bailiff.

Earliest recollections of the family in England were of John Woderoue of Oxford, in 1273, and of a Robert Woderoue of Huntingtonshire, about the same time.

As nearly as may be determined, most of the American Woodruffs can be traced back to John Woodroffe of Devonshire, early in the sixteenth century. One of his sons, David, was the first sheriff of London in 1554, and David's son, Sir Nicholson, was first Lord Mayor of London in 1574.

One of Sir Nicholson's grandsons, Matthew, born in 1612, was in the direct blood line of R. W. Woodruff.

Matthew was among the first Woodruffs to bring the family name to America. The date of his arrival is lost in the annals of time. The first record we have of Matthew was when he moved from Hartford, Connecticut, around 1640, some miles west to a settlement which later was incorporated as Farmington.

Matthew was a pioneer, one of those men with vision to see beyond the hills. To the west of Hartford-Weathersfield-Windsor, which had been formed into a single commonwealth, lay wilderness peopled by Indian tribes. Many of these were thought to be hostile. Among them were the Mohawks, one of the fiercest of the Indian tribes. These resented the intrusion of their country and bore no love for the white man.

Some of the men who went west from the settlements to scout the Indians brought back glowing reports of a fertile, open valley bordering on Indian territory west of Hartford. Matthew was among the settlers who led the way from Hartford in 1640 to the Tunxis meadows. They selected or purchased large portions of the meadows and built homes on the uplands nearby. Others joined them and in 1645 the community was chartered as Farmington.

Matthew was a leader and prominent in civic affairs. He lived out his life there. In 1682 when he passed on in the town he had helped create, he left three sons and three daughters. The third son, Samuel, was in the long line of great-grandparents of Robert Woodruff.

Samuel lived out his eighty-one years at Farmington and in Southington, which in the beginning was a part of Farmington, but later became a separate community. True to tradition, pioneer blood ran in his veins. He was

Southington's first white settler. He spent much of his life outdoors as a hunter and trapper. He was endowed with great physical strength and one of his delights was a wrestling match.

Just like another Woodruff far down the line, Samuel loved people and they loved him. His charm and friendliness kept him on the best of terms with the Indians. He hunted and trapped with them and spent two or three seasons in one of their villages. Once when there was threat of an invasion of the white settlement from a distant tribe, the local Indians came to Samuel and offered help to repel it. They came without being asked and said they could be counted on whenever and wherever he needed assistance of any kind. The Indians knew him as the leader of a military unit which had been organized to protect the community.

Samuel was a deeply religious man and one of the most respected in the state. He organized the Congregational Church in Southington and for thirty-eight years was one of its deacons.

Several generations of Woodruffs lived in Southington, where many of the family members distinguished themselves in business and civic affairs.

George Wyllys Woodruff was the first of the clan to venture southward. In 1832 he moved to Smokey Ordinary, Virginia, with his two sons, George Waldo and Charles Henry, and ten years later migrated to Macon, Georgia, and then to Columbus.

Like other Woodruffs before him, George Waldo was always looking for new fields to conquer. As saturated as he was with a restless pioneer spirit, we can imagine his father found him a willing companion when he proposed moving to southern lands; and a willing helper wherever they set up a place of business. When George Wyllys established his stores in Macon and then in Columbus, George Waldo clerked for him in both places.

Years later George Wyllys became lonely for the land of his birth. With his son Charles Henry he returned in 1848 to Southington where he lived out his last months. He died a few days after Christmas in 1849 in the town of his birth.

George Waldo remained behind to make his permanent home in Columbus. This was Robert Woodruff's grandfather.

He had well chosen the land where he would put down his roots. Columbus was a thriving town when George W. settled there with his father in 1842. In those fourteen years since it had been laid out on the site of an Indian village, Columbus had grown from a frontier settlement to a bustling city.

The year the town was founded, its first steamboat, the Steubenville, came three hundred sixty miles upriver from the Gulf of Mexico, to establish the site as head of navigation on the Chattahoochee River.

That same year, the *Columbus Enquirer* was started by Maribeau Bonaparte Lamar, who later moved west and became president of the Republic of Texas.

A bridge was built across the river in 1833, and Columbus quickly grew into the hub of industry for the region. The textile development began with the establishment of Columbus Cotton Factory in 1838, and this was followed by other manufacturers and businesses. Trade and traffic up and down the river expanded.

George Waldo Woodruff first went into business for himself in 1848. With a Mr. Merry, he opened a clothing store at which they were very successful.

George W. Woodruff married Virginia Bright Lindsay of Columbus on April 23, 1850.

The restless spirit blossomed again. In 1853 the family moved to Juniper, ten miles east of Columbus. The country around this community was heavily timbered, lumber was in demand for construction in the growing South, and George W. set up a sawmilling operation with Henry R. Goetchius, father of one of his friends. Like his other partnership, this was also successful. It ended some six years later when the Woodruff family returned to Columbus to further expand its horizons.

In 1859, under the name of Browne, Woodruff and Clements, they established the Empire Mill, a grist mill for corn and wheat. This was by far the most successful of George Waldo's ventures, and with it he built two fortunes, one before and one after the Civil War.

During the war, Empire Mill was operated largely for the benefit of the Confederate government. So great was their faith in the "cause," the partners put everything they had into Confederate money. The mill was destroyed during the invasion of Yankee troops and their individual fortunes wiped out when the South lost the war.

It was a common characteristic of the Woodruff clan that it accepted and lived through periods of great adversity as well as it thrived on prosperity. The war had ravaged the land and destroyed the standard of living, but not the strong, fierce pride of its people.

After the war, with all resources gone, Riley Browne, one of the partners in Empire Mill, used his personal credit and reputation to rebuild the mill. Then the partners borrowed enough money from friends to purchase a carload of corn and wheat. With this small start, they resumed operation and in the many years that followed, Empire Mill produced a second fortune for its owners.

There is an interesting and pertinent note on Virginia Lindsay Woodruff, Robert Woodruff's paternal grandmother. She was deeply religious and devoted much time to her church and to those serving the church. She dedicated her life to doing things for other people. During the war she organized the Soldiers' Aid Society and worked in hospitals and soldiers' homes. For one period she accepted the responsibility as manager of a soldiers' home. She contributed generously to any and all causes she thought were worthy, and had an especially tender spot in her heart for both sick and old people. She wanted no thanks for these contributions to the needy, and probably did most of them anonymously.

Dedicating one's self to others in trouble is another trait that ran strongly through the Woodruff family.

George Waldo and Virginia Lindsay Woodruff gave to the world six children. Of these, Ernest, the third son, was born in Columbus in 1863 while the war lords raged across the land. He grew up during the period of reconstruction, when pennies were tight and dollars were tighter. These were hard times for the South. The days of luxurious living were indeed "gone with the wind," and most people existed frugally. It was necessary to readjust their sense of values, roll up their sleeves and get back to the job of rebuilding the South. Because the dollar came hard, it was more thoroughly appreciated. Young Ernest learned early to value money and to make few decisions until he was reasonably well assured of the results. This lesson stayed with him throughout his life. Even in later years when he occupied a prominent financial position in the affairs of Atlanta, he would go home for his meals while his contemporaries and those working under him at the Trust Company, where he was president, were having sumptuous luncheons at nearby exclusive clubs or in the best eating establishments.

Earnest started his business career as a flour salesman for his father's expanded Empire Mill. His sales region included a sizeable portion of west Georgia and east Alabama, and often he needed a full week to make his rounds by horse and buggy. Sometimes he would cross back and forth across the river by ferry. As did his son Robert who followed in many of his father's footsteps, Ernest loved hunting and often on his sales rounds would take along his dog and devote an occasional afternoon to shooting quail, which were said to have reached their peak of abundance shortly after the Civil War.

Ernest married Emily Caroline Winship of Atlanta in 1885 and carried his bride to live in Columbus, where he remained a salesman for the Empire Mill until 1893.

Like the Woodruffs, the Winships were an old English family that has been traced back to the days of Queen Elizabeth. As with the Woodruffs, the name was said to have several spellings, such as Winshope and Windcheep, as well as Winship. The first record of the family in America dates back to Edward Winship, who was born in 1611 at New Castle, England. He migrated to Massachusetts in 1634, some fourteen years after the Mayflower, when America was still raw wilderness, and its few citizens had to be sturdy to survive.

The first Edward Winship to the new world settled in Cambridge, Massachusetts, and lived there in his last half-century while he acquired large land holdings. He was active in both civic and military affairs and was one of the most prominent men in the commonwealth of Massachusetts.

Two centuries and five generations after the Winships chose America as home, Joseph Winship came to Georgia to live.

Joseph was born in New Salem, Massachusetts, in 1800. He spent his growing-up years on his father's estate. He might have remained a New Englander all of his days, following in the family footsteps, had he not been imbued with a restless spirit and a burning ambition to find and make his own place in the world.

Joseph left security and a good life behind him in New Salem, acquired a rather menial position as an apprentice in the boot and shoe trade, and traveled south with his employer to Georgia, with a brand new life of opportunity and accomplishment before him.

This was Robert W. Woodruff's maternal great-grandfather.

Joseph Winship lived out his life looking for and conquering new challenges. As a salesman and manufacturer, he changed towns and jobs a number of times. When he made a success of one occupation, he went looking for another. He spent his first two Georgia years in the shoe trade at Monticello, then got into merchandising in nearby Jones County. From there he moved to Clinton, also in Jones. Clinton was an important town long before Macon, and rather famous for the cotton gins manufactured there and sold throughout the southern states.

Always looking for new horizons, Joseph moved to Forsyth where, with his brother Isaac, he built a tannery and shoe factory.

When this was established and successful, he sold his interest to his brother and went back to Clinton. There the cotton gin business got into his blood and in 1845, he gave up his merchandising business and moved to Morgan County, where he built his own cotton gin factory. When this was highly successful, he turned the factory over to his two sons-in-law in 1851 and moved again, this time to Atlanta.

After he was settled in this growing city, he set up a factory to manufacture freight cars. This expanded rapidly and was so successful that Joseph found it desirable to develop an iron foundry which grew and eventually expanded into the Winship Machine Company.

In 1856 the car factory was destroyed by fire. By this time the Winship Machine Company had grown so large and required so much attention that the car factory was never rebuilt.

During the Civil War, Winship Machine Company devoted most of its services and products to the Confederacy, so naturally it was a Sherman target when he ravaged Atlanta.

After the war, and as soon as the factory had been rebuilt and was again operating successfully, Joseph sold his interest to his two sons, Robert and George, whom he had taken into partnership some years before and who were now running the company. Robert was the father of Emily Caroline, Robert Woodruff's mother.

Joseph moved to Macon in 1866, but came back to Atlanta where he died in 1878.

Around the turn of the century, Winship Machine Company became a unit of the Continental Gin Company.

Ernest Woodruff, Robert's father, carried on the tradition of the generations of Woodruffs behind him. He was an empire builder. He belonged to mankind and fit snugly into that category of those included by his son who, much later in life, observed, "The future belongs to the discontented."

Ernest was a far-sighted organizer, a super salesman. As long as he lived, he looked for new worlds to subdue. When Joel Hurt, who had married Ernest's sister, Annie Bright Woodruff, offered him a position with the Atlanta Consolidated Railway Company, he left his job as a flour salesman for his father's mill in 1893 and moved to Atlanta with his wife and two young sons, Robert and Ernest, Jr.

Ernest's rise to prominence in the business world was almost meteoric. He seemed to know instinctively how to reach down into the heart of a problem and come up with the right answer. He rose from vice president and general manager of the Atlanta Consolidated Railway Company to vice president in charge of the Atlanta Railway and Power Company, which in 1902 combined with the Georgia Railway and Electric Company.

All of this, of which Joel Hurt and Ernest Woodruff were integral parts, has its own fascinating history.

The first street railway line was built in Atlanta in 1871. It was known as the West End line and extended over several downtown streets. By 1888 it had expanded to eighteen miles of track through the city's main thoroughfares, with fifty cars powered by two hundred fifty horses and mules.

The first electric street railway operation in Atlanta was masterminded and built by Joel Hurt, and began operation on August 23, 1889, almost four months before Robert Woodruff's birth.

When H. M. Atkinson organized the Georgia Electric Light Company in 1891, he set the stage for a very real power struggle between his company and the Hurt interests in Atlanta.

When Hurt announced plans to consolidate the streetcar systems under the name of Atlanta Railway and Power Company, so that his company could build a steam-electric generating plant to supply electricity for his street cars, to furnish power to the City of Atlanta for lighting its streets and to individual customers as well, the newly formed Georgia Electric Light Company was caught in a bind. Georgia law provided that a street railway company could supply light and power service to the public without an amendment to its charter, but an electric light company was forbidden to get into the streetcar business.

Quietly Atkinson organized another company, which applied for franchises to put down rails on more than fifty Atlanta streets.

This was the opening gun of a battle that involved the courts, politicians, newspapers, bankers, investors and a host of others over a two-year period before the two organizations were finally consolidated into the Georgia Railway and Electric Company. A quarter of a century later this became the Georgia Power Company.

Ernest Woodruff, who had gone to work for Joel Hurt in 1893 as vice president and general manager of the Atlanta Consolidated Railway and shortly thereafter as a director and counselor of the newly established Trust Company of Georgia, was in the thick of this fight. He had inherited, just as he passed on to his son, the courage to accept and face any challenge. Through his diplomacy, wise counseling and financial wizardry, he was largely responsible for effecting the merger, bringing the bitterness to an end, and somehow affording a satisfactory profit for everyone involved.

The year he came to Atlanta, Ernest was elected a director of the Commercial Travelers Savings Bank. That same year the name of the bank was changed to the Trust Company of Georgia, and in 1904 Ernest Woodruff succeeded Joel Hurt as the bank's president. During the eighteen years under his leadership as president, the Trust Company developed into one of the South's most trusted and solid financial institutions.

All of the stories told about Ernest Woodruff and his dealings seem to point up that much of his genius lay in reorganizing and consolidating companies for better management and greater financial gain. With his salesmanship, for instance, he brought together three small companies that sold ice in the summer and coal in the winter, mostly to residences and small businesses, and organized these into the Atlanta Ice and Coal Company. Over the years he acquired other small companies in this business in a number of cities in and around Georgia. Some of these were on the verge of failure. One by one they were added to the Atlanta company, and later all consolidated under the Atlantic Ice and Coal Company, which grew into a multimillion dollar organization.

Mr. Ernest was warmhearted and generous with his family and with his friends. He was strictly honest and fair in his business dealings, but crusty and as tough as a hickory nut. Many of the jobs he thought too involved or mean for others to handle he took upon himself.

The story has been told many times and in various ways about a house which had been acquired by the Atlantic Ice and Coal Company and was to be converted into an office. The house was located in one of Atlanta's red light districts and was a popular meeting place for certain of the citizens. Although it was closed up and ostensibly put out of business, many of the questionable characters continued to visit and use it.

No signs or warnings apparently could keep them away, so Ernest took it upon himself to remedy this situation. He enlisted the help of a close friend and another salty character, Colonel

Robert P. Jones—father of Bobby Jones, the famous golfer. Together they sat many an evening on the porch of the old house, with shotguns across their laps, to frighten away the intruders. The ruse was effective, though everyone who knew Ernest and Colonel Bob was aware that they would never have gone so far as to shoot a trespasser.

As president of the Trust Company, Mr. Ernest, by one means or another, brought a prodigious number of industrial firms to Atlanta, as his son was to do in later years. He served several of these companies on their boards of directors, and many of these prospered in their southern home because of his awareness of business conditions and his almost infallible judgment of character.

Robert Woodruff's relationship with his father was a never-ending pattern of affection, rebellion, respect, defiance, devotion, tolerance, and admiration.

In some respects they were so nearly alike it was only natural that at times they could not get along. Robert lived his own life as a rugged individualist, but even as a young man he was sometimes lavish beyond his means. This distressed his father, who by no means was a miser or penny-pincher but who had been raised in a hard school that called for thrift and prudence in all of his dealings. He wanted his sons to be like him in this respect, though at least some of his counsel fell on unwilling ears.

The story is told that in Mr. Ernest's final years during the World War II era, when Coca-Cola was severely rationed because of the sugar shortage, the elder Woodruff was a patient at Emory University Hospital and the only way in which a delivery of Coca-Cola could be made to his room was through a regular home delivery service then operated by the Atlanta bottling plant. When Ernest learned that the price was one dollar per case, he ordered the service stopped, saying that he had always been able to drive up to the Atlanta plant's loading platform in his chauffeur-driven car and buy a case for eighty cents.

That same trait caused him to shop the store windows when visiting in New York City, looking for the least expensive clothes. In the 1930's, his wife remarked that he would never pay over two dollars for a white shirt.

His frugal traits were reflected in a letter written in 1921 at the time he gave eighty-four shares of stock in the Atlanta and Lowry National Bank (later consolidated with the Trust Company of Georgia) to his three sons, Robert, George and Henry. Mr. Ernest wrote:

> "In prosperous fortunes be
>   modest and wise,
> The rich may fall and the lowest
>   rise,
> But insolent people fall in
>   disgrace,
> Are wretched and no one pities
>   their case."

Later, on the occasion of a gift of Trust Company stock to his three sons, he wrote:

"The wonderful success of the Trust Company was made at the expense of many personal sacrifices made during the choicest years of my life, and my greatest wish is that you boys will learn to resist the temptations and evil influences that never fail to accompany success and wealth."

Woodruff often said, "My father and I were never able to get along. He didn't approve of anything I did. Very frugal himself, he considered me extravagant far beyond my means and this may have had some bearing on his attitude toward me. He was much harder on me than on his other sons.

"I always considered him dictatorial. He never discussed any situation to get the other fellow's view. When he wanted something done, he gave an order and would tolerate no opinion but his own. I suppose I resented this."

This was one of the lessons Woodruff learned from his father. Throughout his business career, he usually asked the opinion of his associates and subordinates and got things accomplished by suggestion rather than by direct order. In this way, those working with him felt that they had a voice in any decision and doubled their efforts to see that the project under consideration was successful.

Although they did not agree on all subjects, Robert very highly valued his father and his sense of this value increased as the years went by.

At the fiftieth anniversary dinner of the Trust Company of Georgia in 1941, Robert Woodruff pointed out that his father was the only ex-official still living who had been active when the organiza-

tion was formed back in the early 1890's. He said of his father:

"His business career started during the panic of the nineties when business acknowledged defeat.

"His active career had its climax of success in the panic of 1929-1930 when the strongest institutions were beaten and destroyed.

"In all these eras he survived and his institutions survived.

"He never acknowledged defeat.

"He was a champion in every sense of the word.

"The two people he was hardest on were himself and his oldest son. Underlying his hard methods was a sound philosophy. He saw many men fail because they had gotten soft and had yielded to the luxuries of life. He didn't expect to have that experience himself, nor did he want his sons or associates to have it. That was the philosophy that actuated and dominated his life.

"Underneath that exterior was a warmth and loyalty that was unexcelled anywhere with anybody. No one was more loyal to his friends. No one would stick closer when a friend was in trouble. No one appreciated friendship to a greater degree or valued it more highly.

"It was these qualities that everybody did not see but they were there with him in full measure."

These traits were further emphasized in a letter written to Robert Woodruff by Mrs. Edith Honeycutt, who attended his father during the last three years of Mr. Ernest's life. After a visit to the

Robert W. Woodruff Library for Advanced Studies on the Emory campus, she wrote:

"How perfect it is and how fitting in honor of a man who is a tower of strength among men. If your father had been able to communicate his feelings to you, that is what he would have said. How he admired and respected you. One could not have spent three years with him, as I did, without learning many things about his feelings, verbal and nonverbal. He loved his three sons and even talked on one occasion about the little one who died.

"You were the challenge he loved, admired and respected—sometimes I felt that he almost envied you as though you were doing all the things he could ever have hoped for, the things he would like to do himself.

"His defense to cover up his feelings was to be hard, severe, firm and non-bending, but beneath he was sweet, soft and very lovable, and such a gentleman. Once someone told a slightly off-color story in his hospital room. Instead of laughing he reminded them that a lady was present."

Ernest Woodruff's creed by which he lived and which—at least most of it —he passed on to his sons, was:

"To live quietly within
my means,
To think soberly in great
themes,
To practice charity toward
all men,
To speak thoughtfully at all
times,
To work constructively and
be happy,
To dwell consciously in the
presence of God,
That I may serve Him and my
neighbor in all that I do."

Among the gifts that Ernest Woodruff passed on to his sons were integrity, the capability of hard work, a devotion to people, and a far-sighted wisdom which was at times almost prophetic. With these as tools, he built several empires which stand today as monuments to his ingenuity and vision.

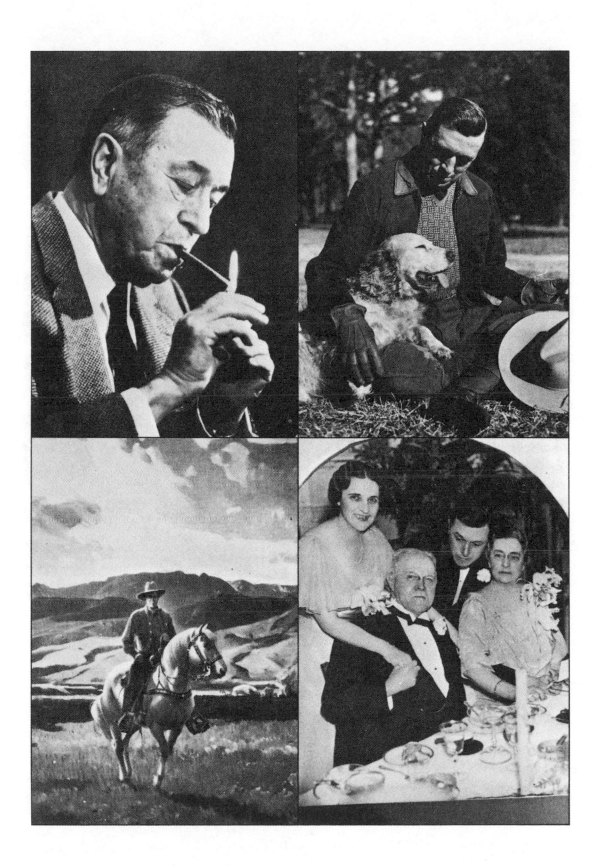

ICHAUWAY

Chapter 1
R.W.W.
The Man

The formal program was over. The guests, who had sat almost breathless through more than two hours of music, speaking and dinner, were once more abuzz with conversation, laughter and the tinkle of glasses.

Mr. Woodruff stood up.

At his sudden appearance on his feet, a hush settled over the assembled guests. In the silence he looked slowly around him and the room could almost feel the dynamic force of The Man.

Toastmaster Bobby Jones looked up from his place at the table.

"Sit down!" he commanded irreverently. "This is your night to listen."

Woodruff hesitated, glanced at Jones, then smiled meekly and again took his seat at the table.

The time was the evening of December 6, 1959. The place was the Mirador Room of the Capital City Club in Atlanta, where five of his close friends were honoring him with what has been described as the most brilliant stag social affair ever held in Atlanta. Gathered were one hundred forty distinguished guests from over the nation and from other parts of the world—all friends and intimate associates of Robert W. Woodruff through the years—to wish him a happy seventieth birthday.

Later that evening, after the party, Bobby Jones asked him, "What were you going to say if you had been allowed to speak?"

"Only that I wish my mother could have been here," Woodruff replied quietly. "She's the only one who would have believed all those nice things being said about me."

Tall, handsome and debonaire for all of his seventy years, tanned by sun and wind from much living outdoors, Woodruff had stood at the door to greet each arriving guest with his customary charm.

In the hour before dinner and in those which followed the ceremony honoring the man who had already become a legend in his lifetime, the guests mingled and talked and laughed together. No introductions were necessary. No man in the room was an outsider in the circle of friends.

There was one topic of conversation—Woodruff.

The program—if such it might be called—consisted of short, simple statements by Bobby Jones, Ralph Hayes, Ralph McGill and Robert B. Troutman, touching upon the character of the man they had come to honor. These were followed by a dramatic recitation of his career from the electronic elocution of a Coca-Cola bottle that stood eight feet tall. They told of the many fascinating highlights over the years, the high points, the low points and the stumbling blocks that only a touch of genius could have turned into stepping stones.

The tributes paid to him by the four speakers on the program, and the recounting of the chronology of the man and The Coca-Cola Company he had led and directed for almost forty years (at that time) were impressive and inspiring. But that evening, the real meat of his character was brought out by the little groups that gathered and intermingled in the huge Mirador Room. The stories and incidents about the man being honored had been told and retold hundreds of times. Every person present was as familiar with them as he was with the happenings in his own life, but time and repetition had in no way impaired the charm. In these lay the substance and the flavor of the Woodruff they all knew. They bespoke the moral toughness, the gentle humor, the capacity and vision, his sometimes ascetic look at life, and of many lesser traits that added up to human.

As Robert Troutman so aptly put it at that seventieth birthday dinner —"Bob Woodruff—'star-dusted saint, mud-spattered sinner'—our friend and the friend of every man everywhere."

The stories repeated by Robert Woodruff's friends wherever they gather and retold in a stack of newspaper columns, magazine stories and in books, have become legend. One is almost afraid to recount them for fear of plagiarism. They must, therefore, be considered in the same light as historical facts, which are also a part of legend.

Naturally, with a large number of associates in The Coca-Cola Company present at the birthday dinner, much conversation among the clan was staged around those activities of the company, where the head man was involved. All were aware that he ran his organization with a velvet gauntlet. Few major decisions were made without his approval. He was consulted on advertising, marketing, quality control, litigation—everything. That was the way he wanted it. He even insisted on seeing all of the mail addressed to him.

To illustrate the point, a favorite story of Harrison Jones, who spent most of his business life in one capacity or another with Coca-Cola, was about one routine meeting of the executive committee, of which Woodruff was chairman.

All committee members were there on time. They waited for a while for the chairman to appear and were beginning to be concerned when word arrived that Woodruff had been detained and would not be able to attend.

For a few more minutes the committee sat quietly, digesting this news. Then the company president stood up and rapped for attention.

"Gentlemen," he announced, "this meeting is adjourned for lack of a quorum."

Another story involved an old friend, L. F. McCollum, president of the Continental Oil Company. He and Woodruff were having dinner one night in New York when McCollum stated that the only job which might possibly attract him away from his company was the presidency of The Coca-Cola Company with Woodruff as chairman of the board.

"You're hired," Woodruff said.

They made the round of night spots, toasting their new partnership, and late in the evening Woodruff asked, "Just how do you propose to run your new job?"

"With an iron hand," his friend stated. "I'll take the burden off your shoulders. I'll make the decisions and call all the shots."

"You're fired," Woodruff said.

Once B. C. Forbes came down to interview him for a story in *Forbes Magazine* on Woodruff and The Coca-Cola Company. The two men spent a pleasant hour together in Woodruff's office. Forbes left, very pleased with himself that the Boss of Coca-Cola had been so gracious, cooperative and easy to talk with.

"Then," he reported later, "when I sat down to my typewriter in the hotel room, and started to write that story, I found it was me, and not him, who had been interviewed."

Someone has said that the man who is successful punches no clock to keep him confined from 8:00 until 5:00, but thinks about his business all the time. Robert Woodruff has always followed this pattern, and no doubt dreams at night about how to improve his company and its products. Often he sits hours before he goes to bed, mentally chewing at some problem from all angles, trying to find a solution without complications. The odds are that this is something he has already discussed with a number of people. He always gets as many constructive viewpoints as possible, and puts them together like a jigsaw puzzle.

Someone once asked Lawrence Calhoun, Woodruff's chauffeur, if the Boss had discussed with him a major change he was considering in the top management of the company.

"No sir, not yet," said Lawrence, "but he will."

Whether he's at work or at play, Coca-Cola is never far from his thoughts. It's been like that for more than half a century.

One of Ralph McGill's stories that evening at the seventieth birthday party confirmed that wherever he was, Woodruff never stopped thinking about his job.

McGill and several other friends were on their way home by automobile from Ichauway Plantation, Woodruff's farm in southern Georgia, where they had been for a few days of quail shooting. They stopped at a small country service station for gas. Like most such stations, this one kept a supply of crackers, candy, cigarettes and soft drinks for its customers.

While the cars were being gassed and checked, the group stood around, drinking Coke and making small talk, until finally someone asked, "What happened to Mr. Woodruff?"

They found him at the side of the building, bending over a trash container which was heaped with discarded bottle tops, apparently emptied from the soft drink cooler. He had separated these and was making a count to determine the percentage of Coca-Cola bottle caps. More than half the tops represented his product, but he did not consider this good enough.

"We'll have to get our bottler down here on the ball," he commented.

His uncanny ability to see beyond the horizon and the undeviating course he had set toward perfection for his product and company, were illustrated in a story told by Morton Downey, a famous singer and Woodruff's longtime friend.

Downey, who appeared on all three major radio networks, had done radio shows with Coca-Cola as his sponsor, and he brought Woodruff what he considered exciting news.

"Columbia Broadcasting System," he said, "will let Coca-Cola sponsor all of its newscasts and special events programs. We'll have millions of listeners every day from coast to coast."

Woodruff shook his head.

"Most of the news," he said, "is about killings, muggings, automobile and train wrecks, floods and fires and everything bad. We don't want people to associate Coca-Cola with any of those. It would hurt instead of help."

From that persepctive, Downey knew the Boss was right, as he had been in so many major decisions for the company. Those who worked with him agreed that at times he almost seemed to have a gift of second sight.

"Many times," one of his employees said, "the Boss knows something is wrong, but can't quite tell you why—yet about one hundred percent of the time he is right."

Another close associate declared, "There have been countless occasions when we made an investment or started a project when all facts, figures, predictions and common sense were against it. Yet Mr. Woodruff's intuition saw or sensed something that we did not. We made mistakes, sure, but almost always the move paid dividends."

In this connection, one of the stories told went back to the time when Woodruff was on the board of directors of General Electric Company. Because of his vision and astute business judgment, he was on the boards of several of the nation's largest companies. The president of General Electric proposed the construction of a quarter billion dollar manufacturing plant in Kentucky to make home appliances. The board of directors would have turned this proposal down, had it not been for Woodruff, who showed them where it made good sense.

The factory was built and turned out to be one of the most profitable investments General Electric ever made. While Woodruff was on the G. E. board, he influenced the establishment of a dozen or more new General Electric manufacturing plants in the South.

"There have been plenty of times when I didn't make the right decision," Woodruff says.

He told about one call he had from Charles H. Strub back in 1932, in the middle of the depression. Strub said, "Bob, you and I are going to build a race track at Santa Anita in California. All I need from you is seven hundred and fifty thousand dollars."

Woodruff told him, "Charlie, with times like they are, if I were to send you seven hundred and fifty thousand dollars, the officers of my company, my family and my friends would individually or collectively have me confined to a padded cell."

"It's the chance of a lifetime." Strub persisted.

"Why don't you get the money out there?" Woodruff asked. "You're surrounded with guys who've got it. Just sell them shares. First thing to do, though, is to see Marion Davies and get her to buy—however small—into your track. That'll keep William Randolph Hearst from fighting it through his papers. Let me know how you come out."

A few weeks after that Strub called Woodruff and told him the Santa Anita track was oversubscribed. "I still want you with me," he said. "How about coming in for five thousand?"

So Woodruff bought a small piece of the Santa Anita track, more as a favor for an old friend.

"I wish I'd taken more," he said. "The profits from the first year's operation paid back the entire investment. The money that track has made is unbelievable."

Woodruff has gone through his entire life with a never-changing philosophy about work. He believes that work is not only man's obligation, but one of his most important privileges. Accomplishment is a necessary ingredient of happiness. Unrest, depression and evil are the children of idleness.

One of The Man's resounding contributions to literature and to the morale of his nation appeared in *The American Magazine* in 1941 when most of the world was at war, and clouds were dark on the American horizon. That was the year one hundred Japanese planes practically destroyed the American Pacific fleet at Pearl Harbor, one day after Woodruff's fifty-second birthday.

With his prophetic vision Woodruff was looking ahead to the grim years in America when he wrote in part:

When the southern soldiers reached home after the Civil War, they found their currency valueless, their property gone, their way of life destroyed. In those hard circumstances, some went to pieces; others drifted to foreign countries; a few chose the easy way out.

But most of them just took off their army coats and went to work.

And that, it seems to me, is the story—and the salvation—of this country.

There have always been enough people willing to see us through our crises by taking off their coats and going to work. This nation has worked out of its troubles.

Today, in another darkening hour, it is learning again that its greatest need is just to get down to work.

The Pilgrims celebrated that first Thanksgiving because they had labored to produce a crop that would see them through the winter, whether a supply ship came or not.

Out of the spinning wheel grew the whirring mills.

The narrow trails of pioneers are now broad highways.

Fitted stones have now become the towers of skyscrapers.

By rivet and girder, by motor and dynamo, by forge and crane, great cities and huge industries have risen on the firm foundations of human effort.

(But) the real wealth of this country isn't in the gains already made.

It lies in the limitless values still to be established; in substances yet to be dug from the earth, drawn from the sea, taken from the forests; in scientific discoveries still to come from the laboratories; in the growth of businesses that demonstrate, by management and production, an ability to foster the common wealth.

In developing these values, there is no substitute for work.

I like to recall how Bill Arp, a Georgia soldier and homespun philosopher, summed up his personal situation at the end of the Civil War. "I killed as many of them as they did of me," Bill drawled. "Now I'm goin' home and make a crop."

Showing through this bit of philosophy of work is Woodruff's patriotism. His love for his country and his belief in it was a passion with him. When the United States declared war in 1917, he offered his services as a private citizen, was assigned to the Ordnance Department and did a superior job in developing equipment and men. In 1918 Woodruff resigned from White Motor Company and was commissioned a captain in the Ordnance Section, Army Reserve Corps, where he served until the war was over.

His patriotism went further than his service in the armed forces. Later when given the opportunity to buy sugar on the black market for his company, he turned it down. "If you can't be honest with your government," he said, "who can you be honest with?" He abided by the rules. He played an honest game. His integrity and the integrity of his product meant more to him than any amount of profit the company might make.

Those who worked for him generally agreed that Woodruff was the best possible Boss. Until The Coca-Cola Company grew to such proportions, he knew most of the people working in the building, much about their family lives and their other interests. Never was he accused of being harsh or ruthless with his employees. He was, however, a tough competitor in the world of business and expected every man in his organization—as they said in the old West—to ride hard for the brand. He worked long hours himself and most of his men followed the example above and beyond their recognized obligations. They did it as much to please the Boss as for company interests. Some employees did not make the grade. When a man failed to carry his share of the load, he was generally transferred to another department and given every chance on the basis that it was better to build a man than to discard him. The theory was that if he couldn't make it after all the help the company could give him, he'd quit of his own volition, which generally happened. Those who did work hard and with intelligence were properly rewarded.

On the other hand, when the occasion warranted it, the Boss could be tough — very tough. One of his high ranking officers and close friends made a deal that had a bit of personal advantage to the officer. He did this without consulting Woodruff or the board of directors. Woodruff, quick to sense and recognize such things, called him in.

"I know exactly why you did that," he said, quietly. "Since it's already done, we'll let it stand. But if you ever make another such move without proper approval, the board of directors will rescind your action and rescind you along with it."

He never mentioned the matter again.

He had that way of quietly making a point, with even more force than if he'd used explosive language. Sometimes this went hand in hand with another Woodruff trait that he never made obvious, but included as a part of his pattern. Usually he arranged to have a third person present when he discussed any business or personal matter which might in any way be considered sensitive, touchy or controversial.

Richard Tift told us of one such story to which he was a witness. Tift had helped him acquire the properties that went into Ichauway Plantation, and later was a consultant in plantation matters. He was perhaps as familiar as anyone with the detailed operation of the plantation.

On one of Richard Tift's visits, Woodruff suggested they call in and have a talk with Roy Rogers, who was his first plantation manager, and who had taken a few extracurricular duties on himself without discussing them with either Tift or the Boss. In a few words Mr. Woodruff summed up what he wanted to convey.

"Roy," he said, "the first year you were at the plantation, I owned it. The next year we owned it together. Now you own it all by yourself."

No further explanation was necessary. It was Woodruff's way of saying inoffensively that he would direct the agricultural and hunting programs at Ichauway. Roy Rogers never forgot that message, and never again made plans without consulting the Boss.

Because of his leadership and the devotion of those around him,

Woodruff's company prospered. In keeping with his philosophy, he gives the credit to others. He dismisses his success with a wave of his hand.

"I've been lucky," he says.

Not all the Woodruff stories told by friends centered around his business judgment and activities. One after another illustrated the different facets of his character and personality. One of the stories E. J. Kahn, Jr., tells in his delightful book, *RWW,* strongly illustrates two of Woodruff's deeply-rooted traits; his love of all living creatures and his embarrassment when anyone tries to praise him.

Woodruff and Dick Gresham, on their way to Ichauway Plantation late one night, were driving along a dark country road when a dog suddenly darted in front of the car. Woodruff wrenched at the wheel to avoid hitting the animal and the car skidded sideways and almost overturned. When it was under control once more, Dr. Gresham wiped the beads of sweat off his forehead.

"That was close," he said. "You almost killed us to keep from hitting the dog."

"It might have been the pet of some child," Woodruff replied.

Gresham nodded.

"That," he commented, "shows your real inner self."

"You're a fool," Woodruff said.

Those close to him will tell you that he wouldn't have run over the dog anyway if it could have been avoided, even if he had known the animal was a mongrel. His reaction was instinctive. Horses and dogs have always been as human to him as people, and he regards them with a similar devotion.

One of my favorite stories about Robert W. Woodruff involved a horse and his anxiety for its welfare. I find much pleasure in telling this one.

A friend and I were hunting with him one winter afternoon, when the skies became overcast and a cold drizzle set in. We stopped hunting and sent a message to plantation headquarters for cars to pick us up.

By the time our transportation arrived, the mist of rain was laced with sleet and Woodruff decided that the weather was too bad for the horses, hunting wagons and the men on our shooting teams to make the hour-long ride to the main barn and kennels. He suggested that the pointers be brought along with us to the kennels and the horses stabled in an auxiliary barn located nearby.

Cars were waiting to transport us to the warm fireside of the big plantation house, but Woodruff remained at the barn, checking on the details of buttoning up for the night, to see that the crew and pointers had a ride home, that the gear had been stored in the saddle room, that all horses had been watered and properly fed.

The plantation foreman turned the bar handle to lock the last stall door, walked around one horse left outside and crawled through the logs of the corral.

"Everything seems to be in order, Boss," he reported.

"You've still got a horse out," Woodruff said. "Where are you going to put him?"

"We don't have a stall for that one," the foreman replied. "He's a mount used by one of the handlers. He's accustomed to being outside."

"Don't you have any kind of protected space?"

"There's nothing but the feed room," the foreman said.

"Then put him in the feed room," Woodruff suggested. "You can't leave an animal out in this kind of weather."

"The feed room's filled with grain and hay."

"Move the grain and hay."

The crew went back to work, stacking bales and bags under the corner of an open shed and, when the feed room was cleared, led the horse inside.

I exchanged glances with Lee Talley, our other hunting partner. No words were necessary.

Woodruff's abiding warmheartedness is characteristic. Legion are the stories where he put down a helping hand to someone who needed it.

"People in trouble concern me greatly," he said a number of times.

Volumes could be written about his lesser charities, but they probably never will be, because only Woodruff knows about the majority of them. An illustration is the time he learned that one of his writer friends was in financial straits. He called the editor of a magazine in which he had an interest and asked that the writer be given a lucrative assignment. The writer never knew that Woodruff had a hand in this.

Another of his friends, who had been high in political circles most of his life, retired. Being an honest politician, he had acquired no estate and the future looked bleak. Behind the scenes, Woodruff arranged for him to be offered a position with good pay and enough activity to keep him interested but not overworked. He came in to ask advice. Woodruff was noncommittal.

"Is it something you'd like to do?" he asked.

"It certainly is," his friend replied.

Woodruff asked what it involved and a lot of other questions, the answers to which he already knew, and said, "Well, you do what you think best."

His friend took the job. No one ever told him how he got it, and he went to his grave not knowing that Woodruff was responsible.

A Negro church burned down at one of the crossroads just off plantation lands. The congregation could in no way afford to replace their temple of worship. Woodruff contracted for a new church. He did this through an outside source, in an effort to keep the congregation from knowing he was involved.

The members were not long in guessing the name of their benefactor. Out of respect for his wish to remain anonymous, the church elders wrote a letter—not to Woodruff—but to God, thanking Him for such a wonderful neighbor. Although they did not call him by name, they were thoughtful enough to send a copy of the letter to Woodruff. This is one of his cherished keepsakes over the years.

His life has been replete with such incidents. While he was building an empire around Coca-Cola, he took time out to dedicate himself to his fellow man.

Shortly after he and Walter White, his old boss at the White Motor Company, purchased Ichauway Plantation and built a country-type home on a bluff overlooking Ichauway-Nochauway Creek, he was standing in the yard of the plantation house one afternoon when an old Negro who had been a farmer on the place for many years drove up in his wagon and stepped to the ground.

"I just wanted to meet the new Boss," he said.

As they talked, the Negro's hands began to shake and the tremor spread over his body as if he had been seized suddenly with a violent case of the ague. When the old man climbed on his wagon and rode off, Woodruff asked the plantation manager who was standing nearby, "What in the world is the matter with that fellow?"

"Malaria," the manager replied. "More than half the people in the county have it. It's prevalent not only here, but throughout the region."

Further inquiry revealed that approximately sixty percent of the people in the county were affected with malaria and that most of them were not financially able to consult a doctor.

From his Atlanta office, Woodruff sent a supply of quinine to his superintendent, with instructions to get the word around that this medicine was available to anyone in the county who needed it. Stories were printed in the local newspapers, urging citizens to take advantage of Mr. Woodruff's offer and a number did, but not enough to make satisfactory progress toward the control of the disease.

More drastic measures were needed. Woodruff arranged through his network of connections to have a malaria control clinic set up on the main road through the plantation, where the clinic was centrally located in the county and easily accessible. Buildings went up for the resident medical personnel, offices and laboratories, and with the help of the Malarial Research Foundation and Emory University, a staff of doctors, nurses and technicians was assigned to the station.

The program was several fold. At Woodruff's suggestion, county-wide tests were made to determine the areas of worst infection, exactly the type of malaria carrier, the peak of mosquito breeding season and location of greatest abundance of this insect; and control concentrated in those areas. The clinic provided medical supplies, at no cost, to all persons affected by malaria. The doctors did not wait for the people of the county to come to the clinic, but held meetings and made house calls from community to community until Baker County, with sixty percent of its citizens affected by malaria only a few years before, was free of the disease.

Woodruff footed a substantial portion of this medical bill out of his pocket and considered it one of his most worthwhile projects.

No one probably realized at the time how far-reaching the effects of this work done at the station in Baker County would be. The information compiled here proved invaluable in the control of malaria and other basic diseases throughout much of the South. Even more dramatically, this data was a factor during World War II where our fighting men in the South Pacific carried on one of their most bitter campaigns against the scourge of malaria and helped to win it with the medical procedures developed on Woodruff's south Georgia farm.

Robert W. Woodruff is a deeply religious man and one of his guiding philosophies is a Bible verse in the King James version—St. Luke 6:38:

"Give and it shall be given unto you; good measure, pressed down, shaken together, and running over, shall men give unto your bosom. For with the same measure that you mete withal, it shall be measured to you again."

Not only does he believe that implicitly; he has lived by it all of his life. He said that on many occasions it was proven to him time and again. Many think that his complete dedication to others was one of the foundations of his incredible business and personal successes.

Those who worked under his direction will tell you there's another angle to this particular portrait, and that in many respects he was a very demanding boss. He expected the best effort they could give, and from those efforts he expected the most satisfactory results. Where The Coca-Cola Company was involved he was often severe to the point of being a tyrant. But this was business, with the ultimate aim the complete success of the company.

Many men are able to give lavishly of material substance, and do—too few make the effort to give of themselves, which is the greatest gift of all. Over many years, after a long, tiring day at the office, Woodruff often fought the late afternoon traffic to go by the hospital and see a friend; not once, but numerous times as long as his friend was confined. He takes time out of a busy schedule to write notes of encouragement to acquaintances. He remembers birthdays of hundreds of friends and more than often sends a single rose, sometimes in a Coca-Cola bottle. This has become recognized as one of his personal trademarks.

Throughout his life, Woodruff has found pleasure in doing things for others. The records are loaded with such stories, but no one will ever know them all. Many gifts he made anonymously, not wishing "to be so loudly thanked for what he had so softly done."

There are a number of better known stories about how he helped some person or some cause and did it with a typical Woodruff touch. One such came out of Cody, Wyoming, where he was a part-time citizen because of the ranch he owned nearby.

He was having lunch one day with C. E. (Bud) Webster and several other Cody friends, when the subject of the local hospital came up.

"We've got a fine hospital here," said Glenn Nielson, "and some of the most capable doctors. Our big problem is lack of nurses."

"Just what is the problem?" Woodruff asked.

"We don't have adequate living accommodations for nurses," Nielson said. "I've been thinking that if we could add several attractive cottages to our hospital complex, this might be our answer."

"How much would a cottage cost?" Woodruff asked.

"We figure around ten thousand."

Woodruff pondered this for a few moments.

"That sounds reasonable. I'll build one, if Bud Webster'll build one."

Webster turned a little pale. He owned a successful automobile business in Cody, but at the moment ten thousand dollars was a healthy chunk out of his pocketbook. A number of eyes around the table were on him. Another man in the dining room spoke up. "If Bud'll build one of those cottages, I will too."

Webster grinned wryly and nodded. "Ok. Put me down."

Within a few minutes eight cottages, including the ones Woodruff and Webster had pledged, were underwritten, and the nursing situation at the Cody Hospital was solved.

The Man often pledged money to some worthy cause, on the condition that it be matched by other people or from other private sources.

There were times however, when he refused people closest to him.

Once a favorite nephew came to him with a grandiose scheme "that simply couldn't fail." The way it sized up was that they could put in a couple of hundred thousand dollars, and out of this they would make millions. Woodruff studied this for several days and turned the nephew down.

"You'll never get anywhere by chasing rainbows," he explained.

Another close friend, who was also one of the in-laws and in the insurance business, once remarked, "Mr. Woodruff could have opened a lot of doors for me, but he never did."

When word of this got back to Woodruff, he thought a minute and said, "The business atmosphere just wasn't right for it. A sudden explosion of his business at that time would have hurt more than helped him. He made it on his own by growing slowly and he made it big. That's a much better way."

He viewed all such requests from a standpoint of sound business judgment and time usually proved him right. His close associates did not resent this—not for long—for they usually could see the logic in his reasoning. One friend, however, stayed mad for years, because The Man turned down a request that simply would have been an unsound investment. Woodruff grieved over his friend's attitude but did not change his mind.

Once another friend approached him and said, "I need fifty thousand dollars."

"What do you plan to do with it?" Woodruff asked.

"I intend to give it out to so and so and so," he said, naming several charities and worthy organizations.

"I'll give it to those I want to have it," Woodruff replied.

Once he turned down a request for a sizeable donation that would help save a valuable historical building which long had been a landmark. His reasoning was that once the building was purchased, no money or organization was available for its management and maintenance.

As fabulous as it was in every respect, one of the things that impressed me most about that seventieth birthday party was that every person with whom I talked had a definite but slightly different view of The Man. There has never been a cut and dried formula which could fit him in any way. His friends and associates may agree on his basic qualities, but each one sees him from a little different angle and makes his own evaluation of the Woodruff personality.

One employee will tell you that the only answer you can get to a problem that has come up in business and needs a solution is a grunt. His "no" grunts and "yes" grunts sound so much alike that an employee must learn to interpret them and woe to the man who doesn't make the correct interpretation. The next man with a problem that concerns the business says that no matter how large it is, or how small, Woodruff discusses it at length, with a lot of questions, and at the end asks the associate for his recommendation. During this question and discussion period, the Boss has very adroitly brought out some considerations no one else had foreseen. All this leads to the right answer for the problem.

Talk to a dozen people and you'll get a dozen evaluations of Robert W. Woodruff. Discuss him with another hundred of those who know—or think they know—him well, and the odds are very greatly in your favor that you'll get a different reaction from every one.

This is definitely verified in the portraits and sculptured busts which have been made of him over the years. Each one captures a different Woodruff. Yet each is accurate for that particular Woodruff the artist could see and thought he knew. There has been much argument among his friends as to which portrait and which bust was the best. Woodruff has never liked any of them.

The artist doesn't live who could put the entire personality of The Man on canvas or in bronze. There is no way he could even be duplicated in flesh and blood and brain, except by the Master Artist. As Boisfeuillet Jones has said a number of times, "There isn't anybody anywhere like him—and there probably shouldn't be."

The people who run his plantation and those who work on it at Ichauway see an altogether different side of the Boss. He is firm in that he wants the farm operated in tiptop shape, the buildings kept in repair, the horses and dogs given special attention, the plantation personnel contented and certain that they'll never want for anything they need. They often put in long hours and go out of the way to please him. The only place where he feels relaxed in driving an automobile is on the plantation roads. He finds much pleasure in driving through the magnificent pine forests, and along the farm roads to watch the crops through various stages of growth, and in riding over the horse and cattle pastures to look at the stock. In the spring and summer his bird dogs welcome him enthusiastically, as though they know that hunting season is not too far away.

The dogs and horses, as well as the people on the plantation, have a special place in his heart. He remembers in detail every fine bird dog he has owned, and is full of little stories about each one. To keep the memory even more vivid, his favorite pointers and setters have been put to rest in a dog cemetery just outside the "circle" of plantation homes—which includes his own—that extend around a spacious lawn, graced with magnificent live oak trees. Each dog has its own headstone with its picture and epitaph. Many quail families are raised on and around the lawn each year. This, he feels, is how the spirits of the great dogs gone on would like to have it.

Many of the dogs in this plot of hallowed ground were named after friends with appropriate inscriptions. There is "Lloyd George—The Old Master"; "Preacher Dick—Faithful To The End"; "Major Buddy Raines—Great Sportsman"; and "Ichauway's General Ike—Gentle In Manner, Strong in Deed." Out of hundreds of dogs which have passed through Ichauway, sixteen are buried here.

Woodruff often said that Lloyd George was his all-time favorite. "Together," he said, "we had some of my finest days in quail woods."

One of his favorites in the cemetery was Chinquapin Dan. This old pointer was a prime example of Woodruff's philosophy that the main reason for being afield is to help the horses and dogs have a good time. This isn't just lip service. He lives by it.

About the only thing that wasn't almost human about Dan was that he couldn't pronounce English words. He made himself clear in other ways, though. If you made a clean kill, he'd actually laugh with you. If you missed several times, he'd come back to sit on his haunches, look up at you, and there was no mistaking the sympathy in his face and eyes.

Dan lived for thirteen years. Over most of those he was a constant companion of the Boss during hunting season. He gave Woodruff as much pleasure in the field as any dog he ever owned.

The Man returned that pleasure in the last two hunting seasons of

Dan's life. Age had taken its natural toll and the old dog was half blind, and his nose slow to pick up the scent of quail. But his enthusiasm and love of the hunt never diminished. Woodruff continued to carry him on the dog wagon, in the place of young, vigorous dogs which would have found more quail and given the Boss and his guests better shooting.

It touched the chords of your heart to see the old pointer go about his job of finding quail. When the handlers put him down, he would stand for a moment on shaky legs. He could no longer take off with spirited bounds that carried him sailing over sedge and briars. He would limp at first, then walk and begin to trot, to get the stiffness out of his aging muscles. After he warmed up he would lumber along with his old flash and style that indicated he was giving his best effort to locate a covey of birds.

Dan knew as well as his trainer when he began to tire. Even though it must have been painful, he didn't want to stop hunting. To keep from being picked up, he would range as far as possible from the wagon and suddenly develop a totally deaf ear to the dog whistle. Even though he might be limping so badly that it must have been torture for him to walk or run, the trainer would have to catch him, pick him up and bring him back to the wagon.

Allowing him to hunt was Woodruff's way of saying "thank you" to an old friend that had given him so many pleasant days.

The Man's concern for others has been one of the ruling passions of his life. Anyone in trouble has a special appeal for him. Shortly after he acquired the plantation, he heard that one of the farm workers who had lost a leg in an accident some years before was saving most of the money he earned to buy an artificial leg. Woodruff talked with this employee and learned that the savings account was being built up so slowly that it might be years before there was enough to purchase the artificial limb. He immediately sent his employee to Atlanta and had him fitted with the best leg available.

He went a step further. He took the fellow off the farm and put him to work at odd jobs around the kennels, horse barn and yard.

Few of the children on the plantation would have gone higher than the low grades in school except for Woodruff. He saw to it that those who wanted a college education were able to have one. After their graduation, some went off to try jobs in business and industry. Many eventually came back home to the plantation, to work for "the Boss."

A man usually judges other men by what he himself would do. A liar expects everyone else to deal in prevarication. A thief is likely to keep one hand on his own billfold. Completely honest, Woodruff implicitly trusts the men around him. A vast majority live up to that trust. The few who did not have brought out another strong facet of the Woodruff character. He may take momentary offense at someone who has wronged him, but it doesn't last long. He recognizes that the human flesh, and sometimes the spirit too, is weak, and quickly forgives any transgression. Often he blames himself for not recognizing weakness before placing such a person in a position of trust.

There was the case of an associate who was in such a position that he was able to steal a large sum of money from the Boss. When the auditors checked, the figures were there in black and white. It was an open and shut case of larceny after trust. Instead of swearing out a warrant and putting the fellow under arrest, Woodruff retired him on a pension and gave him a home and farm.

"It was more my fault than his," he said.

In another case at the plantation, one of the men considered a faithful worker began to keep the wrong company and went bad. After several months, in which he disrupted the work and caused much dissension among the other plantation workers, he was moved off the place. This one, too, was given land on the other side of the county and set up in the farming business.

Woodruff's instructions to his plantation manager were, "Be sure that he never suffers for anything, that he and his family never go hungry, or have to do without a doctor or medical care."

And his erstwhile employee never did, as long as he lived.

Some of The Man's friends say that he has the reputation of helping more people than anyone who ever lived. While this appraisal might be a subject for vast research, it is generally conceded that not only his friends, associates and often acquaintances have shared in his goodwill and thoughtfulness; his vast philanthropies have gone a long way toward helping his fellow Americans have a better life. These will be discussed later.

Bobby Jones, the famous golfer and Woodruff's intimate friend over many decades, said that the only problem Woodruff never learned to master was his golf game. A splendid physical specimen, he could ride or walk all day on a hunting trip, he had all the body motions of an athlete; he handled a gun or fishing rod as though he had been born with one in his hand. He even practiced until he acquired the exacting fluid movements of the perfect golf swing but low scores in the game seemed to elude him. He loved golf. Over the decades he belonged to a dozen or more exclusive golf clubs all over America and many times he played them all, but could never score well enough to put him in the top ranks of the golfing world. Ralph McGill, a friend who belonged to the editorial world, called golf his "hair shirt."

Woodruff followed Bobby Jones through all of his phenomenal golfing career, when the incomparable amateur established records which have never been broken. After the Jones "Grand Slam" in 1930, in which he won the four major championships that year—the American Open and Amateur Championships and the British Open and Amateur Championships—he often played golf with Jones and a group of friends. Their favorite courses were the old East Lake Country Club in Atlanta, where Bob Jones had started playing at the age of six; the Augusta National, and Atlanta's Peachtree Golf Club, both of which Jones had a hand in originating and developing. They played a number of times at the old St. Andrews, in Scotland, where Jones had won some of his championships, and where he had endeared himself to the hearts of all the Scotsmen.

Woodruff enjoys telling a number of fascinating stories about St. Andrews. One time he says he slipped with Jones and two more companions to the old club for a private round of golf. They registered at the club house, and paused there for a bite to eat. While they were eating and changing into their golf togs, word spread that Bobby Jones was to play again at St. Andrews. Every store in town closed, hung a sign on the door— "Bobby Jones is in town"—and the entire community turned out to welcome him and follow him over the course.

"I knew," said Woodruff, "that I could not play as well as those fellows with me, so we persuaded the club pro to take my place, and I became one of the throng of Scotsmen who followed Bob around."

Another time he was playing at Gleneagles with Jones. They had a large gallery. On one of the holes, the Maestro chipped a ball up on the green to within eight feet of the cup. He got a solid round of applause. Woodruff followed the shot with what he says "was one of my best" and came to rest only a couple of feet from the cup. Only one old Scotsman standing behind him seemed to applaud. Woodruff turned, took off his cap, and said "Thank you."

"I wuz only knocking out me pipe," the Scot replied.

Once Woodruff was playing at St. Andrews without Bob Jones and without a gallery. On a long par five hole he hit three good shots and stopped right in front of the green. He turned to his caddy, a weazened oldster who had been caddying at the old course most of his life.

"That was three pretty good shots, don't you think?" he asked.

"When I caddied for Bobby Jones," the caddy replied dourly, "he was here in two."

Woodruff studied him a moment.

"Who's Bobby Jones?" he asked.

The caddy stared at him out of icy blue eyes, as though he couldn't quite believe his ears. With his eyes still on Woodruff, he backed off a step and then another step, took the bag off his shoulder, and laid it on the ground. He turned and walked back toward the club house without a backward glance.

Part of the pleasure Woodruff got out of a golf game was in making and winning a bet. It was never much—a dollar or a golf ball—but he worked as hard to win that as if he'd bet his entire fortune on a shot or a single putt.

He never failed to set up a game in a foursome so that the odds would favor him. That was his business impulse showing through. Bobby Jones in one foursome, gave an example.

Woodruff was shooting good golf, and as guests he had two other fellows who were also good golfers. Woodruff knew the other players wouldn't have a chance if he took Jones as a partner and he wasn't going to play against the champ. He considered a moment.

"Give us a stroke a hole and play our best ball," he said to Jones.

So that's the way they played the game.

"I shot a sixty-four," Bob Jones said, "and it was the best score I ever had on that course. I got the hell beat out of me."

Woodruff almost always won, but after the game he always paid the caddies and bought the drinks, which cost him many times the price of the golf ball or the dollar he collected on the game.

All of his life he loved to gamble. It was part of the competitive spirit that made him one of the most successful salesmen in American history. He gambled for pleasure and because of a perennial ambition to beat the odds. He found a kindred soul in Abie Cowan, who had worked for him when he was associated with White Motor Company, and together they visited some of the world's finest gambling resorts such as Havana, Las Vegas and Monte Carlo. No one will ever know how his lifetime wins and losses might average up. His own estimate is that "I broke about even."

One of the famous stories about Woodruff was on a visit to Monte Carlo. He was playing roulette and had a sizeable stack of chips on a number that came up. The croupier raked Woodruff's chips into another player's pile and paid off all winners except Woodruff. "I'm sorry," said The Man, "but I had chips on that number and you failed to pay me."

The croupier's response was to reach up and spin the wheel again. Woodruff rose from his seat, reached over and picked up the ball and put it in his pocket.

"Still sorry," he said, "but you won't spin this wheel again until you pay me."

That happened many years ago, but he is still remembered as the only man who ever stopped the wheel at Monte Carlo.

Many nights in hunting season, a poker game went on around the huge dining room table at Ichauway. The stakes were high—in dollars rather than in nickels and dimes and quarters. Most of the players were wealthy friends, so winning or losing a few thousand dollars was of small importance in their financial affairs. If Dick Gresham, Woodruff's personal preacher, happened to be there as an observer, one of the players often turned over his winnings as a contribution to Gresham's church. If one or two players of more modest resources lost money they could ill afford to lose, Woodruff would devalue the chips and announce at the end of the game that the chips were worth nickels, dimes and quarters instead of ten, twenty-five and fifty dollars. This rarely upset any of the winners. They knew why he had made this decision.

The poker games were gradually phased out after the second World War. Gin rummy had come into its own and this took the place of the poker table at Ichauway. The players could set their own stakes, as did Woodruff who usually let his opponent evaluate the points on which the winner would be paid off. The Boss of Ichauway enjoyed gin rummy as much as he had enjoyed the poker table, whether it was for pennies or dollars.

The gin rummy sessions were also gradually phased out after Woodruff's two strokes in 1972 so crippled his hands that he could not properly shuffle the cards. The only gambling left to him were bets on such sports events as football, baseball, golf and horse racing. These were with friends only, and never amounted to more than a dollar or two. Then as often as not, when the loser tried to pay off he would say, "Give me a check. I want to frame it to show that once in my life I won a bet from you."

In gambling, as in all of his activities, his driving force was to win. Not dishonestly, for he always played by the rules of the game, but he was not adverse to arranging the odds in his favor. He did this in gin rummy, as well as at golf. In a four-handed rummy game, he would select the best player as his partner.

If he went through a losing streak, the friends playing with him could count on a long night, until one finally revolted and said, "Well, gentlemen, I've enjoyed the game, but now I'm going to bed."

"How about one more game?" Woodruff would reply.

Sometimes they played that additional game. Sometimes they didn't.

The gin rummy stakes generally were never more than a cent a point, or not even that much, unless one of his wealthy friends insisted, then The Man would go the limit with him, with sharp brown eyes that did not miss a trick and remembered every card that had been played in a game.

He gave up the gin rummy sessions after his stroke, but for a while insisted that his friends have a game or two after dinner, and as a kibitzer seemed to enjoy the game almost as much as if he were holding the cards. He'd stand behind one player throughout a game and watch every card. "What'd you play that one for?" he asked. When the player wordlessly pointed out the cards remaining in his hand to explain why without giving information to his opponent, Woodruff would shake his head. "No wonder you can't win," he'd say, and wander off into the next room, looking for a cigar.

Woodruff drank most of his life, but never to excess, nor did he have much respect for a man or woman who did. In his plantation gun room hung a wood engraving with these words, "He who drinks and drinks with grace, is ever welcome to this place. He who drinks more than his share, is never welcome anywhere."

At the age of eighty-three, Woodruff decided to cut down on his daily intake of alcoholic beverages. He discussed it with Dr. Garland Herndon, his doctor. Dr. Herndon suggested that he limit himself to two ounces of alcohol before lunch and another two ounces in the evening before dinner.

"I tried his prescription," Woodruff said, "and figured if I couldn't have more than that, I'd rather not have any at all."

He didn't cut out alcohol entirely. His guests are welcome to whatever drinks they want, and occasionally he joins them with a glass of wine or Cuba Libre. He rarely takes more than one.

Since he can remember, he has been an outdoorsman. Before he reached his teens, his Grandfather Winship and his Uncle Joel Hurt took him under their wings and taught him the basics of hunting and shooting, which they considered necessary to whatever education he might or might not get in other fields. Avid sportsmen themselves, they wanted the youngster to grow up with a gun in his hands, to appreciate the work of fine bird dogs, and the pleasure of being in the field. Young Robert was a natural and with both his grandfather and uncle he spent many pleasant days in the woods and fields on the outskirts of Atlanta. They enjoyed the companionship every bit as much as he did.

One of his boyhood ambitions was to be a big game guide. This was

probably a result of his friendship with William F. (Buffalo Bill) Cody, a famous western character when young Woodruff was growing up.

Young Robert met Cody through Charles A. Wickersham. Wickersham was president of the Atlanta and West Point Rail Road, and a close friend with Ernest Woodruff, Robert's father. When he was much younger, Wickersham had helped to build The Burlington Railroad through the West. On this job he contracted with Cody to keep his crews supplied with fresh meat. The contract did not specify what kind of meat, so Cody employed enough hunters to keep Wickersham's 1,200 laborers and supervisors in buffalo meat, which cost only the price of a bullet and time with a skinning knife. Out of this contract Cody reaped a handsome profit from 4,280 bison furnished the crews, and the title "Buffalo Bill," which proved to be an even more valuable asset.

With his colorful personality Cody was much more of a showman than he had ever been frontiersman or plainsman and he put together a wild west show, one of the first of its kind in the nation. He toured the country with his show of supposedly wild Indians, wild cowboys and wilder broncos and became the idol of every red-blooded American boy. Robert Woodruff was no exception.

When the wild west show moved from New Orleans to Atlanta, Wickersham took young Woodruff with him on his private car to meet Buffalo Bill Cody in Montgomery and bring the noted westerner to Atlanta. As with everyone else who met Robert, Cody was almost as fascinated with the youngster as the boy was with him, and regaled him with colorful tales of the West. For a long time afterward, Robert had visions of following in Cody's earlier tracks and becoming a big game guide, where a man had to be tough and competent and often must depend on his ingenuity and resourcefulness for survival. He was fascinated with that kind of life because it offered the sort of challenge to which he had been geared by nature and his ancestors.

In spite of all his successes, Woodruff never quite gave up that dream. Many years later—in 1941—he purchased Buffalo Bill Cody's old TE Ranch at the foot of the Absaroka Range west of the town of Cody, Wyoming. Here he satisfied much of his love of the western outdoors.

Even before he acquired the ranch, with the help of Max Wilde, a guide and outfitter who lived near the TE, he carried friends on big game hunts back into the Thorofare country south of Yellowstone Park, into a vast mountain land made famous by Cody for many years before Woodruff. His parties took elk, mule deer, moose, grizzly bears and mountain sheep. Woodruff's many trophies collected over the years attest to his abilities as a mountain man and with a big game rifle. These eventually found a home and are on display in the huge dining hall and assembly building Woodruff built for the Atlanta Area Boy Scouts near Covington, east of Atlanta.

Some of those who went on these hunts will tell you that had Woodruff chosen to follow this trail instead of a business career, he would have been as well known in this profession as he has been as the guiding star of a world-wide organization known as The Coca-Cola Company. No one knows. When a man comes to a fork in life's trail, he often wonders where the trail he didn't take would have led him.

Woodruff's love of the out-of-doors, of dogs and horses, of guns and hunting, much of which was instilled in him by Grandfather Winship and Uncle Joel, has stayed with him throughout his life.

Through the years, when he was jetting to prominence in the business world, he took time out to ride the train to south Georgia and hunt quail. He would take his dog with him.

"In those days," he said, "a fellow could really get acquainted with his bird dog. It almost became a part of him. My pointer would ride with me on the train and stay with me in the room at a hotel. He was a good companion and we had some great days together in the field."

One of his favorite hunting companions was Roy Rogers. A graduate of the University of Georgia Agricultural College, Roy was employed by the U. S. Department of Agriculture and lived at Baxley, in the heart of some of the state's finest quail country, but their hunts carried them over much of the southern part of the state.

The Man's love of horses and dogs and quail hunting eventually led him and another favorite friend, hunting partner and business associate, Walter White, to purchase enough tracts of land to put together a thirty-thousand-acre plantation along the Flint River, a dozen miles southwest of

Newton in Baker County. They named it Ichauway, after the large black-water creek flowing through it.

The two partners had only one shooting season together at Ichauway. As the second season approached, Walter White lost his life in an automobile accident. Later Woodruff's generous offer to purchase his partner's interest from the White heirs was accepted and he became the sole owner.

For fifty years Ichauway has been his mecca away from the problems of industry and running a worldwide organization. He went there to relax, but seldom did in a strict interpretation of the word. The plantation was another stage for the restless forces within him. Wherever he happened to be, he was perennially the organizer, the planner, the director of the show. His great concern seemed to be that his guests might become bored, or might not enjoy themselves. He kept them busy at some activity. Each night he laid out the next day's schedule as he sat at the round table in the gun room with his guests and plantation manager. The program might include an early morning hunt for wild turkeys, quail shooting over his highly trained bird dogs, lunch in the woods in some remote corner of the plantation, or in the log cabin at the skeet range, a dove shoot in the afternoon, and either a card game or a fox hunt after dinner.

He outlined for his manager where the hunting teams of handlers, dogs, horses and hunting wagons should be at what hour, and in detail how each team should hunt the course assigned to it. If the afternoon was devoted to a dove shoot, he invited in enough neighbors to properly cover the field and even if the collection of gunners numbered as many as twenty or more, he personally assigned each man to a stand, according to the gunner's ability with a scattergun.

Where no turkey hunt was planned, he often rode horseback with a guest for an hour before breakfast over one of the scenic plantation roads. Usually when steaming dishes were brought out from the kitchen in the big plantation house for lunch in the skeet cabin, his guests would break clay targets for an hour to sharpen the shooting eye, before or after lunch. If there were a spare hour or two in the day, those visiting the plantation went on a tour of the woods, farming operations and pastures where the cattle were kept. There were, in fact, few spare hours.

One of the prized bread and butter notes in Woodruff's files was from his old friend Max Gardner, who was prominent in the political affairs of the nation as governor of North Carolina and U. S. ambassador to the Court of St. James. Gardner wrote after a visit to Ichauway:

"Dear Bob—I'm back at Shelby with a full night's sleep to my credit, with no fox hunt up to midnight last night, no turkey shoot at 3:30 this morning, no dove shoot at 7:00, no long horseback ride to the luncheon rendezvous, no quail shoot this afternoon—and with no arrangement about the kind of horse I should ride tomorrow, nor when I should shoot skeet or how much of the plantation I should inspect with you on another fresh horse—with all these in mind and a firm determination to sleep and rest for a week, I want to thank you from the bottom of my heart for your dogmatic hospitality."

Woodruff was indefatigable. No group of guests remained at the plantation for longer than a few days, but for him this routine went on week after week, except for those days he had to return to his business office, or to attend a meeting somewhere in the United States of one of the innumerable boards of directors he was on, and to which he devoted the same tireless energy.

His plantation visits were mostly during the quail season in the fall and winter. In the summer he usually joined Mrs. Woodruff at the TE Ranch, where she spent a sizeable portion of the summer each year. Even there he made all the arrangements of when his guests should ride and where. They made long horseback rides, up the creek trails into the mountains, or over the TE Hills to a cabin known as the "Cow Camp" because the cowboys often worked cattle out of this camp and spent the night to save the three-hour ride to the main ranch house.

One of the few guests who ever rebelled against the riding schedule was Bobby Jones. The day after Jones got to the ranch, Woodruff organized a six-hour ride along some of the more rugged trails through the TE Hills. The next morning Jones, unaccustomed to that much exercise in the saddle, could hardly crawl out of bed.

After breakfast, Woodruff announced heartily, "Well, what would you fellows like to do today?"

"You can make any plans that you want to for me," Jones replied, "as long as they don't include a horse."

Most guests, however, put up with the torture. They knew that their host's only purpose was to help them enjoy the ranch and the western mountains, so they suffered in silence. A few may have come close to complaining, like Abie Cowan, who was on one of the hunting trips into the Thorofare.

Travel between the ranch and Bridger Lake on the Yellowstone River required a full day in the saddle, over trails that skirted immense canyons where a misstep would send a horse and rider crashing hundreds of feet down the perpendicular canyon walls. When they reached the Bridger Lake camp late in the afternoon, Cowan had to be helped out of his saddle. He clung on to the saddle horn, trying to move his shakey legs under him and glared over the saddle at Woodruff.

"If I go up on that ridge over there in the morning," he said, "and find a paved highway, I'll kill you as dead as you'll ever be."

After watching The Man operate at Ichauway and at the ranch, his old friend, Richard R. (Red) Deupree, who was associated with Procter and Gamble for seventy-five years, in that time working himself up from office boy to chairman of the board, said of Woodruff, "He's a natural baron. If he were posing or being artificial about the way he runs things, it would be most unattractive. Because it does come to him so naturally, it's fascinating."

Deupree pointed out that it was Woodruff's disposition to direct the energies of those around him. His methodical mind was programmed for perfect working order of whatever program—work or play—in which he was involved. He left few things to chance. All activites must have a plan. Arranging the schedule so that every guest would get the most out of his or her visit there was part of his relaxation.

As he is to many of his closer associates in The Coca-Cola Company, Woodruff is affectionately known by all the plantation personnel as "Boss." From the youngest toddlers lisping their first words to the oldest toddlers who move slowly with the dignity of their years, they speak to the Boss with the familiarity which indicates that he is one of them. Not a soul on the plantation stands in awe of the Boss. And there's not a one who doesn' t find an immense amount of pleasure in his word of praise or his smile. Instinctively they know that their problems are his problems also, for he makes them so. They don't worry him with their troubles, but somehow he seems to know. He doesn't deal with them directly, but through his plantation manager or one of his other men in charge of running Ichauway. But they realize that usually the Boss is behind whatever help they get.

All of this might be summed up in a letter he once received from Mattie Heard, who had catered a number of dinners in Mr. and Mrs. Woodruff's Atlanta home, but who spent most of each hunting season at Ichauway, in charge of the kitchen and the meals. For almost a quarter of a century she was the cook at Ichauway. She drew her helpers from the plantation women. To Woodruff she once wrote, "God knows it is a pleasure to work for a friend who is considerate of you. I am asking my other friend, the Lord, to always be with you wherever you are. I know He will because He said that what you do for the least of my little ones, you do for Me. I am one of them and always tell Him about you."

All of his life, Woodruff had the most amazing talent for turning up where he was least expected at that particular time. He might drop in on a friend or employee at home at unusual times, or into someone's office to see what was going on.

The story is told that once during a World Series baseball game, he walked into a part of the building where his presence was entirely unexpected and found a group of employees clustered around a radio, listening to the play by play account. They were caught flat-footed, and waited for the axe to fall.

Woodruff looked over the group a moment, without smiling, and asked quietly, "What's the score?"

"Two to one, favor the Yankees," someone replied.

"That's what it was when I left my office," The Man replied. "Looks like the Yankees might win it."

Once Dr. Garland Herndon, Woodruff's physician, and I were quail hunting partners at Ichauway. The day was bleak and raw, with an occasional sprinkle of rain. The doctor and I had some good shooting in spite of the weather and were getting in and out of our wet saddles rather frequently.

"My hind end is getting a bit soppy," I suggested. "Let's ride the hunting wagon between covey rises for a while."

Dr. Herndon was quick to agree, so we turned our horses over to the groom and stepped up to the comfortable seat of the spring wagon. Even before the dogs could find another covey of birds, a car drove along the narrow plantation road and stopped within fifty feet of the wagon. Naturally it had to be the Boss, and naturally he would come along at just the wrong time for us.

"You boys are taking it pretty easy," he observed, with a twinkle.

"Dammit," Doc said, "we've been drowning in the saddle all morning."

"Just thought I'd check," he said, "and see if you wanted to get out of this rain."

The dogs had pointed again, so we declined his offer of a ride to the plantation house and hunted out the remainder of the morning from the top side of a horse.

Bill Etchells, the manager of Ichauway Plantation, tells an incident that happened shortly after he came to the plantation to take over the dogs and hunting activities.

He was hunting with a high echelon company official when a tremendous covey of quail flushed wild in front of the dogs and flew across a road.

"Let's go after them," the guest suggested.

"The Boss told us to stay on this side of the road," Etchells said.

"He won't mind," the guest replied. "I'll take the responsibility. If he does happen to join us, you won't have to worry. I'll explain."

They crossed the plantation road to where the singles had gone down and were in the middle of this feathered bonanza when Woodruff, who seemed to have a sixth sense for showing up in the right place at the wrong time, drove up to join the hunt.

"I thought I told you to stay on that side of the road," he said to Etchells.

"A large covey flushed wild over here from the other side," the manager explained rather lamely.

"That is no excuse for departing from the course that I outlined," the Boss said crisply.

"That man who said he'd tell Mr. Woodruff it was his decision to cross the road," Etchells said, "ain't opened his mouth, and I got the full load. You can bet one thing. I ain't never crossed another road when the Boss told me to hunt on a certain side."

Over the years The Man often dropped in unexpectedly on one of his bottlers to see how the operation was going when none of the Coca-Cola inspectors or quality control men from the main office were around. Woodruff tells one story about an intended visit to a bottling plant in a certain town through which he was passing. He called the local bottler and said, "This is Bob Woodruff."

"Yeah, and I'm President of the United States," said the bottler and hung up.

Those close to Woodruff know that in spite of his powerful approach to life, his fearlessness in tackling any problem, his incredible successes in all his fields of operation, one of his outstanding qualities is a rare sense of humility. He makes no conscious effort at it; it seems to stem from a deep awareness that physically every man is flesh and blood, that his time as such on earth is limited and in this fleeting space he can be no more than custodian of other physical matter which by one means or another adheres to him. He always shunned the spotlight of personal publicity.

All of this was not because he thought he could accomplish more by working behind the scenes, but primarily because he is instinctively aware that "whatever a man thinketh in his heart, so is he."

This was possibly the reason for a number of other very definite characteristics that mark The Man. Always very much in the heat of the industrial battle, he wanted to remain in the background. Often he said, "There is no limit to what a man may accomplish if he doesn't care who gets the credit." He followed this implicitly.

When some employee fell by the wayside, he was more than likely to take the blame. "We should have handled him a little differently," he'd say.

One of the first things that Woodruff said when he took over The Coca-Cola Company in 1923 was that he wanted every man connected with Coca-Cola in any way to make money. Most of them did—far more than they ever dreamed of making. Some of them developed into millionaires.

59

Throughout most of his life Woodruff avoided personal publicity. He refused interviews about his exploits and transactions. He allowed some writers who were also close friends to touch on phases of his personal life but those reporters were always careful not to pinpoint him too closely. His innate judgment told him that the masses of people who had to struggle for their daily bread were adverse to men with wealth and prominence and he knew this might be reflected in the sales of the soft drink company which he headed. Once when *Time* magazine wanted to use his picture on its front cover, he talked them into using a bottle of Coca-Cola instead.

He had several reasons for this. One was that he did not want sole credit for the accomplishments of his company, where so many people were involved. Another was that when some writer exploited his wealth and his charities, he received literally mail sacks full of letters, asking for donations to every conceivable cause, good and bad, requesting money to help on problems of individuals and families all over America. Some simply said, "You've got it and I need it." He received many threatening letters, promising bodily harm unless he sent checks in varying amounts.

Woodruff makes his own donations to causes he considers worthy. He maintains an organization of men trained in the field of human needs. These are his administrators of the several very wealthy foundations with which he is connected. They study the stacks of requests from charitable and other institutions to determine where the money will do the greatest good for the largest number of people. Woodruff says that one of his most difficult jobs is to intelligently give away money. We'll give more specifics about his charities later in this book.

For the first eighty years of his life he refused to accept citations, commendations, college degrees he hadn't earned, memorials, and honors of all kinds. He gave his gifts anonymously for he wanted no praise for his good works. Naturally word slyly got out as to where most of the anonymous gifts originated and his friend Mayor William B. Hartsfield once said, "The identity of Mr. Anonymous is the worst kept secret in Atlanta."

Recently he has begun to accept recognition for his many charities and the many honors heaped on him from all over America. One of his reasons for this change of heart was that as "Mr. Anonymous," he often received credit for the good works done by others who also wished to remain anonymous. This was one of his ways of remaining honest with himself.

Woodruff has smoked most of his life. He started before the Surgeon General declared how injurious tobacco was for the health and never gave up the habit. He seldom smokes cigarettes and never inhales. His choice is fine cigars and pipe tobacco. He passes out many more cigars than he himself smokes. His choice with coffee early in the morning is the pipe. This is also his choice before retiring at night. One of his greatest pleasures at the end of a day, whether he is at home, at Ichauway, or traveling elsewhere, is a few pipefuls of tobacco with a favorite friend in front of a lighted fire. Sometimes late at night he invites someone in for a pipeful before going to bed. They sit and talk of inconsequential matters and expound philosophical bits of wisdom. Or they sit quietly, with no word of conversation expected or necessary, but with a slow, deep current of understanding that demands no exchange of communication.

His cigars are a daytime pleasure and these are ever present wherever he is. He has been affectionately known to many of his intimate associates as "Mr. Cigar" and a few were brash enough to address him in this manner. Friends bring him boxes of foreign brands from all over the world, and other world famous cigar smokers who admire him sometimes send boxes of their favorite brands—people such as Winston Churchill and even Fidel Castro. These he shares with his other cigar smoking friends, just as he shares all else he owns.

Woodruff always contended that a man lost a lot of life's enjoyment by taking himself too seriously. His sense of humor is rare and delightful. Once Bobby Jones handed to him a poem that Jones had written, and as far as is known, the only bit of verse the golfer ever contributed to mankind. It went something like this:

> "If your nose is close to the grindstone rough
> And you hold it down there long enough,
> In time you'll say there's no such thing
> As brooks that babble and birds that sing.
> These three will all your world compose,
> Just you, the stone and your goddamned nose."

Woodruff studied it, took it home with him, and the next day handed to Jones a poem he had composed in reply. His poem:

"If you sing with the birds
And play in the brook
While the grindstone turns
On the other fellow's hook
You'll find your place
At the table was took."

I had occasion to sample two of his examples of humor. One was in Cody, Wyoming. We had come in from the ranch to have dinner in town. Tom Molesworth, a Cody businessman, and Max Wilde, the big game guide, went with us to a restaurant noted for its western beef.

"Would you like to have a steak?" Woodruff asked me. "They have some of the best here."

"Never turned down a good steak yet," I assured him.

"What size steak would you like?"

"They don't come too big or too raw for me," I bragged.

The waiter took the other orders at our table, and The Man got to his feet. "I'll go back to the kitchen," he said, "and see what looks good."

You wouldn't believe the piece of steak Woodruff had them put in front of me. I'd wagged my tongue too much. It was so big, it hung over the sides of the largest platter I ever saw and was thick enough to stop a .45 caliber bullet. It was so rare that if I'd had my branding iron along, I'd have put Woodruff's brand on it and turned it loose in the TE Hills. My three companions were watching me.

"I'll eat this thing," I said, "if I have to stay here until Christmas."

I put down as much steak as I could hold—with no side dishes—and hardly made a dent in that piece of meat. It would have foundered a grizzly.

"Wrap it up," I said to the waiter. "I'll take it home. This is my winter's supply of beef."

I have no idea what that steak cost Woodruff, but I'm sure he got as much enjoyment out of that dinner as any I've ever had with him, with the exception of one.

We were in New York together, and had dinner with two of his old friends, John Olin of Olin Industries, and Edgar Queeny of the Monsanto Chemical Company. Olin wanted to show a country boy how the city folks lived, so we went to one of New York's most exclusive clubs. Woodruff watched me with a half amused smile while I tried to show how cosmopolitan I was by drinking too many cocktails and too much wine with courses I couldn't even pronounce.

We had after dinner drinks and the waiter brought the check.

"Give it to me," I said.

"I'll sign it," Olin replied placidly.

"Let me pay it," I said.

"I'll sign it," Olin repeated.

"Waiter, bring me the check," I insisted.

Woodruff said, "Let the sonofabitch have it."

For the first time I got a glimpse of the amount that totaled up to about one hundred fifty dollars. I had all of thirty-five dollars in my pocket and until that moment felt rich. My three companions laughed and I'm sure it was at the terror-stricken look on my face. It was only then that I felt relieved. I'd been acquainted with Woodruff long enough to know that he never would leave me on a hook such as that. Not long enough anyway for the establishment to put me to washing dishes in the kitchen to pay for that meal.

Almost any of his friends has some story to tell of his humor and quick wit, with which he was careful never to hurt the feelings of any individual.

One of the stories Atlanta Mayor William B. Hartsfield used to tell was how he and Woodruff teamed up for a joke on Abie Cowan, a special friend of both men. Abie was in a regular Saturday night poker game at the Capital City Club. Gambling was technically illegal in Atlanta, so Hartsfield called Herbert Jenkins, his chief of police, and asked that he bring two uniformed policemen and meet him and Woodruff in the lobby of the club.

With Woodruff and Hartsfield standing outside, the two burly policemen walked into the room where the poker game was in progress.

"You're all under arrest," one said.

"For what?" someone inquired.

"For gambling," he was told. "Games of chance are illegal."

63

Abie Cowan looked up at the officer. "Ain't nobody in this poker game taken a chance in four hours!" he said.

Woodruff and Hartsfield could suppress their laughter no longer and the little hoax was discovered.

Woodruff loved a good story, but was never much of a story teller himself. Outside of "damn" or "hell," I never heard him use one of the ugly or obscene four letter words which apparently are commonly accepted today by at least a segment of our society. His humor was more sly and subtle and often very pointed. Once when an associate in his company wrote him a glowing but overdone letter that outlined Woodruff's accomplishments, and praised him highly, he replied succinctly, "Flattery is like chewing tobacco. It tastes sweet, is very satisfying, and does no harm unless you swallow it."

One of the great touches of that subtle humor has been quoted in almost every article or book ever written about him, when he said, "It has never been my desire to have a yacht, a racehorse or a mistress—in that order."

Although he listened to but seldom dealt in jokes, he loved to tell a good story on himself or on one of his favorite friends. A couple of these that he repeated were about President Eisenhower.

He was in the reviewing stand with Eisenhower during a presidential inauguration. Groups and bands from all over America were in the giant parade. One of the bands was from Georgia Military Academy, which Woodruff has said "was the only school I ever graduated from."

Woodruff had had a hand in the creation of that band when he was a cadet at the academy. From his older friends he had collected enough donations to buy the instruments that got the band started. In appreciation of his efforts, his fellow students had unanimously named their group the "Robert W. Woodruff Band" and painted the name on their drums. Each Georgia Military Academy band over the years has kept it prominently displayed there.

When they marched proudly by the reviewing stand, the President turned toward Woodruff, standing nearby, and called, "You're the only fellow here who brought his own band."

Another Eisenhower story had to do with the location of the plantation and the creek running through it.

When General Ike was the supreme commander of the Allied Forces in World War II, he was routing bombers over Germany where they would drop their loads of bombs, fly on to Russia and there take on fuel and another load of bombs to drop on Germany on the way back to England. One of the gunners who was assigned to such a flight came to see General Ike.

"Can't you give me something else to do?" he asked. "I can't go to Russia."

"Why not?" he was asked.

"I'll never get along with these people. I can't even speak the language!"

"Boy, where are you from?" the General asked.

"I come from a farm down in south Georgia," the gunner said, "near where the Ichauway-Nochauway and Chickasawhatchee creeks come together."

Ike grinned.

"You'll do all right with the Russian language," he said.

Woodruff had humorous stories to tell about most of his close associates. One of these over many years was Abie Cowan. Abie was often known as the Court Jester, for his stories and his observations kept Woodruff and his friends entertained over many years.

When the big house at Ichauway was full of guests, Abie claimed that as low man on the totem pole, he was always assigned one of the upstairs rooms that had no fireplace. This he designated as "Siberia" and it remains Siberia today.

One of Woodruff's favorite stories about Abie was the time, as comparative youngsters just starting out in White Motor Company, they occasionally slipped off together and made a trip to Cuba, where they went the round of the night spots and gambling casinos. Both loved good cigars and always brought back a supply of the Cuban product with them. Ernest Woodruff, Bob's father, regarded these trips with much displeasure. To him, his son was squandering money on pleasure, when he should have been at home tending to his job.

After one such trip to Cuba, Abie happened to meet the elder Woodruff on the street. On an impulse, Abie offered him one of the fifty-cent cigars they had brought with them from the island. Ernest was as much a connoisseur of fine tobacco as his son. He smelled the cigar, lighted it and after a couple of puffs, asked, "Where did you get this and how much did it cost?"

Not wishing to admit his and Robert's Cuban playboy trip to Mr. Ernest, who was always annoyed by his son's extravagance, Abie waved in a negligent gesture.

"Oh, at a little shop down the street. It only cost a nickel."

Ernest reached for his billfold and pulled out a fifty-dollar bill.

"At that price it's a damn fine cigar," he said. "Go back and buy me a thousand."

Over the period of half a century, the guest book at Ichauway Plantation is filled with names of presidents, governors, senators, fellow plantation owners, giants of business and industry, famous sports writers, movie and television stars, and others from all walks of life. Woodruff recalls many of these with amusing little stories.

He likes to recall how Eisenhower, as President, drove the security guards assigned to protect him crazy, when he gave them the slip at George Humphrey's plantation on the Georgia-Florida line to spend the day with Mr. and Mrs. Woodruff at Ichauway Plantation where no one could locate him.

With a twinkle in his eye he remembers the conversation between Morton Downey, who represented Coca-Cola on the radio for years, and Miss Nell with two of her guests in the plantation house. Downey was toying with the piano keys and listening to the talk between the women on how girls in the present generation were not schooled in the basics of cooking and keeping a home and what a shame it was.

Downey turned around on the piano bench and during a lull in the conversation among the ladies, said, "There's only one thing I want the girl I marry to know how to do."

"What is that?" asked Miss Nell.

"Un-make a bed," Downey said.

With much pleasure Ichauway's Boss recalls one of the first quail hunts Grantland Rice, the noted writer of sporting events, made to the plantation. Rice had never shot quail and distinguished himself by missing almost every bird that flushed in front of him. Finally one of the quail, instead of following the rest of the covey, flew up to the nearby limb of a pine tree.

"There's a good chance for you to break your record," Woodruff said. "Take careful aim."

Rice did, but his shot string missed the bobwhite. It merely moved over on the limb.

"Try again," the Boss instructed.

The second wad of shot was also too low. They saw it cut needles under the feet of the quail, which had had as much as it could take and flew off. Woodruff looked at the sports writer who merely shook his head.

"It was teed too high," Rice alibied.

Later, on an early morning hunt, Rice killed the largest gobbler ever taken at Ichauway. It remains mounted in the big dining room.

Edgar Bergen was one of the longest-remembered guests at the plantation. For years he sold Charlie McCarthy, Mortimer Snerd and Coca-Cola over the networks. On the night of Bergen's visit, Woodruff collected most of his farm personnel into the big house and Bergen put on one of his best shows for them, with ventriloquism and many tricks with a magic bell and cane. The older plantation members still recall it.

The next morning Woodruff gave a turkey hunt for his distinguished guest. The events that transpired are among the prized stories of Woodruff's eighty-nine years.

The ritual of a turkey hunt was to rouse the guests long before daylight and give them coffee only. Then in total darkness they gathered outside the plantation house and were assigned to mule-drawn wagons with boards laid as seats from side to side across the wagon bed. Each guest held on to his gun that he kept between his knees with the barrel—unloaded of course—pointed skyward. The wagons, filled with turkey hunters, rolled off in the darkness toward the turkey woods. Morton Downey's description of this ride into the darkness was that "it looks like an uprising of the peasants." Bergen, in the middle of one of the wagons, looked around him.

"It looked like a necktie party," he said, "and I got a little nervous. It suddenly occurred to me that I was the only damyankee in the crowd."

In the turkey woods, the gunners were assigned stands. Bergen, who had never participated in such a hunt, was told, "When you shoot down a turkey, go to it immediately, for it might get up and run off."

The night before, plantation hands had listened at various places and heard the turkeys fly up to roost. At daylight they spread out behind the birds and at flying down time, walked through the woods, singing and beating on trees, to drive the turkeys over the standers.

Bergen missed the only gobbler that came over him. He shot ten feet behind it, but the bird cupped its wings and glided to earth a hundred yards away. Bergen threw down his gun and was going after it, but the guide in the same blind restrained him.

"You missed that one clean," he said.

Almost every gunner on this morning hunt killed a turkey except Bergen. After the hunt, the birds were laid out, each was identified by the gunner who had shot it down and a name tag tied on the leg of the gobbler. One tom turkey remained unclaimed. The plantation manager held it up.

"Who does this belong to?"

Abie Cowan spoke up quickly. "That's Bergen's bird."

Bergen shook his head. "Not mine. I missed."

"You just thought you did," Abie insisted. "You killed it."

"Did you get a turkey?" someone asked Abie.

"My two," he replied rather pointedly, "have already been tagged."

One of the guests on the hunt was a state game conservation officer and the situation began to dawn on the other hunters. Abie Cowan had downed three gobblers and the state legal limit was only two. To keep himself out of trouble, Abie was palming his illegal bird off on Bergen. Bergen suddenly caught on and he arose to the occasion. The ventriloquist picked up the untagged turkey by the neck, looked it straight in the eye and demanded in sonorous tones, "Turkey, who killed you?"

With a deft twist of Bergen's hand, the head of the dead gobbler turned slowly and appeared to study each of the group of gobbler hunters. Then it swung back to the face of the man who held it and nodded its head.

"Why Mr. Bergen," it declared in a high-pitched Charlie McCarthy voice, "you know plumb well you is de one who done kilt me."

Everyone laughed, including the conservation officer and the plantation manager said, "I guess that settles it."

Woodruff always found goodnatured humor in the story of a million dollar set of steer horns that he kept in his trophy room at the TE Ranch.

Once his father had given a sizeable gift of Coca-Cola stock to his other two sons. To Robert he said, "You've got enough Coca-Cola stock. I'll give you something else." His gift was the magnificent set of horns from a long-horned steer.

"The stock he gave to each of my brothers," Woodruff said years later, "grew in value with the growth of The Coca-Cola Company, and today is worth about a million dollars to each one. So I have to conclude that this set of horns is worth about a million to me."

The pilots and other personnel who handle The Coca-Cola Company aircraft were discussing the Boss's subtle sense of humor. He invited a group of them to a dove shoot at Ichauway. All of the airmen but one were good shots and brought in a limit of doves, but this fellow had never shot at the fast flying birds and seemed unable to bring one down.

After the shoot, all were gathered around, reporting their kills to the Boss who made little notations on a slip of paper. To each in turn, he asked the same question—"How many did you get?," although he already knew the answer. To the lad who had brought in no doves, he said quietly, "And did you have a good time?"

Throughout his life, Woodruff has been a master salesman. Examples of his ability to sell others on his ideas, his products and himself would fill volumes. As a youngster he certainly must not have been aware that he was developing this special talent when he charmed older people into doing things for him. Possibly the real meaning of the word and the study of the art did not materialize until later when his livelihood began to depend on his ability as a salesman. His experience in this field, which developed as a truck and heavy equipment salesman for White Motor Company, was only one of the virtues that made him successful in most of his ventures, notable of which was the creation of a world empire in Coca-Cola.

A few times he has expressed himself on the matter of salesmanship. Once to the board of directors of Metropolitan Life Insurance Company, of which he was a member, he said, "Only a person who is genuinely sensitive to the aspirations and problems of other human beings can become a great salesman. It is the salesman, more than any other person, who encounters the motivations of mankind. There is the motivation of love of family; the desire for comfort and security; for pleasure and romance; the urge to keep up with the Joneses; generosity and greed—these emotions and many others are grist in the salesman's mill."

Many men who had dealings with him have characterized Woodruff as "the most persuasive man I ever knew." One of these was Freeman Gosden, the Amos of the Amos and Andy show that delighted radio and TV audiences for many years. E. J. Kahn, Jr., tells this story in his biography of Woodruff:

> Gosden and Woodruff were devoted friends, played golf together and shared many experiences. After a round of golf one afternoon at the Augusta National Woodruff suggested, "How about the two of us going down the road about five miles to that little restaurant?"
>
> I told Bob (Gosden recalls) "I don't want to go, because I know they have a couple of roulette tables in the back room, and we will end up there surer than hell."
>
> He said to me at this point, "I think we should leave the club about 7:30."
>
> I again told Bob that I didn't want to go.
>
> He said he thought we should not wear the club coat because it would not be in good taste to wear it off the premises.
>
> I said, "Bob, as far as I'm concerned, it's not a question of club coat, the premises or anything else. I am not going to that restaurant. First of all, those roulette tables are wired, and if you put your hands on two different places while the wheels are spinning, you can get a shock."
>
> He said, "I'll take my car and chauffeur."
>
> I said, "Go ahead. I'll see you tomorrow."

He said, "And another thing—you'd better bring your raincoat."

This went on for another five minutes. Finally I was so exasperated, I looked him straight in the eye and said, "Listen, Bob, I have known you for about twenty-five years. I am very fond of you. I enjoy being with you. I know that you always have your way, but by God, this is one time you're not going to. I know that I have nothing you want, and I want you to know that you have nothing I want, and if this is going to break up our friendship, then let it break up, but let me tell you once and for all that I am not going to that gambling joint."

At exactly 7:55 I was leaning up against a roulette table, watching "00" come up when I had practically every other number covered. Yes, when you're with Bob, you're going to have a good time, but the way he wants you to have it. But I love him—I guess even more today than I did before I lost seven hundred fifty dollars.

Another story that Woodruff told on himself that's typical of his accuracy in sizing up a situation and his ability to convince others was an incident at the Saratoga race track.

Woodruff was visiting Donald Ross at Saratoga Springs and they spent much time at the track together. Ross knew a great deal about the operation of the track and one day at lunch when he and Woodruff were comparing it with other noted American race tracks, Ross said, "The Saratoga track is one of the best run of any I know. There's no way, for instance, that any person could ever get in except with a ticket or proper identification."

"I can get in," Woodruff said, "without either."

"A hundred bucks says you can't," Ross replied.

Woodruff took the wager.

He walked through one of the open back gates where no ticket was needed and into the compound where the horses were stabled.

"I moved around there for a while," he chuckled, "examining the stalls and speaking to the grooms and other people there as if I owned the place. I made certain that the man taking tickets at that gate into the track could see me and made some motions as though I were giving instructions to some of the attendants. I waited until a surge of crowd collected to go through and I got right in the middle of it. People were pushing to get through and when the man who was busy taking tickets asked for mine, I said, 'I'm just going inside where I'm supposed to meet a fellow.'"

The gate keeper did no more than glance at the tall, distinguished man with the appearance and voice of authority and nodded him on through to where Donald Ross was waiting to collect his bet. Woodruff collected from Ross instead and then walked back outside to purchase his ticket.

One of the things that disturbed Ernest Woodruff about his son was that Robert always seemed to live far beyond his means. A very frugal man himself, many of Robert's activities and expenditures seemed nothing less than wanton extravagance.

Even though he made his own way, with little help from his father, and even though he went through some lean periods in his earlier years, Woodruff always "lived well"—as one of his friends so aptly expressed it. In his early years he belonged to an expensive and exclusive hunting club that he could ill afford, but it gave him the opportunity to meet some of the men high in the circles of business and finance. He joined the Atlanta Athletic Club as a golfing member in 1912 and later in life held memberships in a dozen of the most exclusive golfing clubs in America. His travels were not always for business, for he hunted and fished over a large portion of North America. He entertained lavishly, for he loved people and liked to have them around him. He visited the race tracks and gambling places where sometimes he won and sometimes lost. Never did he neglect his job or his business, and never was he out of touch with it for long.

Ernest Woodruff took a dim view of these extracurricular activities. He could see only financial catastrophe, for instance, when his son bought large tracts of land in south Georgia and put them together into a hunting preserve. His feeling might have been somewhat modified by the fact that Walter White, Robert's partner in the plantation, was wealthy enough to hold it together. Then when White was killed and Robert bought out his share with a sum that strained his financial resources, the elder Woodruff sadly shook his head. This was doom with a capital D, and the elder Woodruff never changed his mind that the plantation would fail.

A year or two later when he was a guest at Ichauway, he admitted that it was indeed a lovely spot, with the best quail shooting he had ever seen.

"Wouldn't you like to own part of it?" Robert asked.

"I'm going to own it all."

"How do you plan to do that?"

"I'll buy it at the sheriff's sale," Mr. Ernest said with a twinkle, "when you go broke."

Ernest wasn't the only one concerned about his son's lavish way of living. Once the younger Woodruff accidentally discovered that two of his employees, Lawrence Calhoun, his chauffeur, and James Roseberry, his butler and personal servant, shared a joint savings account. They had built it into what for them was a sizeable sum. Being curious, he asked about it.

"The way you spend money," they told him frankly, "you won't have any to see you through your old age. Somebody's got to think about taking care of you."

As do most individuals with complex personalities, Woodruff sometimes shows a stubborn and cantankerous streak, possibly the result of a lifetime of fierce competition. This has mellowed notably during his later years. It was never vicious or mean—just ornery—and possibly a balance wheel to keep him down to earth and human. At times, too, this has been an obvious device to keep from showing his true emotions.

A few of those close to Woodruff have heard him wax sarcastic because of seemingly insignificant things, as a misplaced newspaper or coffee poured at the wrong time. Most of these moments came when he was under great pressure with some business or personal problem. Never did they last long.

Few of his friends or employees have seen Woodruff angry. He has a quick temper but normally keeps it under wraps, especially around people who are not his intimate associates. Those close to the Boss find it rather refreshing to see him exhibit such human tendencies.

A few years ago Woodruff and one of his men who worked closely with him would occasionally disagree on some trivial matter. There were no harsh words, but each would become so upset they'd stop speaking to one another, like a sort of cabin fever under modern conditions. When they had to do business, they'd relay messages through Woodruff's secretary. This might go on for two or three days before the pieces eventually fell into place again and the two resumed business as usual.

Most of this was behind him when his age stretched into the eighties, though the spark is still there. It occasionally flares.

The birthday celebration at the Capital City Club was the last such party Woodruff ever allowed anyone to give him, though several were proposed, one on his eightieth. Since his seventieth, The Man has preferred to celebrate his birthdays quietly with a few friends, usually at Ichauway Plantation. As emeritus head of the vast Coca-Cola empire, at whose helm he has served or advised as chief navigator for more than half a century, he receives gifts from all around the world and congratulatory messages in almost every written language. This pleases him naturally, but his pleasure goes far beyond that. He is the only man of this writer's acquaintance who reverses his birthday custom and gives gifts to others on that day. The satisfaction he reaps in passing out appropriate remembrances to employees and friends close to him is so apparent that it is heartwarming to see. There is no doubt that his birthdays mean much more to him than ours do to us.

Woodruff was at his plantation home in the early 1970's when he suffered a mild stroke which was followed by another stroke more severe that affected his right arm and hand and right leg. As he had faced all the crises of his life, Woodruff met this one bluntly and head on. His right leg was so weak that his balance was affected, but with dogged determination he learned to walk again without a cane, and one received the impression of his raw courage when he walked as far as he could go along the road around the plantation circle.

Any lesser man might have given up and spent the remainder of his life in a wheel chair. Not Woodruff. He continued to exercise his legs and arms until he could again get into the saddle for short rides along the plantation trails. He got a portion of his exercise by driving his car over the isolated roads at Ichauway to look at his crops and cattle.

He never spoke of it, but he was somewhat distressed when he voluntarily gave up his shooting. He had always been a remarkable marksman with the scattergun, and even after he began to recover from his stroke, he tried shooting again, but in quail woods he was too unsteady on his feet and in a dove field, he could not pivot and swing with the birds. He continued to carry a gun into the dove fields, and to be a member of the quail hunts, but as a spectator, either from the hunting wagon or from the saddle for a while.

He accepted this as stoically as he had faced problems throughout his life, and has never ceased from trying to remedy it.

Except where he thinks that he might hurt some friends' feelings by not attending, Woodruff avoids meetings and parties where a large number of people are present. He wears a hearing aid and it's hard for him to carry on a conversation against so much background noise one usually finds at those places. He loves company and finds much enjoyment with smaller numbers of friends or acquaintances.

Some of his friends wonder if he doesn't hear more than he admits. "He hears what he wants to hear," said one. "A couple of fellows and I were talking with him not long ago, and suppose we were talking rather loudly, because he couldn't seem to quite understand what we were trying to say. One of the fellows said in a quiet voice, 'Maybe he needs a new battery in his hearing aid.'

"'The battery's all right,' Woodruff came right back. 'Luther put in a new one just this morning.'

"And before that we'd been talking loud enough to be heard across the street."

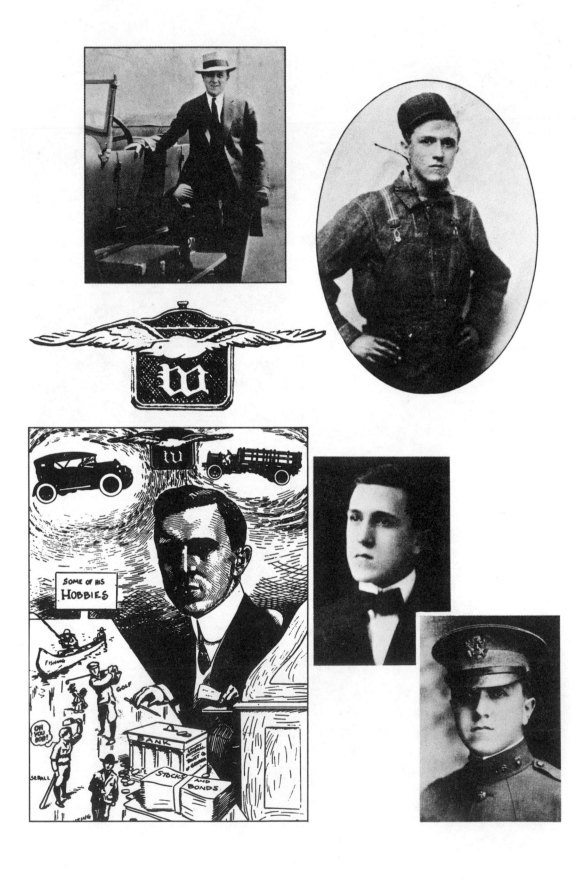

Chapter 2
Growing-Up Years

In 1889 a number of notable events were added to the footnotes of history.

Over in Paris, at the six-month long Universal Exposition, Carl Benz, generally recognized as the father of the modern gasoline automobile, exhibited his Benz and started mankind on a new era.

The Eiffel Tower, miracle of the new steel age, built for the exposition by Alexandre Eiffel, noted bridge builder of the century, was opened.

Here at home, twenty-two hundred lives were lost in the Jamestown flood. Between the white man and Sioux Indian Nation was trouble which developed a year later into the battle of Wounded Knee, the last major conflict between the Indians and U. S. troops.

In a modest frame house in Columbus, Georgia, on the sixth of December, Robert Winship Woodruff came into the world as the first born son of Ernest and Emily Woodruff.

Robert Woodruff remembers little about those first few years in Columbus, other than the fact that his father was a salesman for the family grist mill and worked a territory that included a large segment of Georgia and Alabama downriver from Columbus. His father traveled by horse and buggy and was away from home for days at a time. Often he carried his bird dog and gun in the buggy and brought home a "mess" of quail.

Robert's recollections were sharper at three and a half years of age when his family moved to Atlanta. In 1893, Ernest Woodruff's brother-in-law, Joel Hurt, offered him a position with the Atlanta Consolidated Railway Company. Ernest accepted and the family moved from Columbus to Euclid Avenue, near the end of the street car line on Waverly Way. Some years later Ernest built a spacious brick home at the corner of Edgewood Avenue and Waverly Way. The family moved into the new home when Robert was in high school. A few years ago the house was restored and is now a private residence.

Euclid, Edgewood and Waverly Way made a rough triangle. Enough land was set aside there for a park. This, according to Woodruff, was named for Hugh Inman, who had loaned money to build the street car line to this residential development. There was another appropriate reason for the name of the park. Woodruff remembers that Inman was one of the early environmentalists who felt that some lands, even in the heart of the city, should be set aside as playgrounds and places of relaxation. Young Robert learned his lesson well, and much later in life donated a number of such parks to the people of Atlanta.

Young Woodruff grew up in the homes on Euclid and Edgewood with his two brothers, George and Henry. His brother Ernest, Jr., who had been born in Columbus, lived only about three years. Woodruff's younger brothers called him "Buddy." His father and mother addressed him more formally as Robert.

Handsome, debonaire and persuasive, young Robert was a salesman almost from the time he could walk. Few were the individuals he could not, in one way or another, influence. One of these few was his father who was a rather stern disciplinarian with his boys because he wanted them to grow into strong, self-reliant men. He did talk his father—possibly with help from his mother—into buying a pony that he could ride to school. To feed his pony, a bay gelding named "Pat," he also promoted a modest allowance out of the family. Then he made friends with Jim Key, the hostler who kept the stables where Asa Candler housed the horses that pulled his wagons to haul ingredients, supplies, and Coca-Cola syrup. Jim Key liked the youngster well enough to board the pony free. This gave Robert a bit more pocket money out of his allowance. It also paid off well for the old stable hand. When Woodruff took over the presidency of The Coca-Cola Company two decades later, he gave Jim Key a job for life.

Young Robert was gregarious. He loved company, as he has done all of his life. He liked to have his friends around, but sometimes this was not convenient at home. Then he would take his persuasive ways over to his Aunt Ida's, who lived nearby, and convince her to give a party for him.

Robert entered the Edgewood Avenue Grammar School when he was six years old. As he was to do throughout his life, he captured the hearts of those to whom he was drawn by one reason or another. When he finished his grammar school term in 1903, he received a note from Mrs. W. F. Johnson, one of his teachers.

"I have been greatly pleased," she wrote, "to note the effort you have made since coming to my little summer school and if you will only continue in this line, some day you will be a man to whom your parents will point with pride."

Robert cherished that note and kept it in his memoirs. Twenty years later, when he was established as president of The Coca-Cola Company, he wrote to Mrs. Johnson:

"There is hardly a day passes that I don't think about you, not only with affection but in grateful appreciation which I feel you are due for any good fortune that has come to me in the business world.

"I should love for you to accept the enclosed check (fifty dollars) each month to buy yourself something with it so that you will be reminded of me. It gives me great pleasure and satisfaction to do this and I hope you will accept it in the same way I intend it.

"You see you had a great many pupils, lots of whom were much better than Robert W. Woodruff, but I had only one Mrs. Johnson."

Mrs. Johnson replied: "The sentiments of your letter are much dearer to me than thousands of times the amount of the check. An ex-teacher values such sentiments expressed by you more than anything in this world. I live each day in the past and your dear letter has put new life into me. May God bless you and yours for your kind words. They are very dear to me. I could not love you more were you my own son."

In 1904 Robert entered Boys' High School, about two and one-half miles from his home. Here he could not seem to find the handle as he had in grammar school. With his innate honesty, he says that the reason he "flunked out" at Boys' High was that neither the studies nor the teachers particularly interested him. He spent only a few months there, then in 1905 transferred to Georgia Military Academy at College Park for the remainder of his high school years. He claims this was one of the best moves he ever made and that "GMA was the only place from which I ever graduated."

Georgia Military Academy, founded by Colonel John Charles Woodward, was only half a dozen years old when Robert entered. Some of the facilities were still primitive. The first year there was no "inside plumbing," but these conditions were improved over the years young Woodruff attended the school.

Woodruff quickly became friends with Colonel Woodward and was attracted to the other instructors. One of his favorites was his Sunday school teacher, Mrs. Alonzo Richardson, who was also one of Atlanta's prominent social leaders. Mrs. Richardson was known as the "sweetheart" of the student body.

Though he was attracted to the school, its instructors and most of its students, Robert's first year at GMA was one of the most frustrating periods of his life.

While he was at Boys' High, Dr. Thomas P. Hinman, whom Woodruff has classified as a "good golfer and a good talker," sold Mr. Ernest on the idea that his son's undershot jaw had his teeth so out of line that the "bite" would affect his health in later years. He convinced the elder Woodruff that his boy should wear a set of the cumbersome braces. At that time the entire conception of braces was new enough to be in the experimental stage and all of his life Woodruff has been positive that he was one of Dr. Hinman's guinea pigs for these medieval instruments of torture. They had to be tightened every two or three days and Robert endured excruciating days and nights. He says he'd have pulled them out and destroyed them, but the doctors had foreseen that contingency. The braces were firmly attached and irremovable. Woodruff believes they may have been one contributing factor to his lack of interest in high school. Since that day he has looked with a suspicious eye on all but a few close personal friends in the dental business.

The braces greatly influenced Robert's life, but in an unexpected manner. What happened over the next three quarters of a century bears out **author Don Byrne's great lines: "What we think at twenty-five was a trifling accident, at seventy-five we know to have been an enormous gesture of God."**

Strong, quick and alert, and interested in sports of all kinds, Robert could have developed into a professional athlete. With such a hazard as the braces, he couldn't play games, so he stepped into a leadership role in most campus activities. He took over as manager of the football team, as business manager of the *Gamilicad,* the school publication, and as manager of the dramatic club. He became prominent in other clubs and societies in the school, among them the bugle corps, which was to bring out another of his qualities rare for one of his age. He was involved with so many school organizations and in so many activities that he was named manager of the board of managers, so that he could take on all business responsibilities for that group. Even in those days, his capacity appears to have been unlimited.

His simple physical charm, personal magnetism, inclination to take command of any situation and other assets responsible for his meteoric rise to such incredible heights in the business world were already in evidence at GMA. This was strongly indicated when young Robert volunteered to raise money for a school band. This was one of his early experiences in "always taking the initiative in situations which really were none of my business, but where people needed help."

"Of course," he said with a smile, "I had another motive, too. As long as I was out trying to raise money for the band, I didn't have to go to classes."

He seemed to gravitate to anything or anybody in trouble. This was one of the foundations on which he built his life. He admits that this was one reason that influenced him many years later to take a job with The Coca-Cola Company at less than half the salary he was making with White Motor Company.

Characteristically he met head-on the job of fund raising for his school band. From this early age he never dodged a confrontation with anyone, or with any issue. Inborn were both the courage and the confidence that he could handle any situation. If he knew trouble was on the way he never waited for it, but went directly to the source, carrying with him a bold approach and complete honesty, regardless of the consequences.

He went about his first job of fund raising by tackling the highest sources. He promoted donations from bankers and other executives he knew as friends of his father's. He got a list of the merchants who sold supplies to the school and most of these were eager to make contributions to a good customer for a worthy cause.

This was only one of his lessons in public relations and salesmanship during his school years. In the summer months when school was out, his father gave him the job of making a house to house canvass, selling coupon books with which housewives could purchase ice from the Atlantic Ice and Coal Company, one of the Woodruff businesses. Shrewdly, Ernest thought it best not to tempt his drivers by allowing them to handle too much cash.

"I met all the madams in the red light district," Woodruff said with a grin much later in life.

Probably his best and most important job of salesmanship while enrolled in GMA was to help his school out of a serious financial difficulty.

Robert heard about this and went in to see and talk with Colonel Woodward. The head master admitted that the Atlanta National Bank held a mortgage on the property. He wasn't able to pay it and the bank was about to foreclose. This would put the school into bankruptcy.

Here again shows that character facet which dominated Woodruff's life—of wanting to help anyone in trouble and taking the initiative and doing something about it. Without telling anyone, he took it upon himself to pay a visit to whom he remembers as James S. Floyd, vice president of the bank, located at Peachtree and Mitchell Streets. When he was ushered into Floyd's office, the vice president looked him over and asked, "What do you want?"

"I understand," Robert replied, "that Colonel Woodward is unable to make a payment on the note owed by him and GMA and that you are about to foreclose."

"That's true."

"I want you to be easy on him," Robert said.

"And who are you?" Floyd asked.

"I'm a student at GMA," young Woodruff replied, "and Colonel Woodward is my friend. I'm going to see that he doesn't get into any trouble and that nothing happens to him."

"You're nuts," Floyd said. "Why don't you get out of here?"

"I'll borrow the money myself from some other bank," Robert said, "and pay you off."

Floyd snapped, "Why don't you just do that, then?"

"I've talked to Mr. John K. Ottley and Mr. Tom Glenn," Robert said.

"They'll endorse Colonel Woodward's note, or they'll take it off your hands at any time."

"I didn't say that I had talked to Mr. Ottley or Mr. Glenn specifically about the note," Woodruff commented with a sly smile, when he was telling the story recently.

Floyd pursed his lips and studied young Woodruff.

"All right. Go get the money."

Robert turned to leave and was half way to the door when Floyd called, "Wait a minute."

The boy stopped and turned around.

"I've decided to renew this note," Floyd said.

"Why?" Robert asked.

"My better judgment," Floyd said, "tells me to."

"I guess I didn't have any more sense," Woodruff once said, "than to tackle almost anything that came up. I'd get it started, then put some capable person on the job to keep it going or to finish it. He'd have to be the kind of fellow who was entirely trustworthy, and that I didn't mind turning my back on, because I knew he'd get it accomplished. Then I'd go on to something else that needed being done."

This too started early in his life. At GMA, where he was the moving force behind the *Gamilicad,* he enlisted the help of Richard C. Gresham, a school mate, and made him editor of the school paper. Gresham was more than a year older than Woodruff and was at GMA as a stepping stone on his way to the naval academy. The two boys became fast friends and often slipped into town to visit Gresham's father, who had the food concession for trains and terminals throughout most of the Southeast. They could always count on the elder Gresham to give them a free meal of steak and potatoes.

Young Woodruff and Dick Gresham became fast friends and remained close as long as Gresham lived. He changed his mind about going to the naval academy and studied for the ministry instead. Even before they graduated from GMA, Gresham took upon himself the assignment as Robert's spiritual advisor, and through the years Woodruff claimed him as his personal preacher. This relationship between the two men was sometimes jokingly referred to by their friends as the "reverend and the reprobate," and years later Gresham became known as the "Bishop of Coca-Cola."

Woodruff's personal files contain sermons written especially for him by his personal pastor. They date back to 1908 and were Gresham's contribution to the spiritual life of his friend. Though Woodruff was technically a Presbyterian, he contributed regularly to Dr. Gresham's First Baptist Church in Moultrie, where Gresham took the pastorate in 1929 and remained until his retirement. Moultrie was less than an hour's drive from Ichauway Plantation and the preacher was able to spend many hours with Woodruff when he came down for a visit or during the hunting season. Woodruff occasionally drove over for one of his friend's Sunday services.

Dick Gresham lived by the highest spiritual code, but he didn't wear his religion on his sleeve. He was one of the "regular fellows" who came to the plantation. He participated in the hunting and most of the other activities. He was said to be the only man who ever shot a wild Canada goose at the plantation.

E. J. Kahn, Jr., tells a delightful story about one visit of the reverend to Ichauway. This was back in the days when poker playing occupied some of the evenings. The preacher didn't participate, but he enjoyed standing around to watch and indulge in the fellowship of such a gathering.

Kahn points out that Gresham's flock was not financially affluent and occasionally the minister had to struggle to keep his church functioning properly. At one time the preacher was at Ichauway when a poker game was in progress and when it came to an end, the banker Thomas K. Glenn had won around five hundred dollars. Knowing that the pastor's church was strapped, Glenn offered it as a contribution.

"He won't take that kind of money," Woodruff said.

"The hell I won't," Gresham replied. He put it in his pocket and it helped his church over a tight spot.

In these formative years Robert was torn between two desires. One was prompted by his love of the outdoors, of horses and dogs and hunting, and possibly his association with William F. Cody. He wanted to be a big game guide in the western lands. The other was to be a successful business man—so successful that he would (as he put it) "make a million dollars."

When a man hesitates at the forks of a trail, then decides upon one path over the other, there is no way to even imagine what his story would have been had he chosen the other pathway. Maybe a preordained destiny decides for him. Young Robert took the million dollar route.

When he graduated from GMA, Colonel Woodward, with more vision than he realized, said very seriously to Ernest Woodruff, "Don't send Robert to school any more. You'll ruin him."

Disregarding this suggestion and the advice that "college is a place where stones are polished and diamonds are dimmed," Ernest enrolled his son in Emory University when it was located at Oxford, Georgia, in 1908.

For all the education Robert received at Emory, he could as well have been working in the icy mines of Siberia. He had no interest in his studies. He had few close friends among the students. He pledged to the Kappa Alpha fraternity, the one to which most of the Candlers belonged. KA headquarters were in the upper part of Stone's Store in Oxford. From his father Robert received a forty-dollar-a-month allowance for all of his expenses other than actual college costs. From the very beginning one of his lifelong traits was living luxuriously. With his powers of persuasion he established good credit at Stone's Store and in the four months he attended Emory, he ran up his bill at the store to astronomical figures as related to his allowance. Woodruff says that when he took over as president of The Coca-Cola Company, fifteen years later, he learned that he had never paid all of his bill to Stone and sent a check to the store, even though the proprietor had long before written it off.

Robert was unhappy at Emory. He felt it was time to get out of school and go to work. His letters home complained about as many things as he could think of to complain about. The roof leaked and water ran into his room. He caught cold. He said his eyes hurt so badly that he couldn't see to study, though he was trying hard. He didn't have enough spending money. He and his father constantly bickered about his expenses. He continuously wrote to Mr. Ernest asking to come home. He found his father, perhaps on to his son's tricks, unyielding. The elder Woodruff wanted his son to have a college education and wrote some caustic letters, advising him to apply himself to study instead of devoting his time to social correspondence.

Robert continued to complain about the trouble his eyes were giving him. Late in January Woodruff Senior wrote to Dr. James E. Dickey, president of Emory College, and suggested that since Robert's eyes were bothering him, it might be wise to take him out of school for the time being and let him make a fresh start later. President Dickey's reply was succinct and to the point:

"I do not think it advisable for him to return to college this term as he has not done satisfactory work and cannot therefore make up what he would lose before returning again. He has never learned to apply himself, which together with very frequent absences, makes it impossible for him to succeed as a student. Should you decide for him to continue his academic career, I would suggest that he begin all over again, starting at the point where he is qualified to work, and then go forward."

Young Woodruff had no intention of suffering through four years of college. He was ready to get into a trade and make his own way in the world. His decision was directly against the expressed wishes of his father, who said, "I intend for you to have an education. You must remember that it's only three generations from shirtsleeves to shirtsleeves."

"That being the case," Robert retorted, "I'll take my shirtsleeves now."

He never went back to Emory, though many decades later after he had donated vast sums of money to the growth of the university, its hospital and clinic, Emory made an attempt to claim him as one of its own. In recent years they dedicated a new library building to Robert W. Woodruff. In making the announcement of this dedication, the university trustees, possibly with tongue in cheek, stated that "Mr. Woodruff entered business before his formal graduation from Emory."

The student body at Emory University also dedicated its 1947 yearbook to him with the statement that "he represents those qualities which an alma mater seeks to develop in every student: a combination of keen intelligence, effective leadership and breadth of culture."

Robert's venture into business was delayed. Charles A. Wickersham, who was president of the Atlanta and West Point Rail Road and who had introduced Robert to Buffalo Bill Cody, was a close friend of the Woodruff family. He loaned them his private railroad car for a vacation trip into the West. One of the stops was Yellowstone Park. In those days visitors to Old Faithful and other park sights made the all-day trip from the nearest railroad into the park by stagecoach.

Woodruff never forgot that trip. Even then his young mind was looking over the hill, behind the hill and into the valley beyond. Whether or not he enjoyed the picturesque stagecoach, he doesn't remember. What impressed him was the long slow ride into and then out of the park. This remained very much in his memory and years later, when he was associated with White Motor Company, he tried to sell buses to the company operating the stage and inn in Yellowstone Park. They wouldn't listen. With the slower stagecoach, the guests had to spend a night at the inn. This was money in the pockets of the concessionaires.

So Woodruff took his case before the park commission in Washington and there sold his buses for transportation to and from the national park.

Robert's keen sense of humor was developing even in those days. One picture of the Yellowstone trip imprinted on his memory concerned his Aunt Mamie and her husband, George Walters, who were along. "Mr. Walters," Woodruff said, "always had a special penchant for saying the wrong thing. On our way into the park, he suddenly exclaimed, 'Look at that pretty doe deer!' All eyes turned just as the animal squatted to relieve a call of nature."

In February, 1909, after his father had long since despaired of his son acquiring a college education, Robert entered the business world by getting a job with the General Pipe and Foundry Company. He says one reason he took this job was that it was only five or six blocks from home and he could walk to work. He was too proud and self-reliant to ask his family for carfare. He was determined to make it on his own. His salary was sixty cents a day, less than half his allowance when he was a student at Emory.

His position with Pipe and Foundry was apprentice machinist. The first job given him was shoveling and sifting sand. He was kept at this for about a week, probably to test his staying powers. Then he began to get his training on a lathe and other machine tools.

He stayed with this job for about a year, and then was given an assignment with General Fire Extinguisher Company as an assistant stock clerk.

This was more a matter of promotion, since General Pipe and Foundry was a branch of General Fire Extinguisher. His superiors recognized in young Woodruff that he was capable of greater achievement than shoveling sand and working on a lathe.

His next step upward was another promotion from assistant stock clerk to salesman for General Fire Extinguisher. A charming story that is typically Woodruff was told of this transition by biographer E. J. Kahn, Jr.

The first day he reported for work on his new job, Robert drove up in a seven-passenger Stephens-Duryea automobile. Kahn says that Joseph M. Tull, "his immediate superior, who had no automobile at all, was enormously impressed. The good rich life was evidently beginning to appeal to prudent Ernest Woodruff's oldest son. Tull also recalled later on that, while Ernest was having his ascetic mid-day snack at the luncheonette in the Trust Company building, the young fire extinguisher salesman and his new boss would repair to the M&M Club atop the Candler building for a two hours' repast built around broiled guinea hen."

Ernest's ultimate wish for his oldest son was that Robert should follow in his footsteps as a banker, and after watching him operate successfully as a salesman with General Fire Extinguisher, gave him a job as purchasing agent for his reorganized and growing Atlantic Ice and Coal Company, at a salary of eighteen hundred dollars a year.

With his developing facets of salesmanship, the instinct to meet issues squarely, honestly and unafraid, his slight touch of flair for the dramatic and his uncanny power of seeing into the future, young Woodruff brought new conceptions and ideas to Atlantic Ice and Coal. One move that he made as purchasing agent had much to do with changing the course of his life.

One of his jobs was to buy all mules, wagons and other equipment used in hauling ice and coal to the customers. The company, its owners and managers were satisfied to do things the old fashioned way. In this respect, even his father showed a lack of long range vision. The company was making a profit, so why change? Robert did not have this limited point of view, even as a youngster just starting out in business. He wasn't satisfied with the short-sighted thinking that even with the expanding population in a growing city, all they would ever need was a horse and wagon to deliver their goods. Trucks were faster and a more economical way to deliver ice and coal. As he did all of his life, he gave this a lot of thought, and possibly, as he has always done, talked it over with a number of people whose opinions he valued. He neglected, perhaps purposely, to discuss it with his father.

He definitely made up his mind to go along with the truck purchase after attending an automobile show in New York. He went to Walter White, president of White Motor Company. Both he and White belonged to Norias Shooting Club.

"I couldn't afford to be a member at Norias," Woodruff said. "It strained me financially, but some mighty important men of the day belonged to the club, and I knew my association with them wouldn't hurt."

Woodruff sold Walter White on the proposal that it would be vastly to the advantage of the White Motor Company to exhibit a fleet of trucks that had replaced an outmoded delivery system for an Atlanta business concern. There was the added possibility that Atlantic Ice and Coal might eventually equip all of its branches with White trucks, after its purchasing department had proved what a saving in time and labor they would be for the company. He would also see that word got around to other businesses in the area as to the efficiency of motorized equipment over the old style way of doing things.

Reports are that Woodruff bought a fleet of fifteen White trucks at — or close to — manufacturing costs.

The story is that when Ernest got the news of his son's wild extravagance, he almost collapsed. In those days, autos were scarce and trucks were scarcer. No one trusted the new gasoline monsters too far, and buying more than one at a time was unheard of. But the sale stood and Atlantic Ice and Coal developed into a much more efficient operation, with a real saving in delivery services.

When Woodruff was at Atlantic Ice and Coal, William Hartsfield was his part-time stenographer. Hartsfield was studying law and when he left Atlantic he opened a law office. Later, in 1922, he got into politics as city alderman and still later served as mayor of Atlanta for several terms.

Woodruff was his right hand consultant through those years when Bill Hartsfield was at the helm of big city government. The Mayor made few decisions without consulting his old boss at Atlantic Ice and Coal.

It is often said that Atlanta had two mayors through the terms of Hartsfield and Ivan Allen, Jr. The other was Woodruff. Both of these mayors would have been the first to admit it.

This early association with Hartsfield was the beginning of a friendship which was to prove very productive for the City of Atlanta. Ivan Allen, Jr., came along later through a very troublesome period for Atlanta, and at that time he worked closely with Woodruff through this period of stress for their city.

The same year Woodruff went with Atlantic, he married Nell Kendall Hodgson of Athens. The Hodgsons were an old, wealthy and socially prominent family in Athens, and some reports have it that they were rather concerned that their beautiful daughter was marrying a young upstart from Atlanta, who had no college education and whose sole means of support for their daughter was his inadequate salary as purchasing agent for a company that delivered ice and coal.

When Robert Woodruff and Nell Hodgson were married, they were given a wedding present of one thousand dollars by his father. Instead of depositing it in Ernest's Trust Company Bank, Robert opened an account with the Chase National Bank in New York. He was still looking far into the future. This was the beginning of a long and fruitful association with Albert Wiggin, who later was prominent in affairs of the U. S. government.

Mr. Baker, manager of the Ice and Coal Company and Robert's boss, had told him that after he was married, the company would raise his salary from one hundred fifty dollars to two hundred fifty dollars a month so that he could adequately support his new wife.

When, after two months, he didn't get the promised raise, he went to Mr. Baker and asked why.

"The board of directors," his boss said, "objected to giving you the raise."

"You mean my father vetoed it?"

"Yes," Baker said, forthrightly.

"You may tell him," Robert said, "and I will too, that I'll love him the rest of my life. I'll associate with him as a companion and a friend. I'll do anything I can for him, except one. I'll never do another lick of business with him as long as I live."

Woodruff went to Walter White.

"I've been fired," he said. He told his friend the story of his promised raise in salary.

Later Walter White commented, "I thought I had a sucker when I got hold of the youngster and started selling him trucks. I ended up with a deal in which my profit would not have bought the shirt I almost lost."

To Woodruff, at the time, he said, "If you can sell half as good as you can buy, you've got a job at the salary you want."

He put Robert on as a salesman with the southeastern department of White Motor Company with headquarters in Atlanta, at a salary of two hundred fifty dollars a month.

Ernest still had hopes that his son would follow in his banking footsteps. He thought that by getting into the automobile business Robert was down-grading himself both socially and financially.

"You are making a terrible mistake," the elder Woodruff said. "That is not the type of job you should have. Why can't you get into some more worthy business?"

"He never approved of anything I did," Woodruff said later.

To his father, at the time, he replied, "I don't know of any truck or oil people in trouble. I know at least a dozen bankers in the federal pen."

This probably didn't improve relations too greatly between father and son.

As a salesman with White, Woodruff made his mark. He not only placed trucks with many Atlanta companies, but went out into the counties, met with county commissioners and persuaded them that they could do a better job on the roads with mechanized equipment. Most of Georgia's roads were dirt and most were kept graded and passable with scrapes and other machinery drawn by mules or teams of mules. Much more was done by hand.

Apparently he was very persuasive and his presentation of the economics involved was sound. He showed where the use of trucks and other mechanized gear was not only less expensive in the long run, but would keep the roads more passable, which was also good politics.

White trucks became a familiar sight on Georgia roads.

He quickly developed into Walter White's top salesman, and within three years was made manager of the company's southeastern department.

Walter White must have congratulated himself many times on his choice of this company employee. Perhaps he was a little appalled, too.

"What's the secret of your salesmanship?" he once asked Robert.

Woodruff gave him only part of the answer. It is probable that at the time even he did not realize the combination of abilities which were being welded into a powerful personality. Being a very humble individual, the odds are big that he has never thought of himself in this light.

"I don't waste any time," he said, "with the wrong fellows. The most important time any man just starting out as a salesman can spend is getting to know the right people. Then you have got to genuinely like them. But it must be genuine. Sham stands out like a red light."

Woodruff learned too that he must be extremely tough at times.

When he was made manager of the southeastern department, Cecil B. Cowan, an Alabama boy, was working with White Motor in the Montgomery branch office. He was a good salesman. Woodruff needed someone of his capability in the Birmingham office and selected Cowan to take the job.

"I don't want to move up there," was the reply. "I like it here."

"Well, you can stay there, then," Woodruff said, "but there's no need for you to report to your office in the morning."

"What does that mean?" Cowan asked.

"If it means what you think it does," Woodruff said, "you'd better start looking for another job."

It was stated as a simple fact. There was nothing harsh or brusque about it. Cowan got the message.

Cecil Cowan got his nickname "Abie" by an amusing incident. He was in a hotel along with a group of fellow salesmen, when a drunk, obviously of the Jewish faith, stumbled across the lobby, threw his arms around the startled Cowan, and shouted, "Al-lo, A-bie! A-bie!" For the rest of his life,

Cecil Cowan, an unmistakable Irishman, was called by all those who knew him even slightly, "Abie."

After he'd served a time in the Birmingham office, Abie was moved to the main southeastern office in Atlanta, where he remained until his retirement as vice president with White Motor. Woodruff went on to bigger things, but the two men became close and usually inseparable friends at work and at play for the remainder of Abie's life. Brilliantly witty, he was always the court jester.

Woodruff imparted a lot of his ideas to his staff of salesmen. Although he seldom had to "crack the whip" to get results, his salesmen simply worked their hearts out for him. This was their way of responding to the inspiration and loyalty he gave to them. It was something he would carry through all of his business career. That strange mixture of character ingredients somehow made the men under him and associated with him always anxious to please the "Boss." It went deeper than his personal charm, than his forthrightness, his courage in any situation. He had a deep and sincere affection and interest in people and this was reflected in how they felt toward him.

There was mutual affection between Woodruff and his staff of White salesmen. As his employees and associates have done throughout his business life, they worked their hearts out under his leadership and even though Woodruff was devoting much of his time to the war effort in 1917, his southeastern section won White's efficiency trophy for the highest percentage of increase in annual sales. From the collective salesmen in the company's southeastern section he received this pledge:

"We renew our pledges of loyalty in thought and action to the man who matches every ounce of loyalty with a pound of appreciation; every foot of initiative with a yard of cooperation, and every pint of Pep with a gallon of Tabasco, and every manpower of push with one hundred horsepower of pull—that's Bob Woodruff, the good pal of our play and the leader of our work, to whom we are bound by a chain that may lengthen but can never break."

With sincere appreciation, plus a touch of the dramatic that he always seemed to have at just the right time, Woodruff acknowledged the tribute with a solid gold medal to each salesman. It was made from a special die that read, "Woodruff gives credit to his men."

Nine of the salesmen in his group went on to become branch managers.

He not only worked with them as a group, but as individuals, ironing out the spots they found rough.

"Don't try to sell trucks to an entire county commission," he once told Abie Cowan. "This makes too many people who try to find something wrong with your presentation or your product. Cultivate the commission chairman and work with him. The other commissioners will go along with what he decides."

World War I came along. Woodruff, whose patriotism helped to dictate many of his life's policies, offered his services as a private citizen. These were readily accepted. Because of his background with White Motor and his comprehensive knowledge of trucks and heavy mechanized equipment, he was appropriately assigned to the Ordnance Department, where one of his first important jobs was to help recruit and train nine hundred chauffeurs and mechanics for the Quartermaster Enlisted Reserve Corps. Some of these men were trained by the White Motor Company mechanics in Atlanta.

He went from this training chore to the production of heavy equipment for army use. Calling the top engineers of White, Packard and Pierce Arrow companies together, he and Colonel Hugh J. Gallagher helped to develop a two-ton, thirty-five horsepower troop transport, with plenty of clearance to allow it to get through swamps, mud and water. To facilitate manufacture, orders were placed with the three companies involved and before the war was over, between seventy-five and one hundred of these had been put into use. In the days before assembly lines as we know them now, this was a remarkable record of production.

Probably Woodruff's powers of persuasion, as well as his long hours on the job, had much to do with this contribution to the war effort. Alvan Macauley, president of Packard Motor Company and president of the Automobile Manufacturers Association, got an apartment in his club in Detroit for Woodruff, who spent much of his time commuting between Atlanta, Cleveland and Detroit to get this job done.

One interesting record of this troop transport development was the trial run made by one of the first of these transports between Fort McPherson in Atlanta and Fort Oglethorpe just south of Chattanooga. Lurching over the old Dixie Highway through mudholes and over rocks and ruts, with seventeen soldiers crowded in the back, the truck made a record run of one hundred thirty-two miles in five and one-half hours. The soldiers arrived, a little dizzy perhaps, but with their equipment intact and ready to fight. Other trucks and an army car carrying Woodruff that followed the transport were two and one-half hours or more behind the record run. The army was elated at the new means of fast maneuverability of its troops and equipment.

On January 10, 1918, Woodruff was commissioned as a captain in the Ordnance Section, Army Reserve Corps. He resigned from White Motor Company, put on a khaki uniform and he and "Miss" Nell, his wife, moved into the Rochambeau Apartments in Washington. Mrs. Woodruff immediately enlisted in Red Cross work and served out the war as a Red Cross nurse.

Much of the first part of his official army career Woodruff spent in Detroit, where he helped design an armored staff observation car for the army. Then he was moved permanently to Washington and nine months later promoted to major and executive assistant in the motor equipment division of the Ordnance Department. He was in this job for a month before the armistice was signed on November 11 and remained in Washington until January 14, 1919, when he was honorably discharged from the army.

To pursue this brief chronology further, two months after his discharge from the army, Woodruff went back with the White Motor Company as manager of the southeastern section. From that point, his rise with White was rapid. He went to Cleveland in August, 1921, as vice president of White Motor Company, the next year he was made first vice president and put on the board of directors, and in January, 1923, was given the title, vice president in charge of distribution and chairman of the sales committee, White Motor Company.

Possibly his first transaction with The Coca-Cola Company was during this period. In 1921 he sold the company thirty trucks worth one hundred thousand dollars to service the growing number of stores and businesses that distributed Coca-Cola.

In those years with White, he became enamored of Coca-Cola stock and put as much money as he could borrow into buying it. Possibly with his perception to see over the far hill and into the hidden valley beyond, he saw Coca-Cola as a wise investment. Other reasons could have been that he was a patriot at heart and this was a home-grown enterprise, or that he had great respect for Asa Candler, its former owner, who had been his Sunday school teacher. It is certain that he read the glowing financial reports of The Coca-Cola Company. He may have foreseen that some day he might be involved with the company, with their purchase of trucks he visualized as farsighted enough to change their methods of transportation and operation from the old fashioned to the modern.

When Woodruff first went to Cleveland as a vice president of the White Motor Company, he spent his weekends with Walter White at Gates Mills, White's country estate, outside Cleveland. Apparently this was one of the few less satisfactory periods of his life. He doesn't say that exactly, but never talks about it with the same fervor and enthusiasm with which he tells some of his other experiences. He and White were very close friends, as well as business associates. Walter was also an avid outdoorsman and, like Woodruff, had a deep affection for horses and bird dogs. He belonged to the Chagrin Valley Hunt Club, near Cleveland, and one of his hobbies was riding to the hounds; another was polo. These smacked too much of social events for Woodruff, who was a lover of horses and horseback riding, but in more rustic settings and for a better purpose, such as quail hunting.

With much relish Woodruff tells of one experience at Gates Mills. One afternoon White was showing a guest over the estate. Woodruff was along. They stopped by the stables to look over the horses.

"These are fine looking animals," the visitor observed. "How many horses do you own, Mr. White?"

"Well," Walter said, "I don't know exactly."

The groom spoke up. "You've got twenty-nine," he said, "and a couple of colts are on the way."

White nodded and said nothing more about horses until the next morning, when he and Woodruff were ready to depart for their offices in nearby Cleveland.

"I've got to run by the stables for a minute," White said.

"At this time of day?" Woodruff asked.

"I'm gonna fire that sonofabitch," White said. "He knows too much."

That story is well known around Ichauway Plantation. You'll never know how many horses or dogs the Boss keeps there unless he himself tells you.

Both before and after the creation of Ichauway, Woodruff kept horses at his home in Atlanta. He and Miss Nell often rode together, alone or with friends. Horses had had an appeal for him since his pony days, when he boarded his gelding in Mr. Candler's stable. He and Nell went through one period when they competed in and supported horse shows. In 1929 Woodruff was named a director and chairman of the executive committee of the Atlanta Horse Show Association, and in both 1929 and 1930 he served as a director in the National Horse Show Association, but was never deeply engrossed in these events. His idea was that at least sometimes, picking winners was in one way or another biased, or socially or politically motivated, and to have a champion lose out for such a reason went against his grain. Neither did the social aspects appeal to him, and this may have been one of the reasons he was not attracted to fox hunting or to polo when he lived in Cleveland.

His job was to sell cars, trucks and units of heavy machinery, and he and his organization found customers for the products almost as fast as White could turn them out. Under his leadership his forces developed into an organization of super-salesmen who worked more to please him than they worked for their profits. Walter White admitted that many times he stood in awe of his vice president's ability. Their admiration and respect were mutual.

"Walter," Woodruff told me once, "was a tremendous fellow by every measurement. He was a sound businessman and hard-boiled about that. Outside business he was often too softhearted. He was a sort of shy and timid fellow and I doubt that he would ever have made a good salesman.

He was also too modest to be a good public relations man. But he knew his organization and how to make it tick.

"At his death, the tribute from his company described him as a broad shouldered man who carried youth in his eyes and courage in his heart. I know that was right. He was charming and took an interest in everybody and in everything that went on around him."

Woodruff maintained his home in Atlanta, but as first vice president in charge of sales, he kept an apartment in Cleveland, close to the home office, and one in New York, where he knew some of his best sales might originate. Woodruff walked in where even his boss had been hesitant to trod. He didn't mind knocking on the biggest doors. He went to see Walter Teagle, president of the Standard Oil Company of New Jersey, that carried on its business with Ford trucks.

After they had exchanged pleasantries, Woodruff said, "Mr. Teagle, you and Walter White are good friends. Why don't you use his trucks?"

"Nobody ever asked me," Teagle replied.

"We've run surveys," Woodruff said, "and find that the cost of operating a number of other trucks, Ford among them, is much higher than for the White. Do you know what your operating costs are?"

"We'll find out," Teagle said.

He rang for his purchasing agent, and while he was on the way, Teagle asked, "What were some of your sources of information in comparing costs?"

"Gulf Oil was one," Woodruff said. "You can check my figures with them."

Teagle seemed surprised to find how much more his company was spending for truck operation than Gulf.

"Why didn't you check on this?" he asked his employee.

The man turned a shade of red. "Well - why - un -" he stammered.

"Before you make another purchase of trucks," Teagle said to the employee, "check with me."

After this, another big sale was to the Southern Express Company.

"They bought one hundred trucks," he chuckled, "at regular prices. No discount."

For his age, and in those years when economic values were different and taxes less outrageous, Woodruff drew a fabulous salary and commission. What he did not need for the rather bountiful life that he and Miss Nell lived, he put into stocks of companies he envisioned with a future. Coca-Cola was one. In addition, he borrowed as heavily as the banks would let him.

Mr. Woodruff told one story about a note he had signed at the Guaranty Trust Company in New York. He continued to pay interest as it came due, but was unable to take up slack in any of the principal. Once when it came due, he had a memo from one of the bank's officers, telling him to come around and take up his note.

A bit panic-stricken at the thought of having to raise enough capital at a loss to pay off the note, he went directly to the office of William C. Potter, president of Guaranty Trust.

"You know my financial situation," he told Potter, "and that with the way the market is, I'd be flat busted if I paid this off. That is, if I could cash in that much money at all."

Bill Potter reached for the telephone.

"Let's see why our vice president wants this paid off," he said.

The officer came in and Woodruff explained his financial situation. The vice president looked at Mr. Potter.

"Hell," he said, "I didn't want him to pay it. I just wanted him to sign another one. This one's been here so long, we've about worn it out."

In those four years with White, Woodruff was a busy man, traveling between headquarters, branch offices and factory. He spent much time in the top management headquarters in New York. This was in a rundown shop in Queens, just beyond the bridge. He didn't think either the building or its location was imposing enough to represent a company such as White Motor, so he moved his offices to the end of Wall Street and later to the Chase National Bank.

On September 12, 1919, Ernest Woodruff and a syndicate he had organized for that purpose purchased The Coca-Cola Company from the Candlers and other stockholders for twenty-five million dollars.

As its first president, the directors of the newly acquired organization elected Samuel C. Dobbs, a nephew of Asa Candler, who had gotten his start in Coca-Cola by hauling the total assets of the company, which consisted of kettle, paddle, percolator for treating the ingredients, and other supplies, from Marietta Street where the syrup was made to Mr. Candler's store at 47 Peachtree Street.

But The Coca-Cola Company in which Woodruff had invested a good deal of his money was soon in serious financial trouble. Although it had made six and a quarter million dollars in 1922, this wasn't enough to pay operating costs and interest on the money they had borrowed. The future looked even more bleak.

This was generally the state of affairs when the board of directors offered Woodruff the job as president.

Wherever you go you will find

Coca-Cola 5¢

AT ALL FOUNTAINS

to refresh the parched throat, to invigorate
the fatigued body, and quicken the tired brain

ASA GRIGGS CANDLER

Chapter 3
Coca-Cola Before Woodruff

Coca-Cola was an infant of some three years when Robert W. Woodruff was born. As a nation we were little more than a century old. We were near the end of the reconstruction period that followed the bitter Civil War, but still skirmishing with the Indians in the Southwest. The horse and buggy era was at its height and we were a few years away from the horseless carriage and many years away from transportation that would send us winging along the pathways of the heavens.

Coca-Cola didn't burst upon the American scene in a shower of stars. Its birth was an obscure event, unheralded by headlines, known at first to only a select few. One of these was John Styth Pemberton, a local pharmacist who, during the Civil War, had served in the calvary under General Joe Wheeler. Pemberton had moved to Atlanta in 1869.

"Doc" Pemberton set up a laboratory and devoted his last score of years to the creation and promotion of medicines for a score of human ills, as well as other pharmaceutical products. Among some of his best known products of the day were Globe Flower Cough Syrup; Pemberton's Concentrated Extract of Stillingia, a blood medicine; Gingerine, "a prohibition drink"; Indian Queen Hair Dye; Triplex Liver Pills; and Pemberton's French Wine Coca—Ideal Nerve and Tonic Stimulant.

This was the era when soda fountains were becoming popular. The four in Atlanta were well patronized, and Doc Pemberton envisioned the creation of a new drink that would corner the soda fountain market. In the back of his mind was a beverage to sell by the glassful instead of by the bottle, which would be tasty and refreshing.

The nearest one of his manufactured products to this formula was his French Wine Coca which had sold for one dollar a bottle in the drug stores. Pemberton modified this by taking out the wine and adding a pinch of caffeine. This left the taste with something to be desired, so he added an extract from the cola nut and a few other oils, with enough sugar until the product suited his taste buds.

One of the pharmacies with whom he had done a large part of his business was Venables, located on Norcross Corner, which later became known as "Five Points" and was for a long time the hub of the city. Pemberton walked the short distance between his office and laboratory at 107 Marietta Street to tell Joe Jacobs and Willis Venable about his new product.

"I created it especially for soda founts," he said. "Instead of selling by the bottle, we should put it on the market by the drink, at five cents a glass."

"What do you call it?" Venable asked.

"My bookkeeper, Frank M. Robinson, named it," he said. "In his precise handwriting he wrote out the name—Coca-Cola."

They put up the sign and to identify the new product added the word "Drink" above it. Neither the name nor flowing script in Frank Robinson's handwriting has ever been changed.

Pemberton advertised his new mixture as "delicious" and "refreshing," the first use of these words describing Coca-Cola.

The story is told that one morning, a busy soda clerk, to save himself a few steps to the fresh water tap, thinned the syrup with a bottle of charged water closer at hand. It was so different that word spread and soon most of the customers were asking for a Coca-Cola made with charged water. This was the birth of the product as we know it today.

Pemberton, who continued to manufacture syrup in a three-legged iron pot, stirring it with a boat paddle, sold only twenty-five gallons that first year, but more soda fountains were springing up around the city and the prospects were never in doubt to the man who originated the drink. The next year he was granted a registration by the U. S. Patent Office as "sole proprietor" for "Coca-Cola syrup and extract." This was the first trade-marked beverage in the soda fountain field.

There is no way of knowing how far Coca-Cola might have gone under Pemberton, but that year his health failed. From his sick bed, he called a friend, George S. Lowndes, and offered to sell him the business. Lowndes told Pemberton he had too many other business interests, but he did take time out to check with Willis Venable, a clerk in Jacobs' Drug Store. Venable was said to be the last word on anything connected with soda water and soda fountains in Atlanta, having been in the business since 1867. According to Hunter Bell, one of the historians of The Coca-Cola Company, Lowndes asked Venable what he thought of Coca-Cola.

"I've never seen anything like it," Venable replied. "I'm selling more Coca-Cola than any other drink I handle."

"Would you like to own the entire Coca-Cola business?" Lowndes asked.

"More than anything I know," Venable said.

Pemberton sold two-thirds interest in Coca-Cola to Lowndes and Venable for twelve hundred dollars, plus two hundred eighty-three dollars and twenty-nine cents for his Coca-Cola equipment and supplies, which were moved to the basement of Venable's store. With these went the formula for the drink.

At this stage Coca-Cola did not get off the ground. Venable kept the apparatus and ingredients stored in his basement because "it would take more money than I had to put the new drink on the market." Lowndes tried to sell his share in Coca-Cola to other Atlanta druggists, but they saw no future for the drink. It was finally taken off his hands by Woolfork Walker and his sister, Mrs. M. C. Dozier, and the meager equipment moved back to 107 Marietta Street where Walker, who was an old friend of Pemberton's, manufactured the syrup.

On April 14, 1888, four months before Dr. Pemberton died, he and his son Charles signed a document releasing all claims in Coca-Cola to Walker, Candler and Company, a partnership that included Woolfork Walker, Asa G. Candler, Sr. and Joe Jacobs, owner of Jacobs' Drug Store. For this release, Pemberton and his son were paid the sum of five hundred fifty dollars.

It was said that Asa Candler came to Atlanta from Cartersville in 1873 with a dollar and seventy-five cents in his pocket. He went to work for druggist George Jefferson Howard and five years later married Lucy Elizabeth Howard, much against her father's wishes. In another five years Candler and his father-in-law became reconciled and opened the retail drug firm of Howard and Candler. In 1886 Asa Candler bought out Howard's interest and changed the firm's name to Asa G. Candler and Company.

Frank Robinson, who had left Pemberton when its originator sold two-thirds interest in his rights, had gone to work for Candler, who put him to manufacturing the syrup—first at 107 Marietta Street, then in Candler's store at 47 Peachtree Street, to which the kettle, paddle and percolators for treating the ingredients, and other supplies, were moved.

In August of that year, Asa Candler paid one thousand dollars to Walker and Mrs. Dozier for their interest in the drink and became sole owner of Coca-Cola. He was involved in the promotion of a number of patent medicines in which he was at first more interested, but with increased sales, his interest in Coca-Cola developed and he began to advertise his new drink. To the words "Delicious" and "Refreshing" he added "Exhilarating" and "Invigorating."

For twenty-three hundred dollars Asa Candler had purchased a product that less than two decades later his children sold for twenty-five million dollars.

In 1892, Candler moved the Coca-Cola manufacturing operation from his drug store on Peachtree Street to a new address at 42½ Decatur Street, incorporated it as The Coca-Cola Company and launched an extensive program of sales and advertising that expanded his drink from a local to a nationwide product by 1895.

Asa Candler was a promoter as well as a sound businessman. As John Pemberton had done before him, his company issued tickets good for one free glass of Coca-Cola at any soda fountain throughout the United States. In all sections of the country, Coca-Cola representatives visited colleges and schools having teen-age students and made a liberal distribution of tickets, blotters, pencils, calendars and other favors advertising Coca-Cola. By 1905, the number of free drink tickets turned in by the soda fountains and redeemed by the company had passed the eight hundred fifty-five thousand mark.

Candler, ever conservative almost to the point of being a tightwad, estimated that by 1905 the redemption of tickets was costing the company forty thousand dollars annually. This was too much money and he called for a drastic reduction in the number of free tickets being passed out.

This, according to Frank Robinson, cost the company the sale of sixty thousand gallons of Coca-Cola syrup during the last half of 1906, and he strongly urged a renewal of the free drink ticket policy. His recommendation was followed. Thousands of tickets were mailed out to lists furnished by the soda fountain operators, with other advertising material and a special bonus for the fountain operators. The next year, 1908, was a banner year for the company.

Tickets were distributed through 1931, and a quarter of a century later an occasional ticket was finding its way into the Atlanta office for redemption.

It was a good policy followed by the company since the early days. Fifty years later tickets were again used to introduce new drinks as "Sprite," "Tab" and "Fresca," made by The Coca-Cola Company.

It is generally considered that the Coca-Cola bottle originated in 1899 with Benjamin F. Thomas and Joseph Brown Whitehead, two young Chattanooga lawyers. But the practice of putting "ready-to-drink" Coca-Cola in bottles for home consumption was started five years before that in 1894 by Joseph A. Biedenharn, who managed Biedenharn Candy Company, a confectionery and wholesale grocery firm in Vicksburg, Mississippi.

Joseph Biedenharn, the oldest of seven sons, was twenty-eight years old at the time and considered by his brothers the best salesman, always "full of ideas it took to sell goods."

Among the merchandise distributed by the Biedenharns were several brands of soda water bottled by two small Vicksburg plants and popular for parties and picnics. Among their customers were a number of nearby plantations to whom they delivered orders of soda water, along with their shipments of candies, bakery products and groceries.

According to Coca-Cola historian Hunter Bell, "A day came when the Biedenharns had orders from three different plantations for soda water—ten cases for each customer. But when Joe Biedenharn got in touch with the bottling plant that had been supplying him, the owner said he didn't have enough goods even for his own customers. The other plants were too small to help him."

His irritation with the lack of cooperation from the bottlers and his inability to fill the orders led Joe and his brothers to install a used bottling machine and a carbonator in the rear of the store and to purchase enough second-hand bottles to serve their customers. For their washing equipment they sawed a fifty-gallon Coca-Cola syrup barrel in half—one for the washing unit and one for rinsing the bottles. One of the early problems was that few of the bottles, which required no deposit, were returned.

Herman Biedenharn was in charge of the bottling operation. Joe suggested that they put in some Coca-Cola syrup with the carbonated water, and bottled Coca-Cola became a reality.

The sons remembered that H. H. Biedenharn had once told them "everybody has a nickel," so they established a price of five cents—same as that at the soda fountain—and there it remained until the early 1950's.

The first container used was the "Hutchinson" bottle with a permanent rubber stopper inside the bottle. The stopper was topped by a wire loop used to pull this sealer into place. The drink inside was made available by hitting the loop with the hand to drive the stopper down into the bottle. This made a loud "pop," with the result that all carbonated beverages in bottles became known as "soda pop."

Later the metal crown made its appearance, greatly adding to the ease of washing the returned bottles and cleanliness of the drink.

For ease of distribution, the Biedenharns developed two crates—one which held two dozen bottles for local distribution and the other six dozen for shipping up and down the river. The two-dozen crate was much the same as that used three quarters of a century later.

With the sale of his Coca-Cola syrup going so well in the Mississippi Valley, Asa Candler paid several visits to Joe Biedenharn and had gone with him to call on some of his soda fount customers. When the Biedenharns put bottled Coca-Cola on the market, Joe shipped a couple of cases to Candler in Atlanta. The only comment from the owner of the syrup company was that the bottled product was "fine," but at the time he did not pursue it further, possibly because he considered that the foundation of his business would always be through soda fountain sales on which he had concentrated since he became sole owner of the company.

Apparently Candler was unimpressed with the bottling process. He paid scant heed when E. R. Barber, who operated the Valdosta Bottling

Works, put Coca-Cola on the market in bottles in 1897, or in 1899 when Thomas and Whitehead came down from Chattanooga to obtain a bottling contract for his product. One story is that they paid five dollars for the contract, another that they agreed on one dollar which was never collected. There is no record of any amount having been paid. The only territories held out of the bottling contract with Thomas and Whitehead were Texas, where negotiations were underway for a franchise in that state; New England, where Candler had a twenty-year sales contract with Seth Fowle; and the state of Mississippi, which went to the Biedenharns.

The two Chattanooga lawyers chartered their new venture "The Coca-Cola Bottling Company." Joe Whitehead, lacking capital for machinery to equip the plant and put their product on the market, sold half of his interest to J. T. Lupton for twenty-five hundred dollars, and that same year a bottling plant was opened in Chattanooga under the management of Ben Thomas.

Because Mr. Candler's agreement called for the establishment of a bottling plant in Atlanta, the next year the partners expanded their venture to Atlanta and opened a plant at Edgewood Avenue and Courtland Street.

That year also, the basis of the future Coca-Cola industry was established when the partners, lacking the money to finance two plants in the beginning, decided to take in local capital by issuing franchises to bottlers of soda water and other beverages and persuading them to include Coca-Cola in their merchandise. A stipulation in the agreement specified that they would purchase Coca-Cola syrup from the Chattanooga company at a slightly higher price than the partners had to pay for the syrup in Atlanta.

The partners divided the United States between them, with Thomas taking the Chattanooga plant and all the "northern" territory, and Whitehead and Lupton getting Atlanta and the southern business.

In those early days, it was easier to sell a glass or bottle of Coca-Cola than it was to find bottlers and others willing to put it into their line of merchandise. The original partners worked at it assiduously, but soon found that running one bottling plant while promoting others was a two-man job. In Atlanta, Joe Whitehead became intrigued with the ability and personality of a young express agent, Arthur Montgomery, who made regular visits to the bottling plant to pick up cases of Coca-Cola for shipment by rail to surrounding towns. Montgomery left his express job and moved over to the Coca-Cola bottling plant. Part of his stipulation in the contract on his new job was one-third interest that included not only the city of Atlanta, but some fifty or sixty miles of territory around the city.

In Chattanooga Ben Thomas also discovered that running one plant and promoting others required more time than the clock could give him. Instead of taking on a manager, he sold his Coca-Cola Bottling Works of Chattanooga to a couple of friends, James F. Johnston and William H. Hardin, so that he could devote his full time to the creation of new bottling plants to handle the syrup. These came under all types of contracts to suit the finances and convenience of those taking such a franchise. Some were awarded one-fourth interest in a bottling plant, along with the contract; some were sold for cash; some given outright where a man had the money and enthusiasm for the product.

Before the new year of 1902, a total of seven bottling plants were in existence in the United States; by 1909, three hundred seventy-seven.

All equipment and processes for making Coca-Cola developed slowly. From the iron pot and paddle days of making syrup in Pemberton's back yard to the crude bottling apparatus of the Biendenharns, the equipment became more modern and sanitary, and by 1909 a well-organized plant could turn out as many as five to six hundred cases a day. Now with high-speed machinery and modern techniques the modern bottling plant can produce as many as several thousand bottles a minute.

As with any new enterprise, the company went through its own special growing pains. It was natural that a product so popular should be imitated. There was no way to identify it when it lay with other bottles of carbonated drinks of the same color in a tub of ice, some of which were often sold as Coca-Cola. Even though the bottlers affixed paper labels to their drinks, these softened and came off in a tub of ice water, from which most drinks were sold commercially in those days. The story is that one unscrupulous bottler of other soda drinks purchased Coca-Cola syrup at soda fountains and made his own Coca-Cola of an inferior quality, without benefit of contract. Others were marketing a similar product from syrup not supplied by The Coca-Cola Company. In 1916 there were said to be no less than one hundred fifty-three imitations of Coca-Cola. Against one of these—J. G. Butler and Sons—the company entered suit to protect its patents and distribution plan and received a court decision upholding its rights and system.

This was the same year that the distinctive Coca-Cola bottle appeared. Its objective was to get away from the other round drink bottles, all so much alike. Alex Samuelson, who worked for the Root Glass Company in Terre Haute, Indiana, had been trained as a glass blower in Germany. He conceived the idea of a bottle built somewhat like a cocoa bean. This he perfected, but the bulge was so large that the bottle could not be properly handled by the equipment in the bottling plants. So he trimmed it down and it was patented in his name. The new bottle was adopted by a committee of bottlers six to one, and became an instant success with both the plant managers and public. It has been in use since that date and is a recognized shape throughout the world. The bottle itself is registered as a trademark, one of only a half-dozen containers to be accorded this distinction.

In 1916 and the years following, other things were happening which were to affect the future of The Coca-Cola Company.

In 1916, Asa Candler stepped down from managing The Coca-Cola Company, so that he could devote himself to real estate and politics. He remained a director in his company and put in his son Howard as president.

In 1917 Candler was elected mayor of the city of Atlanta. At Christmas that year he equally divided all but seven shares of his stock between his wife and five children. They immediately began looking for a buyer and the next year put the company up for sale.

In September, 1919, almost a year after the end of World War I, the Candlers were able to dispose of their stock. The buyer was a syndicate headed by Ernest Woodruff, Robert's father, whose forte through the years had been organizing and consolidating small companies into large, profitable corporations.

The sale was said to be the largest financial transaction that had ever taken place in the South, and Asa Candler, Sr., who owned only seven shares of stock, was not even consulted. The sale price, fifteen million dollars in cash and ten million dollars in preferred stock, was more than ten thousand times the amount of money Candler had spent to purchase the entire Coca-Cola operation some thirty years before.

The news of the sale so upset Asa Candler that he would not even attend the board of directors meeting at which the sale was approved. With the company turning a profit of five million dollars a year before taxes, he considered that selling was poor business, as indeed it ultimately proved to be. But later he was magnanimous enough to say of the transaction and his family, "When I gave them the business, it was theirs. They sold out a big share for a fancy price. I wouldn't have done that, but they did, and from a sale standpoint, they drove a pretty keen bargain."

The new company almost immediately issued five hundred thousand shares of Coca-Cola common stock at forty dollars a share. As its commission, the Trust Company of Georgia, which handled this transaction, was allowed to purchase stock at five dollars a share, and the eighty-eight thousand shares it acquired in this manner would in thirty years be worth ninety million dollars.

The new stock was not as popular as the new owners of the company had predicted. The company was in trouble almost from the beginning. One of the reasons was the price of sugar. During the early months of World War I, it had sold for between six and seven cents a pound. During the war, sugar, along with other vital products, was severely rationed and, The Coca-Cola Company, following government rules, relinquished its rights to fifty percent of its normal quota of sugar.

The year following the war, with rationing lifted, the price of sugar rose to twenty-two cents and the next year soared to twenty-eight cents a pound. Samuel Candler Dobbs, nephew of Asa Candler, and president of the company, predicted that the price would go even higher and contracted for millions of dollars worth of sugar for future delivery.

No one could have forecast a collapse of the sugar market, but collapse it did, dropping back to eighteen cents a pound. The new Coca-Cola stock went down with it, from the original price of forty dollars to eighteen dollars a share. E. J. Kahn, Jr., tells the story of one Florida bank that figured it was stuck with the large block of stock in which it had invested. To help

rid itself of this liability, the bank directors made as part of a loan require-
ment the purchase of Coca-Cola stock. "The poor fellows," says Kahn,
"who accepted this package deal and hung on to the stock are now among
the world's most affluent husbandmen."

The price-of-sugar problem went much deeper than that. It created
vast dissension between the company and its bottlers. The contract for the
price of syrup to the bottlers had been set on a basis of the pre-war price of
sugar. The sugar contract made by President Dobbs was more than four
times that. There seemed no outcome to this stalemate but bankruptcy.

The Coca-Cola Company tried to raise the price of syrup, but the bottlers would have none of that. They banded together and took the matter
to court, first in Atlanta and then to the Federal District Court in Delaware,
where the new company was incorporated. The courts held that the original contract with the bottlers was a perpetual one.

Long negotiations followed between Coca-Cola officials, the bottlers
and lawyers on both sides. The parent company was able to present a
rather strong argument — "If we die, the formula dies with us, and we're
all out of business." In the end the bottlers accepted a substantial hike in
the price of syrup until such a time when the supply of high-priced sugar
owned by the parent company was exhausted. But at the same time the
contracts were "amended through an escalation clause which would protect the company in the event of future inflationary sugar prices."

In 1919 the syndicate headed by his father bought The Coca-Cola
Company. Woodruff had ended his army career, where he had spent most
of his time as a civilian consultant. Two months after his discharge from
the army he was reappointed southeastern manager of the White Motor
Company and the next year was made a vice president, with offices in
Cleveland and New York. Walter White suggested that he take over as executive vice president of the company, but Woodruff shook his head. "That
doesn't mean anything," he said.

"Would it mean anything," White replied, "if I gave you authority to
sign my name?"

Nell Woodruff heard of the news of his rise in rank to vice president
before Woodruff, who was attending a sales meeting in New York, did. She

wired him: "Congratulations. Am proud of my vice president. Am with you to the limit. Much love. Nell."

This was the year that Woodruff sold a thirty-truck, one hundred thousand dollar order to The Coca-Cola Company. His interest in Coca-Cola, however, went much deeper than the sale of trucks or the fact that his father had headed the syndicate that bought The Coca-Cola Company. He was in hock up to his ears because of the money he had borrowed to buy Coca-Cola stock when it was placed on the market at forty dollars a share. Even then, he was looking over the hill, beyond the valley and into the country beyond. He knew that with his salary and commissions at White he would eventually pay out his loans.

With the long-range mistakes, the general apathy throughout the company and an alarming decrease in the sale of syrup, the directors were fully aware that new blood was needed. Because of his incredible record with White Motor Company and the regard for him in business and financial circles throughout the United States, Robert W. Woodruff was elected to the executive committee of the board of directors of Coca-Cola.

Less than two months later he was offered the presidency of The Coca-Cola Company. He didn't want it. He was making more money with White than he'd ever made in his life. Other more established organizations had offered him fabulous jobs. His friend, Walter Teagle of Standard Oil, had told him that any day he wanted to come with Standard Oil he could name his own salary. Three of his friends, Tom Glenn, Charles Wickersham and W. C. Bradley, all who had taken tremendous stock losses with The Coca-Cola Company, went to New York to persuade him to take over Coca-Cola. They had a sound argument. The company in which young Woodruff owned more than thirty-five hundred shares was about to go broke. It owed millions of dollars more than it could pay, and the situation was worsening. The company needed new blood, new ideas. Woodruff at last agreed to come down and talk with the other directors on the board.

Woodruff made an offer to the board. He would take the job for a salary of five percent commission on the annual increase in sales. He might have had it too, except that his father, who had manipulated men and organizations all of his adult life, was smart enough to veto that idea. So

Woodruff took the job anyway at thirty-six thousand dollars a year, fifty thousand dollars less than he had been making with White Motor Company in salary and commissions.

He always said that he had several reasons for taking this tremendous cut in salary. One was that during his entire life he had been drawn to people that needed him and he knew that his friends—and his father— were in trouble with the company. Another was that he would be back home again, living with people he had known all of his life. He felt, too, that any time he wanted to leave Coca-Cola and go back with the White Motor Company, Walter White would welcome him. Another basic reason was that the revival of The Coca-Cola Company offered a tremendous challenge and Woodruff was never one to turn down any challenge.

He put it more prosaically. "The only reason I took that job was to get back the money I had invested in Coca-Cola stock. I figured that if I ever brought the price of stock back to what I had paid for it, I'd sell and get even. Then I'd go back to selling cars and trucks."

Chapter 4
Early Coca-Cola Years

When Robert W. Woodruff stepped into his new job as president of The Coca-Cola Company, his thirty-fourth birthday was still more than seven months away. Although he was the unanimous choice of the board of directors, this enthusiasm and confidence in his ability had by no means seeped down through the ranks. In spite of his brilliant career of salesmanship and organization with White Motor Company and during his brief army career, skeptics in The Coca-Cola Company agreed among themselves that he was too young and too inexperienced to take on a job of this magnitude. Much resentment came from those who themselves had navigated the company into its stormy seas. Actually hostile were some who had maneuvered for the presidency and were bitter that the directors had moved them aside to choose a young upstart with no experience in the soft drink business to guide the destiny of a company now foundering in its own blunders.

One of the most openly militant was Charles Howard Candler, who was holding the reins of The Coca-Cola Company when Woodruff took over in 1923. Woodruff walked in and Candler resigned, cleared his desk of all personal matters and moved out. Characteristically, Woodruff went to see him at his home.

"The company needs you," he said. "It needs your ability, background and experience. I don't know any more about Coca-Cola than a pig knows about Sunday."

"You'll learn," Candler said.

"Both you and I have a lot of money tied up in stock," Woodruff persisted. "I need you to help me bring the price back to what we paid for it, so that we can get even."

"I think you can swing it," Candler admitted grudgingly, "but you'll have to do it on your own."

"I won't take the job," Woodruff said, "unless you'll stay and help me."

"What do you want me to do?" Candler asked.

"You can help the company most," Woodruff said, "by staying on as head of the production department. As you know, our sales of syrup dropped from nineteen million gallons in 1919 to fifteen million gallons last year. An important job will be to build back that production because we are going to sell the syrup."

Candler agreed to stay on, at least temporarily, as head of the production department.

Woodruff went a step further and persuaded Sam Dobbs, also disgruntled because of changes, to continue with the company as promotion and advertising manager.

In retaining the services of these two men, Woodruff eliminated them as active opponents to the company's welfare and progress. Their goodwill and friendship were far more valuable to him and to the company. He accomplished another purpose, too, of helping to assure other employees he had inherited with his new job that no drastic changes would be made and that there would be no wholesale firing of company personnel. This was one of his first actions to establish confidence in their jobs and in the company and to create an *esprit de corps* that later would be extended on a worldwide basis.

Another early decision was to put together a strong board of directors with hard core businessmen who were tremendously successful in their lines of business. It was hardly incidental that the new board selections were Woodruff friends who had tremendous respect for his business judgment and whom he knew would back his programs.

"These men I'd known over many years," Woodruff said. "I felt that we were gathering some of the top business brains in the country to help pull our company out of its hole. And we were. Their contributions to the success of The Coca-Cola Company were inestimable."

One of the things that disturbed him most was a survey which exposed the fact that not all servings of Coca-Cola were alike. The taste was different from one to another. Some of the fountains and bottlers were cheating a little on the amount of syrup or in other ways that impaired the quality of his drink. In some cases the water wasn't right, the fountains less than spotless, or the plants were unclean and the bottles half-washed. This might spell disaster in the long run. His basic business and personal philosophy had always been the production of a good, reliable product, a fair price and complete honesty in all his dealings.

He knew that one of his biggest and most important problems early in the game was quality control. He took steps to establish this both with the fountains and his bottlers.

Since the largest volume of sales of Coca-Cola syrup was to the fountains, Woodruff set up a training school for his sales organization that called on the fountain trade.

"You are salesmen," he told the group selected for this school, "but you are much more than that. You sell best by being of service to our customers who buy syrup to pass on to their customers at the soda fountains. By service I mean that we must help the fountain people in more ways than just being an order-taker. Help them to dress up and make every fountain as attractive as possible. It must be sparkling clean. This will help their Coca-Cola sales and their other business too. Careful attention must be given to mixing the drinks just right, with the proper amounts of syrup, carbonated water and ice, so that no matter where you buy a Coca-Cola, it will be exactly like any Coca-Cola you might taste anywhere."

Woodruff set his sales staff up on a regional basis along much the same lines he had found successful at the White Motor Company. After the intensive training period, these salesmen which had graduated into "service men" were assigned to regional offices. Inspired by the new concept, and no doubt by the enthusiasm and forcefulness of the new president, they went back to their jobs of calling on soda fountains. The emphasis placed on the quality of the drink sold over soda fountains and making the fountain itself more attractive for the customers paid off. Supported by an intensive advertising campaign, this added effort resulted in an almost instant increase in sales and mounting profits for both The Coca-Cola Company and soda fountain operators.

With a clear conscience, Woodruff might have stopped at this point. He could have considered that his only obligation to the company was to see that adequate syrup was made and shipped to supply the demand, and that the responsibility of creating that demand fell to the people who purchased the syrup and put it up for sale in a mixed drink. Who cared how this was done? Woodruff did. He knew that the man who would ultimately determine the success or failure of The Coca-Cola Company was the consumer who pushed a nickel across the counter for a glass or bottle of Coca-Cola. How many persons pulling that five-cent piece out of pocket and how often, to purchase a Coca-Cola, depended on both the attractiveness and availability of his drink.

Although the return from fountain service far surpassed that from the bottlers, Woodruff, with that intangible something that let him see beyond the hill, arranged a meeting and invited the largest and most successful bottlers. Neither he nor the company had any direct control over this group, most of whom were independent dealers with franchises. Their only dependence on The Coca-Cola Company was the syrup that kept their businesses going and the national advertising program of the parent company. All but a handful of bottlers showed up for his meeting.

Woodruff considered the soda fountain business attractive, but knew that the bottle was the surest, swiftest and most convenient way to build the world empire he had envisioned for his drink.

In keeping with his lifetime philosophy that "there is no limit to how far a man can go if he doesn't care who gets the credit," he put the burden on the shoulders of his bottlers.

"What," he asked, "can you and I do to make Coca-Cola available to anyone, anywhere in the world, whenever they want one, and be certain that it tastes just like the last Coca-Cola they drank?"

This was discussed at length. Under Woodruff's persuasion and magnetism, the bottlers entered wholeheartedly into the spirit of accomplishing the goal Woodruff proposed. To the bottlers as a group and to as many as he was able to talk with individually, he stressed cleanliness and quality, promotion of the product, goodwill and always having the drink available. He stressed too, the ambition that he carried through his business life—he wanted everyone connected with Coca-Cola to make money. How much they made depended on how well they followed the rules. Woodruff was looking far ahead.

He thinks this may have been his most important point. Everyone is in business to make money. Apparently this conception was well-taken. The bottlers responded enthusiastically to the charm of his salesmanship. Little more than a year after that meeting, the bottle sales had skyrocketed. The company had enough money in the bank for a long-term operation and to pay off a twenty-two million dollar mortgage to Guaranty Trust Company in New York.

Woodruff recalls how he and Turner Jones went to New York to pay the note and bring home the secret formula for Coca-Cola, which had been held as collateral by Guaranty Trust. On the way home by train, he and Jones began to wonder whether the sealed envelope actually contained the secret formula.

"It wasn't any distrust of the bank," he said, "but more a matter of caution. Suppose that someone who recognized the tremendous value of that formula had somehow substituted a piece of blank paper for it. I knew I'd never rest until I found out."

Back at home he carried this problem before the board of directors and received authorization to allow the company's head chemist, Dr. W. P. Heath, to check the contents of the envelope. Woodruff and all of his top associates were relieved that the formula was there and intact.

It has been said that the only time the company's board of directors turned down a request by Woodruff was within the first two years after he became president. He asked for an appropriation to expand the foreign market. The board, no member of which had Woodruff's farsightedness, saw little future but abundant headaches in creating a big demand for their product in the distant places of the earth. They were making enough money at home. Plowing those profits back into bottling plants they probably wouldn't be able to control, and political corruption they could not cope with in many countries, made little sense. Woodruff envisioned what later was to become a reality—a worldwide market, with Coca-Cola a household word. He didn't get his appropriation but went ahead anyway.

Selling Coca-Cola outside the United States was nothing new. In 1898 Asa Candler reported to his directors that Coca-Cola was being sold in some Canadian cities and in Honolulu, and plans were being made to market the drink in Mexico. In May, 1899, a salesman had been hired to sell in Cuba and Puerto Rico, and before the year was out over one thousand gallons of syrup were shipped to those islands.

Coca-Cola historian Hunter Bell points out that possibly the first Coca-Cola to reach the European continent was in 1900 when Howard Candler, Asa's son, made a trip to England with ten other Emory college students and carried along a jug of Coca-Cola. In London they located a soda fountain which dispensed carbonated water.

Under young Candler's direction, John T. Ralphs, the fountain manager, measured out an ounce of syrup in each of an array of glasses, poured in the carbonated water and put in the ice. He filled enough glasses to serve the Atlantans and the officials of Spence's Department Store, who had gathered for the occasion. The Britishers were so enchanted with the new drink that Ralphs ordered five gallons of syrup, which was thought to be the first inter-continental shipment.

Bell says that by 1901 shipments were being made to Germany and Jamaica, and that in 1905 the trademark "Coca-Cola" was registered in Canada. The next year the first syrup was manufactured outside the United States and the first bottling plant set up, both in Toronto. In 1907, Hawaiian Soda Works in Honolulu became the first Coca-Cola bottling plant away from the North American continent.

The tide swelled. In the next fifteen years Coca-Cola was being bottled in Puerto Rico, Philippines, Nicaragua, Guatemala, Guam, France and Hawaii.

When Woodruff took over as president, overseas trade in Coca-Cola had been in existence but only on what he considered a most modest basis. It had sprouted more or less as a wild seedling, with little attention, nurturing or promotion. The company supplied syrup to a number of bottling plants in various parts of the world but had little concern for these, except the amount of syrup they were able to use. The export trade simply was not moving fast enough to please Woodruff.

Although his board had given him a thumbs down on any additional appropriation to increase foreign business, he went ahead with what money was available. He organized and staffed a foreign department in New York

City and made his first splash there. His salesmen in this branch solicited orders from both American export houses and foreign importing firms. One salesman devoted all of his time to calling on ships berthed in New York Harbor, selling Coca-Cola to be served on board. Many foreign travelers on ocean liners and crews on freighters got their first taste of Coca-Cola on the high seas.

"A special package," says Bell, "designated as the 'export bottle,' containing the finished beverage, was adopted for overseas shipment. This was an emerald green, straight sided bottle of six-and-a-half-ounce capacity, with red, green and gold paper label. The bottles were packed for export in wooden cases containing five dozen bottles each. It sold for six dollars per case FOB New York City. Transportation and duty charges, as well as profit for the importer and dealer, had to be added; therefore, the overseas consumer paid an exceedingly high price for an export bottle of Coca-Cola."

The initial shipment of the export bottle in 1927 went to Haiti, Liberia, the Gold Coast and Puerto Rico.

Woodruff utilized every means of getting his product spread around the world. He had his export salesmen call on the large steamship companies, and within a short time most of the oceanliners and freighters sailing out of New York carried heavy stocks of Coca-Cola to foreign ports and introduced the drink there.

The idea was sound, for not long afterward the foreign department sold its first railway car lot of the export bottle to a single customer. This shipment went across the water to the Dutch East Indies. This large sale was the cause of a party and much rejoicing by the New York staff.

By every gimmick known to salesmanship, Woodruff and that arm of his company devoted to foreign trade introduced his export bottle worldwide. Wherever it appeared, the drink found such favor that applications began to come in from foreign bottlers to include Coca-Cola in their line or to establish separate plants authorized to manufacture and distribute the finished product.

Barrels of syrup were being shipped to many corners of the world when Woodruff, looking far into the future, made the important decision to supply concentrate instead of syrup to his foreign trade. This cut down costs in many ways and added to the accumulation of profit from the market abroad. The first twenty-five gallons of concentrate to an overseas plant was sent in January, 1927, to Hamilton, Bermuda.

Five years after Woodruff hired salesmen to hammer away at the foreign trade, his New York branch was officially incorporated under the name "The Coca-Cola Export Corporation" and assigned the job of handling the sale and promotion of all Coca-Cola outside the continental United States and Canada. Woodruff was its first president. Over the years several other Export presidents who followed him went on to become the presidents of The Coca-Cola Company and later chairmen of the Coca-Cola board. The export business was one of the finest training grounds he knew and in addition was becoming the healthiest arm of the company.

While creating his foreign department, Woodruff did not neglect the home market. From the beginning of his association with the company, the qualities he stressed most were complete honesty in all dealings by company personnel. Upon this foundation, which has always been his philosophy, stood the objectives of goodwill and the integrity of his product.

One of his first goals was to see that a Coca-Cola made in Seattle tasted the same as one made in Santiago or Singapore. This meant that it had to be put together with specified amounts of the same components, with pure water and in clean bottles. He called it "quality control."

In this, one of the most important ingredients was water. Historian Bell says that in the early stages, especially where plants were located in smaller communities, water from a clear artesian well was generally considered suitable for making Coca-Cola.

Bell says that "when bottlers began to treat water, the 'complete' treatment consisted of filters made from porous stone. The only purpose was to remove suspended matter from the water. Quartz filters followed by paper disc filters were used where suspended matter was especially serious. A few plants distilled all water used for bottling."

As the demand for Coca-Cola increased and volume of production grew, sufficient clean water became a problem. Woodruff put his technicians to work, seeking a faster and more reliable method of water treatment than by running it through porous stone.

Dr. William P. Heath came up with the idea that activated carbon used in the World War I gas masks might successfully remove all odors and tastes from water. His theory proved correct, and by 1930 the activated carbon process was used in thirty bottling plants and planned for more as the cheapest and quickest way to have a clean, abundant water supply.

Woodruff employed an army of chemists and put them to work testing water samples from every bottling plant in the United States, and where the water was not up to standard, doing something about it. Recommendations were made up for each plant to follow in bringing its water to a standard quality.

This philosophy of quality control spread throughout the world, with the Coca-Cola technicians going to whatever trouble was necessary with purification systems available to make the water clean enough for Coca-Cola. One of the most interesting sources of water is on the Persian Gulf side of Arabia. The earth is very rich with oil and drilling a well for water is forbidden, so the only drinking water for the inhabitants must come out of the sea. Kuwait operated the largest desalinization plant in the world to provide fresh water for its citizens and, incidentally, for the Coca-Cola plant located there.

Because he felt quality control was one of the keys to the exploding sales record of his company, Woodruff never ceased promoting it within his organization. Almost everyone in the company who had anything to do with the production of the drink worked for its perfection. Woodruff introduced traveling laboratories, each manned by two chemists. These were kept continuously on the road from one bottling plant to another, making tests of water, Coca-Cola mixture and cleanliness, and making suggestions for how the plant might be operated more efficiently and economically. Most bottlers welcomed the appearance of these traveling Coca-Cola teams.

Empire building is never easy. All along the way the pioneers and those who follow closely on their heels more than often struggle through great difficulties and encounter unbelievable obstacles. This not only applies to nations, but to all human endeavors. Where men make progress, there are always other men making an effort to tear down those things being built.

Coca-Cola was not exempt from this fact of life. As early as the Asa

Candler ownership, promoters of other soda water flavors on the market, inspired by their partial knowledge of its contents, were calling Coca-Cola "dope" and explaining how harmful it is when taken internally.

One favorite trick of the detractors was to place a piece of raw meat in a glass and pour a jigger or two of Coca-Cola syrup over it. After it stood for a while, they'd point to the darkening piece of meat with a gesture of triumph and say, "Just look at that! That dope stuff is disintegrating a chunk of raw steak, just like it'll eat the lining out of your stomach."

These agitators knew as well as the company chemists that Coca-Cola does contain some acid which, although having no effect on living tissue, tends to act as a digestive of meat in the same way as does digestive acids which are always present in the human stomach. The enemies of Coca-Cola made much of this fact, but without seriously cutting into the sales.

The creation of the world's most successful bottling business was one continuous conflict. That it definitely was on its way, even in the early stages, to heights not dreamed of by its creator was evidenced by the growing opposition to the drink and, on the other hand, by the number of imitators yapping around the edges, looking for a piece of the action.

As early as 1909, fourteen years before Woodruff, the beer people were fighting Coca-Cola. By then the five-cent drink had become so popular that it was beginning to cut into the beer profits. The suds industry preached far and wide that Coca-Cola was a "prohibition" drink associated with the Candlers, who were church people. To give it the desired effect, they said, it was loaded with cocaine and caffeine. It was so full of dope that it simply couldn't be compared with a cold, clean, harmless beer.

To offset these rumors, Asa Candler had the state chemist of Georgia analyze Coca-Cola for its content of harmful drugs. The chemist's report, still on record, concluded that Coca-Cola contained no cocaine and that "a cup of coffee contains considerably more caffeine than the ordinary glass of Coca-Cola as served, while tea contains approximately the same amount of caffeine as an ordinary glass of Coca-Cola."

The detractors wouldn't give up, and they found a valuable ally in the person of Dr. Harvey W. Wiley, a medical doctor as well as a chemist. He was head of the Bureau of Chemistry for the U. S. Department of Agriculture. At one time he was a wine connoisseur, but when he was converted to prohibition became rather rabid on the subject. He went so far as to consider all manufactured drinks, alcoholic and otherwise, as poison to the human system.

For some reason, Dr. Wiley was especially unhappy about Coca-Cola. He could do nothing about his dislike of the drink and the company that made it until the Pure Food and Drug Act became a law, and his bureau inherited the job of policing the act. After the enactment of that law, Wiley caused the seizure of a quantity of Coca-Cola on the ground that it was adulterated and misbranded. This was the opening shot of a battle that went through the courts for ten years before it was finally resolved in favor of The Coca-Cola Company.

After the decision, the impounded shipment of Coca-Cola was returned to the company, minus four barrels and fifteen kegs of Coca-Cola, which probably could be classed as an unwritten testimonial to at least some enjoyment the prosecution had gotten out of sampling the evidence over more than a decade.

The early opponents of Coca-Cola even got to the President of the United States — at that time Teddy Roosevelt. Somehow they got word to the President that he should by all means stop the manufacture of Coca-Cola syrup for the sake of the nation's health. The report was that Coca-Cola syrup was cooked under the most unsanitary of conditions such as dirty pots; in an old building that was dusty, hung with cobwebs and littered with all manner of filth. The report was so convincing that Roosevelt appointed a special commissioner to look into the matter. The result, naturally, was a clean bill for the company.

When Woodruff stepped into the presidency of The Coca-Cola Company, it seemed as though his drink was at war with the rest of the world, collectively and individually. Although before he became associated with the company, the Supreme Court had made it clear that "Coca-Cola" and "Coke" were protectable trademarks belonging to The Coca-Cola Company. Literally hundreds of imitations of Coca-Cola had sprung up with names as euphoniously near as possible to Coca-Cola without using the same letter combination of the two words. These quasi-duplications not only appeared over the United States, but were beginning to appear in other lands where Coca-Cola was sold. Almost without exception they included the words "Cola" or "Kola" or variations of these, and many were uncomfortably close to the words they tried to copy. Some of those advertised were Polar-Cola, Take-a-Cola, Coke-Ola, Ko-Kola, Kok-Kola, Coca & Cola, Copa-Kola, Cofa-Cola and Coca-Lola. There were many more.

The imitation flavors tried in every possible way to get as close to the color and flavor of Coca-Cola as they did with the name—a few of the infringers even pawned off their substitutes on unsuspecting druggists, who served the imitations over their soda founts as Coca-Cola.

When he took over as president, Woodruff found the company's legal staff with its hands full. They were busy not only with lawsuits the company had initiated to protect its name and product from infringement, but with a flood of other litigation.

Long before Woodruff, the Coca-Cola bottlers were besieged by both threats and lawsuits from the "fast buck" artists who claimed to have found all kinds of creatures and foreign matter in bottles of Coke. This caused, they insisted, their health to be impaired—for which they demanded heavy compensation.

One of the results of this activity was the organization of The Coca-Cola Bottlers Association, to take out insurance and fight such claims as a group rather than as individuals.

Before and during Woodruff, The Coca-Cola Company was heaped with troubles. He was aware that almost since the turn of the century, the company had carried on a running battle with its imitators and infringers. Possibly the most famous pre-Woodruff lawsuit—that laid solid groundwork for the protection of the trademark—was initiated against the Koke Company of America, which in 1913 attempted to register "Koke" as its trademark with the U. S. Patent Office. The Coca-Cola Company filed its notice of opposition to the registration.

For seven years this contest went through the courts. While it was underway, other companies added Coke substitutes to their lines. By 1916 there were no less than one hundred fifty-three imitations of Coca-Cola on the market. The Coca-Cola legal staff was kept busy. One of their biggest all-time victories, which was to help mow down at least some of the infringers, came in 1920, when the U. S. Supreme Court ruled against the Koke Company of America and handed down its decision that "Coca-Cola" and "Coke" were trademarks belonging solely to The Coca-Cola Company.

Even with this landmark decision, the imitation, and in many cases substitutions for the real thing, continued through the post World War I years, and the lawsuits went on. They seemed to be one of the orders of business, along with the skyrocketing price of sugar, the declining sale of syrup, the sliding price of Coca-Cola stock and the verbal sabotage carried on against Coca-Cola by the other beverage companies.

Woodruff knew all this had led to the decline of the company, and he had no illusions about what lay ahead and what was needed to turn the company around. He found some satisfaction that Coca-Cola was stepping on a lot of toes. To him, this meant Coke was taking the place of other drinks and the other drink companies were not too pleased about it. The beer industry had been after Dr. Pemberton's drink almost from the time it began to be popular around the place of its birth. Woodruff knew that in the years ahead of him, other drink industries all over the world would do what they could to stop Coca-Cola.

The decades proved him right. In South America the coffee interests took up arms against Coca-Cola, as did the distillers of sake in Japan and the tea growers in many parts of Asia. The fruit and fruit juice companies— worldwide—could see Coca-Cola cutting into their sales and profits, and they too threw down the gauntlet. In places even the merchandisers of milk complained of the drink's encroachment on their market.

Possibly the most opposition developed in central Europe from the beer and wine industries. Much of this was promoted by the communists. To them Coca-Cola was the essence of capitalism, and the antagonism of the grape growers and the makers and sellers of wine and beer was grist for the communist mill. They made trouble for The Coca-Cola Company wherever and however they could.

While Woodruff kept abreast of all these developments, he didn't allow them to detour him from his main job of selling Coca-Cola. One of his policies in helping to encounter these difficulties was the selection of the highest quality supervisory personnel from the citizens of each nation with an established Coca-Cola business. The bottling franchises went to reputable and highly respected businessmen.

In some regions steps were taken to combat the unfavorable propaganda. In Switzerland, for example, the communists spread word by every possible means that Coca-Cola was a witch's brew poison, concocted in filth.

At Woodruff's suggestion, the Switzerland bottlers did no "shouting from the housetops" to deny these charges. Instead, they quietly arranged and conducted tours of their plants for hundreds of Swiss citizens. Special invitations for these tours went to men and women in daily contact with the public, such as barbers and beauty shop operators, who were sources of information and gossip with a diversified segment of the population. Seeing a modern Coca-Cola plant in operation proved an effective way to disprove the communist charges.

Woodruff had his Export Corporation stress the fact in every country where Coca-Cola was made and sold that the Coca-Cola plant and product there was not a foreign, capitalistic venture, but a local business dealing on only a limited basis with the parent company. They could prove this by showing that of the total number of employees working for the Export Corporation all over the world—including America—ninety-nine percent were citizens of the nations in which they were employed. Another good talking point was that only a fraction of one percent of the contents in a Coca-Cola bottled in a foreign plant came from the U. S. Everything else connected with the process—plant machinery, bottles, caps, water, trucks—everything—were local products. The only need from the parent company was concentrate and, the only requirements, cleanliness and quality.

Although at the time Woodruff and The Coca-Cola Company did not consider it in such a light, the opposition to Coca-Cola that popped up around the globe was really a tribute to the tremendous job in salesmanship and product quality by the entire Coca-Cola Export organization.

These conflict-of-interest spots have appeared here and there throughout the history Coca-Cola. They still show up, sometimes in the least expected places. Usually the hostility is short-lived; somehow the Coca-Cola people always find a way to circumnavigate it.

One of the interesting conflicts Woodruff remembers was in Sweden. A bottle rinser in a beer factory there, posing as a beverage authority, made the statement that Coca-Cola contained a toxic substance strong enough to break down the health of a man. Without making an investigation, the newspapers jumped on the beer rinser's words and played them up for several years in news stories, editorials and cartoons.

Another incident with a different flavor popped up in Denmark, where the beer industry was politically powerful. It maneuvered and passed an outrageous tax on all cola beverages. This was aimed primarily at Coca-Cola, but it taxed all such beverages in Denmark out of existence until it was repealed more than a decade after World War II.

The fruit industry in several parts of the world did all it could to hurt the competitive Coca-Cola. In some nations where the fruit growers were able to yield enough influence with their lawmakers, the manufacture and sale of Coca-Cola was banned outright.

These stories are related to indicate that the establishment of the Coca-Cola empire was not as simple as the wave of a magic wand, but came about through the far sighted wisdom and inspiration of one man and the dedicated efforts of thousands of other men in his army. Woodruff is fond of recalling what Steve Hannagan, the company's public relations counselor, once said after he had attended his first Coca-Cola convention: "My God! Those boys believe in the Holy Grail!"

Almost from the time it was introduced in France, the French wine industry bitterly fought Coca-Cola on all fronts. In spite of all the growers and wine makers could do to destory the reputation of Coca-Cola and the demand for its drink in France, the company went right on ahead, establishing bottlers and increasing its sales there. It made its greatest gain in World War II—a story that comes later in this book—but also reached the climax of its opposition around the end of the war. Communist agitators and Coca-Cola haters, backed by the wine groups, pushed a bill through the National Assembly to give the minister of health regulatory powers over the distribution of all soft drinks containing vegetable matter. Everyone knew this was aimed directly at Coca-Cola.

This brought a rather unexpected reaction from all over the world.

Some wag observed that the legislation would either be the cause of another French Revolution or precipitate a Franco-American War. Newspapers across the water took up the battle cry. Ban Coca-Cola? That was almost as sacrilegious as trampling our stars and stripes in the dirt. News stories and editorials all over the country demanded that we boycott all French wines and perfumes. One of our political figures said that he and his friends had sworn off French dressing, and one editor—tongue also in cheek—went so far as to declare that we should give up French toast.

James A. Farley, chairman of The Coca-Cola Export Corporation, conferred with Woodruff. Both men were admired and respected in France and had enough friends and political savvy there to have the proposed legislation killed by the Council of the Republic, the French upper house which had to approve all bills passed by the National Assembly before they could become law.

The amazing postscript to this international incident is that only a year or two later, the French wine industry had embraced Coca-Cola and left their communist allies stretched out on the battlefield. Many of the wine people themselves had gone into the Coca-Cola bottling business on the old "If you can't lick 'em, j'ine 'em" basis, and did so well that many gave up wine and went entirely into the Coca-Cola business.

The lawsuits launched by Woodruff's battery of lawyers to protect the Coca-Cola trademark and the drink itself seemed endless. The more successful Coca-Cola became at sales and profits, the more thickly swarmed its imitators in an effort to capitalize on the product's good will and reputation. The realm of Coke was eternally invaded by a flood of new and diversified beverages.

In the middle of all these fireworks, Woodruff and company sold Coca-Cola. He sold Coca-Cola because he had selected as his representatives the highest quality personnel he could find, brought as many of them as possible up through the ranks and inspired in them a spirit that was almost an obsession to sell Coke. He continued to hammer at his chemists and traveling laboratories that each fountain and bottle drink should be of the highest quality and that they should seek eternally to improve even that. He was a genius for detail and his associates kept him informed of every proposed action in the company. No major decisions and few decisions of any kind were ever made without consulting him.

All of his biographers have recognized that he was czar on the throne of the Coca-Cola empire. He especially liked the one that called him the "pro quarterback" on the "Coca-Cola" team. Yet even while he made the decisions, he followed a lifelong policy of giving others the credit for those decisions and for the action necessary to carry out plans and programs.

Woodruff kept a hand on the advertising campaigns. It was his idea to associate Coca-Cola with the nation's top business leaders. From his years in the top echelons of businesses, he knew many of these prominent people and didn't hesitate to ask them to pose singly and in groups with a bottle of Coca-Cola in the hand for "the pause that refreshes." He tied in his drink with the names and faces of actresses, movie stars, stage personalities and such people who were admired and respected all over the world.

He didn't neglect the less affluent. One famous early poster showed a Postal Telegraph messenger boy amicably having a bottle of Coke with a supposed competitor, a Western Union messenger boy. One touch of gladness makes the whole world kin. His ads were designed to show a spirit of friendliness everywhere.

Woodruff insisted on seeing every picture before it went on a national poster or advertisement. Over the years dozens of "Coca-Cola" girls were introduced to match the changing times and dress and styles. Naturally each girl had to be beautiful, but even more important to Woodruff's eye, she had to be wholesome—"The girl any man would be proud to claim as a sister or daughter."

Usually before a poster or ad was approved, Woodruff set it up in his office on a table or the back of a chair. Any associate, friend or acquaintance who came by was asked to study the layout and give an opinion. Any criticism or even hesitation in expressing an opinion was followed up by Woodruff until he had pinned down the objection and reason for it. If it were at all valid, he called his advertising staff into the office.

"If one fellow out of a few doesn't like some point about it, out of the millions who see this there may be thousands who find it objectionable."

The advertising budget increased faster than some thought the company could afford, but Woodruff had the wisdom and vision to place the name of his drink where it would be seen by millions every hour of the day. Attractive signs, outside and inside every place where Coca-Cola was sold, eye-catching billboards (long before they began to clutter the landscape and get unfavorable public reation), ads in magazines and newspapers, national performers extolling the virtues of Coca-Cola on radio, favors of every kind from pencils to playing cards and coolers, all these and many more were used to advertise Coca-Cola. The advertising budget boomed but so did the sale of Coke through all the old sources of supply and myriads of new sources springing up everywhere.

Under Woodruff the profit curve swung upward—fast. In 1924 the company paid off the twenty-two million dollar mortgage held by Guaranty Trust Company in New York. By 1927, only four years after its new president had taken the helm, the company had retired its ten million dollars in preferred stock and paid off all loans, bills and other debts. That year the company split its stock from five hundred thousand to a million shares and set a dividend of five dollars a share on the new stock, payable quarterly to its stockholders.

"It's the only time in my life," Woodruff says, "that I ever felt rich."

A Coca-Cola historical note reveals that everyone seemed to be so elated over the stock split and dividend, and with the continued rise in profits, that the very next year, in 1928, certain directors of the company insisted that the stock be split again. Woodruff shook his head.

"This country," he said, "is living in a sort of fool's paradise. Everything is too easy—flows too freely. Many businesses and many people are in over their heads. Our whole economy is on shaky ground. Our company's financial position is sound. Let's keep it that way. If we and the country survive what surely lies ahead, then we'll make moves to expand and strengthen our position."

Prophetic words! America was living high, and except in a few minds such as Woodruff's, no one had any inkling that a severe depression lurked just around the corner.

The Coca-Cola stock was not split again at that time, but Woodruff did compromise with his board of directors and issue a million shares of

Class "A" stock at fifty dollars a share, with a preferred dividend of six percent, and callable at fifty-two dollars and fifty cents.

As Woodruff and so few others had foreseen, the great depression hit late in 1929. The bottom dropped out from under many businesses in the country. Stocks plummeted. Coca-Cola went down like all the others, but had much less drop in value than most. As Herman Henry Biedenharn had told his boys out in Vicksburg, Mississippi, many years before when they began to bottle Coca-Cola, "everybody has a nickel," and as tight as the present depression was, this was as true in the early 1930's as it was then.

Woodruff never allowed his company to let up in its efforts to sell Coca-Cola. His schedule of advertising and otherwise pushing his drink paid off. Coca-Cola made money all through the depression years, when many other companies were going broke. By 1935, when the depression was beginning to ease, Coca-Cola stock had skyrocketed to three hundred dollars a share and the shares were split four for one.

Late in 1927, Woodruff, who had served on the White Motor Company board of directors during and since his connection with White, was elected to the executive committee of the board. Possibly this was a move ordained by fate. No one could see what lay ahead.

Woodruff and White were more than close business associates over a long number of years. They were close friends, drawn together by their business principles of integrity and keen business judgment, and by their devotion to horses, dogs, hunting and all things outdoors. Together they had shared a dream of owning a southern plantation devoted, among other things, to quail shooting.

In 1928 that dream came true. The two men were like boys putting together a new toy. They looked over a number of sites in north Florida and southwestern Georgia. The place that appealed to them most was an expansive tract along the Flint River between Newton and Bainbridge. The land they wanted was under a dozen or more ownerships, with cultivated fields and a large percentage of wooded land. One of the attractive features of the property was the wide, fast-flowing blackwater creek that wound through its heart. This waterway, like many other historic sites in that region, bore an Indian name—Ichauway-Nochauway.

Woodruff and White spent many delightful days riding over the back roads of their new plantation, visiting with the farmers, many of whom had been born there. One of the complex chores was the selection of a site as headquarters. They considered a stately mansion in the village of Elmodel, a few miles away, but decided this was too far from their new plantation. When the choice of sites boiled down to a stretch along the creek between the Elmodel and Bainbridge highways, each partner favored a different location. They finally compromised on one of the bluffs overlooking the creek about a mile above where the Bainbridge road crossed it. This was to be temporary headquarters until they could decide on the final location and recreate the magnificent old southern mansion setup.

On this temporary site they laid out a house place on a sloping bluff that led down to the creek and drew plans for a roomy but rather simple two-story frame house. In front of this they laid out a road in an ellipse of little more than a quarter of a mile, and around this circle were placed the plantation manager's house and houses for those attendants who would take care of the headquarters duties, which included the stables and kennels on the far rim of the "circle."

This temporary headquarters was built almost fifty years ago. It's still there, much as it was then.

Woodruff and White named their newly acquired plantation Ichauway.

The two friends were able to enjoy Ichauway together for only one season through its period of building and bird hunting. In late October, 1929, only three days before the stock market crashed into America's worst depression, Walter White was killed in an automobile accident between his home at Gates Mills and his office in Cleveland.

In keeping with his agreement with White that if anything happened to either of the friends, the other would acquire both shares, Woodruff paid the White heirs substantially more than each had invested in Ichauway and became sole owner.

"It strained my pocketbook at the time," he often said, "but I've never regretted it."

Mr. and Mrs. Woodruff entertained their first house guests at Ichauway in January, 1930.

With his perception to look beyond the hills, Woodruff had sensed the collapse of the economy and so arranged the affairs of The Coca-Cola Company that it was on solid ground. Walter White's death, coming on the verge of what might be a national disaster, was not only a tragic personal loss, but a potential crisis for White Motor Company and its stockholders. Already a number of top echelon personnel at White were in contention for the president's job.

Since Woodruff had behind him long years of association with White and experience at top administrative levels in the company, as well as his complete familiarity with the whole operation as a member of the executive committee of the board of directors at White Motor Company, the other members of the board turned to him for guidance to help keep the company operating efficiently and effectively.

Woodruff went to Cleveland. He knew that his first order of business there was to put an end to the bickering for the top job at White. All of this could result in only complete disorganization. Before he called the top men together to confer with them as a group and lay plans for the future, he made it a point to talk to each one individually, both as a board member and as a friend.

"We know you'd like to have the job as president of this company," was his theme, "and we know you have both the experience and ability to run it. Right at this moment, it would be a lot harder to fill your job than it would be to fill the job of president. We are facing a severe crisis and this old machine has got to keep on running smoothly. The best service you could give your company right now is by the continued excellent performance in your job."

What he said made sense and each man seemed to realize how petty his bickering for the top spot had been. Woodruff sold them unity around the importance of each position and each man agreed to carry on where he was for the best interest of the company.

The next job was to find a man with the knowledge and administrative ability to fill Walter White's shoes. The board made an intensive search. No such man seemed available.

"Why don't you take it?" one of the board members asked Woodruff.

"Remember me?" he said. "I've got a job."

"You don't have to work full time at it," the other persisted. "Just sort of keep one hand on the reins until we can find the proper man or until the company passes its critical point in this depression."

It was against Woodruff's grain, however, to do any job half way. He continued in Coca-Cola and took on the full burden of White. It appeared that a dual role was nothing new and he took this one in stride. He spent so much time in Pullman cars between Atlanta and Cleveland that he was the most familiar figure on that section of the railroad. With his dominant force, he kept both companies running smoothly. The story is told that once when he was to be away from his office in Atlanta for a few days, he left only one definite instruction: "If my father issues any orders around here, pay no attention to them. Anyone following an order of his is automatically fired."

His employees knew their boss, and that was one instruction that he never had to issue a second time.

Time spent on the trains gave Woodruff opportunity to evaluate and plan the programs for both companies. Walter White was a conservative businessman and his company was financially sound. Woodruff increased that stability by following the game plan White had laid out many years before when Woodruff was associated with him at White Motor. They paid only half the dividends the company could afford to pay and put the other half back for emergency and growth at the proper time.

The far sighted policy proved a lifesaver for White Motor when it went into the depression with Woodruff at its head. The demand for trucks and cars naturally decreased during the lean years. Woodruff found enough cash reserve to keep the White Motor Company operative, but wisely cut back on production to keep it in line with sales. This he did with his usual thoughtful consideration for others.

"During that era," he said, "many companies were laying off employees. This meant that some families might even have to go hungry. At White's we didn't let this happen. We got around it by reducing the number of working hours for all employees. The take-home pay was less, but there was enough so that no one suffered. This also helped us keep our organization intact."

Woodruff's Coca-Cola organization weathered the depression. In fact it came through with flying colors. It grew and progressed. He never let up on advertising, promotion or expanding his operation as fast as conditions warranted. As he had pointed out, few might have enough money to buy a truck or a new car, but everyone had a nickel and Coca-Cola had become an American way of life. The great depression failed to affect the growing tide of Coke sold in bottles and at the fountain, and The Coca-Cola Company showed an increase in sales for every year.

Where most companies put out voluminous annual reports to their stockholders, Woodruff made history in 1930 with his report to the stockholders for that year. Business leaders all over America chuckled about and applauded it, and when such matters come up, it is still remembered and discussed.

"With two jobs on my hands," Woodruff recalls with a sly smile, "I didn't have time to write a history book."

The 1930 Annual Report from Woodruff to his stockholders in The Coca-Cola Company consisted of only one short paragraph:

"I am pleased to report that during the year 1930, total sales as well as net profits of your company have exceeded all previous records; a conservative policy of expansion has been continued; reserves have been increased and the financial position of your company is stronger than at any time in its history. We look forward to 1931 with confidence."

Since Woodruff, the stockholder meetings as well as the reports have been noted for their brevity. Many of these sessions were said to extend over no more than a quarter of an hour and one such meeting took up only half that time. Several stories have been told of stock owners who, arriving a bit early for a stockholders meeting, decided to walk around the block for a breath of fresh air, only to find when they got back that the meeting was over and everyone was leaving.

In 1930, Woodruff found the man he considered right to relieve him of his duties at White Motor Company. This was Ashton G. Bean of Elysian, Ohio, who had been a close friend of Walter White. Bean was prominently successful in the business of manufacturing soda fount cooling equipment —which had indirectly tied him into the Coca-Cola business.

Bean was elected president, but Woodruff remained as chairman of the White Motor Company board of directors for another couple of years, until White Motor worked out a merger with the Studebaker Corporation. He resigned in 1932 and came home to devote his full time to Coca-Cola.

Woodruff remembers 1933 as the year of the big tax scare that resulted in some profound changes in the life and routines of The Coca-Cola Company.

Coca-Cola, as well as other soft drinks, lived under the sword blade of tax, suspended by a very slender thread. This threat went back to the Candler era, and over the years spread through the whole realm of Coca-Cola. As the drink grew popular and prosperous in state after state, it seemed a signal for the lawmakers to start talking about a one-cent tax for every five-cent bottle of soft drink. The government had assessed such a one-cent tax during World War I and this remained in effect until 1923, although the secretary of the U. S. Treasury had classed it as a nuisance tax that cost more to collect than the amount collected.

The government gave up this annoyance tax, but the state legislatures wouldn't let it die. Records in The Coca-Cola Company show that since 1926, two hundred such tax bills have been introduced in forty-six states. Some of the legislators may have been sincere in considering this as a legitimate source of state revenue. From all indications, many lawmakers who proposed such a tax had only one thing in mind. They hoped to be bought off by the soft drink companies for a fat fee to see that such legislation was not introduced, or that it did not pass.

Woodruff knew that a six-cent Coca-Cola was nowhere near as marketable as a five-cent Coke and threw a percentage of his manpower into making political friends and connections in the high echelons of government. Most bottlers followed his example at the local level. In spite of all this, the attempted shake-downs went on. In most instances, the bottlers refused to be intimidated. Only a few years ago, three legislators in one state tried to swindle two bottling companies out of ten thousand dollars each for keeping a soft drink tax bill from being introduced in the legislature. The local bottlers went to the district attorney with the evidence and the blackmailers were indicted.

It was in 1933, however, that tax matters hit a climactic high with

The Coca-Cola Company. This was brought about by a ruling of the U. S. Supreme Court, which concluded that it was within the prerogative of a state to tax the real property of any corporation operating in the state and, in addition, to also impose an intangible tax on all properties and securities of that corporation, including the stock value of all wholly owned subsidiaries, wherever they were located anywhere on earth.

This gave the Georgia legislature a green light to put such a tax into effect. While it wouldn't have spelled disaster for The Coca-Cola Company, such a sum as they would have to pay into the Georgia treasury each year to carry on their worldwide business meant a substantial cut into their financial growth.

Woodruff didn't hesitate in his decision. His political advisors told him that when the state legislature met after the first of the year, this new tax law would pass. Georgia was his home state. He was loyal to it and dedicated to it as a person. A heavy tax came under the head of business. In the last few weeks of 1933, The Coca-Cola Company moved out of the state of its birth. It re-established its corporate headquarters, with all of its worldwide properties and securities which would have been taxable under the new Georgia law, in Wilmington, Delaware. Many other national and international corporations, facing the same tax problem in the states of their residence, were making the move to Delaware, which had agreed to impose a minimum tax rate.

Wherever he lived, Woodruff was always a Georgian at heart. He had an abiding interest in the affairs of his state and of Atlanta where he was reared and continued to maintain a home. Living in Delaware and New York had little effect on the time he visited at Ichauway Plantation. Many of his closest friends were Georgians and he spent a good percentage of his time in the state. He didn't bring a large segment of his Coca-Cola operation back to Georgia until 1946, when the state reduced its intangible tax laws so that both his and his company's business could live with them.

With all of his problems and pressures of business, Woodruff allotted a certain percentage of his time to play. He profoundly believed that the body must remain strong through exercise, just as concentration helped improve the mind and "doing unto others" was good for the soul. In a tremendous schedule, he made time to be outdoors; on a golf course, riding horseback trails, and riding where there were no trails to fish and hunt. In his younger years, he went after big game in the Wyoming mountains; he devoted his lifetime to quail, bird dogs and horses. He spent as many days as possible in late fall and winter at Ichauway, riding and shooting with his guests and seeing that everyone—whether he worked there or was a visitor—had a busy schedule. There was no other way. Woodruff made the plans. Occasionally during hunting season, he might slip away for a day or two of duck shooting or for a try at prairie chickens, or grouse, or pheasants, or any number of winged game species. Several times he participated with other noted Americans in the one-shot antelope hunt in Wyoming.

For several weeks in the summer, he visited his TE Ranch in western Wyoming, usually with guests. They rode the TE Hills, fished for trout in the South Fork that ran through the ranch, looked over his cattle and visited with friends in Cody.

Many of his leisure hours were spent playing golf with Bobby Jones, his close friend and the world-renowned golf champion, and with other friends at golf clubs in which he held memberships from Cypress Point in California to Long Island, or taking time out from a business trip to visit one of the gambling clubs. Woodruff played as hard as he worked, though many times over many years I've heard him say, "One of the worst things a fellow can do is take himself too seriously."

Just as his father did when he was a salesman for Empire Flour Mills in Columbus and carried his dogs and gun along when he made his rounds in a buggy, Woodruff took time out from many of his perennial business trips to hunt and otherwise relax. There were few times, as during his early days in Wyoming before he bought the TE Ranch, that he made big game hunting trips for several weeks back into the mountains and was not available by telephone. Even so, when he was away from business, his associates never bothered him by phone except in matters of utmost emergency.

Fortunately for The Coca-Cola Company, Woodruff found much pleasure in traveling and his contributions to the welfare of his bottlers all over the world are immeasurable. He evaluated and helped in the selection of many of his foreign staff and he was able to work out with them many of their problems. Most of his overseas personnel had a fervid sense of patriotism for the company and its product, much of it inspired by Woodruff. This was to serve the company well through the bitter years of World War II.

The years 1923 to 1943 covered the peaks of prosperity in America and the depths of depression which were some of the most dramatic in the history of our country. During those years Woodruff found time for other activities beyond the boundaries of work and play. One of these interests of rather paradoxical nature included his re-association with Emory University, from which he had retired in anything but glory almost three decades before. In 1935 he was elected to the board of trustees of Emory University and the next year elected to the executive committee. One wonders if the university fathers had that same in-depth perception as Woodruff himself when they selected him as one of them. During that period Woodruff laid the foundation for his incredible philanthropies of which Emory University and its medical center was one of the main beneficiaries.

In 1937 Robert Woodruff set up his Trebor Foundation, Inc. Trebor is Robert spelled backward. Possibly when he did this he had Emory in mind, for that same year he announced plans for a Robert Winship Clinic at Emory. The history of the development of this idea into one of the world's most famous medical centers is told in another chapter.

The next year he persuaded his father and mother to set up the Emily and Ernest Woodruff Foundation for philanthropic purposes.

Woodruff loaned his advice and support to many worthwhile endeavors. He served on business advisory councils, industrial committees, safety councils and on the boards of many national and international corporations.

Even though it seemed that Woodruff's time was fully occupied with affairs outside The Coca-Cola Company, those in his organization knew better. He continued to run the company with a velvet gauntlet, and through all this period Coca-Cola prospered and everyone connected with it prospered.

Then World War II came along to offer Woodruff and The Coca-Cola Company one of their greatest challenges and, should they survive that, possibly their greatest opportunity.

ROBERT W. WOODRUFF AND THE DRINK HE MADE FAMOUS

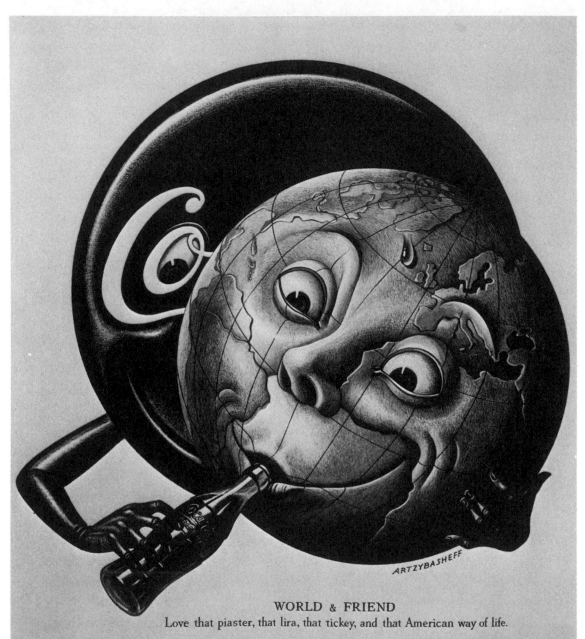

WORLD & FRIEND

Love that piaster, that lira, that tickey, and that American way of life.

TIME, May 15, 1950
by Boris Artzybasheff

Chapter 5
Later Years

The history of Coca-Cola and the story of Robert W. Woodruff are as inseparable as the elements that make air—or water—or Coca-Cola syrup. There would be no way to give a complete account of one without including the other. Someone in the spaces beyond the stars must have preordained the relationship of the two, for it is doubtful that a more satisfactory marriage ever existed on this earth.

Historians who recorded the "Coca-Cola saga" have never deliberately tried to separate the drink and the one-man power behind it. In most of the histories he is there by inference, standing tall in the shadow but not often enough given credit for some brilliant coup that allowed his company and its product another giant step forward. This was in deference to the man himself, who wanted no acclaim, no glory, no notoriety—only to sell more Coca-Cola. The product was more important than any one individual. In that category he included himself.

Once when the editors of *Time* magazine planned to run Woodruff's picture on the front cover, he expressed his appreciation for the honor but vetoed the idea and sold them on portraying a bottle of Coca-Cola instead. It turned out to be a tremendous bit of advertising. He figured that his picture on the cover could have in no way inspired the sale of more Coke.

The Coca-Cola Company maintains a tremendous file of stories which have come in from the far corners of the earth and which reflect the tremendous success of the most remarkable sales campaign ever launched. Woodruff could care less that although these stories reflect the genius and capability of the man behind this accomplishment, he was seldom mentioned. He knew that he had one job—and one only—to sell Coca-Cola.

The historians for Coca-Cola and others who keep such records claim there is no spot on earth where the product is not known. Question this, and they'll regale you with a hundred stories to prove it.

One yarn that went the rounds during World War II—but was not vouched for by the Coca-Cola people—was that when the U. S. Marines splashed ashore to take Iwo Jima, they found a Coca-Cola man ahead of them with a stand already set up in the fringe of trees behind the beach, ready to serve friend or foe.

Stories that can be verified or are on file include several reports from hidden corners of the world where the natives had never heard of the United States, did not know the name of the man who ruled or headed their own country, but were familiar with Coca-Cola.

One delightful account is about a Coca-Cola representative who worked up a daring publicity stunt for his company. He organized an expedition into the Peruvian jungles near Lima. With a photographer and interpreter along, he hoped to bring back a real picture story of introducing Coca-Cola to the "savages."

His party was deep in the jungle—more than two hundred miles from the fringes of civilization—when they found a colorful Indian woman who the photographer thought might be the perfect model.

After she had been assured that the party was on a peaceful mission, the interpreter tried to explain what it was all about and how she could help. She didn't seem to understand until he came to the word "Coca-Cola," which is universal in any language. Smiling broadly, the Indian woman reached into a sack she was carrying and retrieved a bottle of Coke, from which she offered the interpreter a swig.

In the records of The Coca-Cola Company are many similar and often unusual incidents. One considered a classic is the story of Geoff Workman who was known in England as the "Potholer" because of his hobby of living long periods underground. Once he set a world record as a human mole. For three months he lived in a cave beneath the Yorkshire Moors. Among the survival items he carried into the cave were twelve cases of Coca-Cola.

Coke is supplied to the inhabitants of secluded spots in many ways. Historian Hunter Bell says that at one time the only way to supply Coke to the residents on one sector of the high plateau of Jersey Island, one of England's Channel islands, was with heavy, premix tanks. These were brought by boat to a secluded bay and hauled in over a tortuous trail on a wooden yoke, normally used for carrying milk churns.

In one part of Mexico, he says, the Coca-Cola dealer must transport his cases over the mountain trails to the villages, and that Indian dealers in the jungle areas of the Isthmus of Tehuantepec use canoes for transporting cases to their native villages.

Coke is available in the cloud-covered peaks of the Himalayas and in the Andes and in the depths of jungles throughout the world. But these make up only a tiny fraction of this "nectar" that's found in all the civilized nations on earth.

That Coke is so highly regarded by all peoples, that under Woodruff's skillful promotion it appeared to break through every stratum of human society, has been recounted in a number of stories by Bell. One of the delightful little accounts was in a letter from Eddy Gilmore, Pulitzer Prize-winning Associated Press correspondent, to Paul Austin, who came up through the ranks to chairman of the Coca-Cola board of directors. The letter, written from Sussex in 1964, is one of the company's prized possessions. Gilmore wrote:

"Princess Anne, Queen Elizabeth's only daughter, is a student at a very swanky girls' school down here in Sussex. Well, Anne and a daughter of a friend of ours went to the local village not long ago, dropped into a fairly stuffy tea room and when the waitress (who was more or less overcome by seeing the Princess in the flesh) asked what the two girls would have, Ann replied, 'A Coca-Cola please.' The waitress fled in disorder, and the proprietress came out and said rather disapprovingly, 'We don't have Coca-Cola here.' To this Her Royal Highness stuck out her teenage tongue and commented, 'Well, we have it at Buckingham Palace.' She and her girlfriend then swanked out of the shop."

Winston Churchill was a devotee of Coca-Cola but because of British regulations earmarking all Coca-Cola for military use, even Churchill was denied one of his favorite drinks. When the Coca-Cola overseas staff heard that, an employee there managed to wangle a case out of the post exchange and deliver it personally to Churchill at No. 10 Downing Street.

E. J. Kahn, Jr., another Coca-Cola historian, says that when Farouk reigned in Egypt, all of the nightclubs in Cairo reserved a table for him each evening just in case he should decide to visit, and that beside each table was an iced-down supply of Coke. Before a bottling plant opened in Addis Ababa, Emperor Haile Selassie of Ethiopia regularly sent his imperial plane to Cairo for a load of Coke for his palace.

In all of the world's capitals, Coke is available. Even though Germany was at war with the United States and the German propagandists were shouting that Coca-Cola was not only the symbol of American capitalism but a menace to mankind, Hitler is said to have kept his larder well stocked with Coke as long as a supply was available.

In spite of its eternal battle with the beer, wine and fruit industries, Coca-Cola became the prestige drink in many countries, often acquiring a social status much higher than it enjoyed in the land of its birth. It often substitutes for champagne, wine and beer at weddings, garden parties, formal dinners and occasionally religious ceremonies in South America, Asia, Africa and Europe. For Coke there are no barriers of custom, race or religious creeds. Simply and without question it is the "universal drink."

In previous chapters, we told the story of Coca-Cola from its inception, when it crawled onto the American stage; of its slow walk into various parts of the world; and finally under Woodruff, the progress made to expand the horizons both at home and abroad of the Coca-Cola empire. The jet age of Coca-Cola really began when Japan brought America into the war with their shells and guns at Pearl Harbor. Among the casualties at Hickam Field were four Coca-Cola coolers. The date was December 7, 1941. Much of the western world had been at war since 1939.

With America in the war, Woodruff pledged all the resources of The Coca-Cola Company to the war effort. It is possible that the military, knowing that America might be on the verge of getting into the war, checked back on Woodruff's World War I record. They called on him again. The request had absolutely nothing to do with Coca-Cola or with any type of product that might fall naturally into the background and experience of The Coca-Cola Company technical staffs. The Ordnance Department wanted Woodruff to build and operate an efficient plant to load bags of gunpowder for use in artillery cannons.

Woodruff thought this over and even discussed it with several friends in the top echelon of the business world—men whose opinions he highly valued. He realized that what the Ordnance Department wanted was not so much the technical know-how in ammunition, but the kind of precision operation for which The Coca-Cola Company was noted.

Woodruff, a dedicated American, followed through on his pledge to lend every possible effort to the war effort and agreed to take on the pow-der-loading job. One of his specifications in accepting this enormous chore was that his company would handle it with no expectations of profit.

In late January, 1941, almost a year before Pearl Harbor, the company signed a contract to build, equip and manage this powder operation. Wood-ruff and his staff selected a site near the sprawling DuPont powder plant in Alabama, and Woodruff named his new subsidiary "Brecon Loading Company."

Under Woodruff's drive, the plant was completed and went into oper-ation two months ahead of schedule and at a saving of over four million dollars under the original estimate. In this instance the farsightedness of some in the War Department paid off, both in predicting America's entry into the war and in turning the critical powder job over to Woodruff. In less than a month after Pearl Harbor, Brecon Loading Company was in operation.

Woodruff assigned one of his senior vice presidents to the job. W. N. (Bill) Cochran was placed in charge of the operation, which required as much precision as—well—putting together a perfect Coca-Cola. The con-tribution of this Coca-Cola subsidiary was invaluable to the war effort.

The Coca-Cola Company went much further than merely lending some of its top administrators to the military. Woodruff knew how the price of sugar had skyrocketed during and following World War I, and with war clouds again on the horizon, his company had invested heavily in sugar, one of the chief ingredients in the manufacture of its drink.

This time, when America entered the war, the question of price was not nearly as important as the acute shortage of sugar. We were cut off from one of the vast sources of supply, and there was no way the home produc-tion could begin to make up this deficit. There simply was not enough for home consumption and to ration out to our troops stationed around the world. It was Woodruff's decision that The Coca-Cola Company willingly share a portion of its tremendous stockpile of sugar with the home folks and with the men in service.

Woodruff's statement was to the point, "We are delighted to do anything and everything we can toward winning the war."

Sugar rationed on the home front meant the curtailment of all manufactured products using it. The Coca-Cola Company, the largest user of pure granulated sugar on earth, was one of these. It meant that the company would have to greatly curtail the output of its product.

Woodruff's built-in computer sorted out the pieces and put them in order. No matter how complex his calculations were, they arrived at the amazing but simple decision. His company, regardless of cost, would make Coca-Cola available at a nickel a drink to every member of the armed forces, no matter where in the world they might be stationed.

All he needed was the approval and cooperation of the Department of Defense. When he proposed this to the military, they not only responded enthusiastically, but pledged their full cooperation.

Of all the momentous decisions Woodruff ever made in business, this was probably the most farsighted. It fulfilled a sizeable number of important obligations. The first was patriotic. It represented a touch of home to every service man, wherever he might be and under whatever circumstances. A bottle of Coca-Cola represented his country and many of the other things for which he was fighting. No one could ever calculate the number of lives it might have saved. The historians have innumerable stories which verify how important Coke proved to the war effort. They are taken from records in the War Department and in the offices of The Coca-Cola Company.

As an example, Bell tells of the GI from Texas who was stationed at Canada's Fort Churchill to help build one of the many airstrips in the Hudson Bay area after Pearl Harbor. He was half frozen from the forty-two degrees below zero when he walked into the post exchange and struggled to get out of his icy gloves and heavy parka. One of the attendants in the canteen automatically picked up a pot to pour steaming coffee into a mug.

The GI stopped him, and perhaps left him in a bit of confusion, by asking, "You just wouldn't happen to have a Coca-Cola, would you?"

The post exchange did, for it had been sent in by the heated freight carload from one of the bottling plants in Winnipeg.

Kahn tells an even more dramatic story about a GI who was captured and spent a horrible year in German prison camps. He was abused, half-starved and given hard, unnecessary manual labor. Once, on a forced march through a German village, he had made up his mind to give up, lie down and let his captors end his misery with a bullet when a peeling Coca-Cola poster caught his eye. As he walked on, memories started by the poster began to well through him of the drugstore back at home where he had courted his wife, of his wife and child waiting at home for him, and of the good life ahead if he could just come out of the war alive. He said that new strength and hope surged through him and a determination that he would come through.

Hundreds of such experiences are recorded, and probably thousands will never be.

Patriotism was possibly uppermost in Woodruff's mind when he made the decision to supply soldiers wherever they might be with five-cent bottles of Coke, but this was only a part of his decison. With what sugar was rationed to the company, it could make syrup for the home consumption and at least a part of the foreign trade. A virtually unlimited supply of sugar was available for use by, and in products for, the armed forces. This would keep most of the plants in operation.

Woodruff by no means overlooked the tremendous impact his collaboration with the military would have on future markets for his drink, both with the boys coming home from the war and the introduction of Coca-Cola into lands where it might be little known. He was looking far, far ahead.

Although bottling plants were scattered worldwide, in many corners of the globe they were too far removed from military outposts and actual battle lines. To remedy this, Woodruff had his technicians develop portable bottling plants, which had approximately the same priority with the armed services as guns and ammunition. These were hauled by military transport to wherever they were needed to keep the troops supplied with Coca-Cola. The first plants were rebuilt equipment; later, in spite of the shortage of metals and other materials, new bottling units were authorized and shipped overseas. With these The Coca-Cola Company sent along its own "colonels" to supervise the setting up and operation of these plants.

The first "war" plant, according to Bell, went to Iceland, halfway along the great circle route between New York and Moscow and a critical location in the shipment of supplies. The first American, British and Canadian troops arrived on this island in September, 1941, to protect it against German invasion, and the first Coca-Cola bottling plant was in operation by May, 1942.

One of the next plants went to Khorramshahr at the head of the Persian Gulf in Iran. Between these two points, one on the arctic circle and the other only thirty degrees above the equator, the difference in temperature was often as much as one hundred sixty-five to one hundred seventy-five degrees.

And so it went. The Coca-Cola plants doing military service were placed wherever they were needed to supply Coke to the boys in uniform. They were moved at the discretion of the military forces and The Coca-Cola Company. They appeared on all the continents in places never before served by the Export Corporation. One plant was dismantled in India, flown piece by piece over the Himalayas and set up again in China. One of the prized communications in Woodruff's office is the copy of a telegram from General Dwight D. Eisenhower to the High Command Headquarters in Washington ordering three million bottles of Coca-Cola and ten complete bottling plants with all the equipment and supplies. At the time this was a top secret communication, for from it the enemy could have deduced that the Allies intended to invade North Africa.

Another report was when Japan surrendered, a number of Coca-Cola plants were stored away in the hold of a naval vessel, waiting to follow the troops ashore. Japan has since become one of the sizeable markets of The Coca-Cola Company.

Later Eisenhower ordered more plants to follow his troops ashore after the Normandy invasion.

The end result was that sixty-four new Coca-Cola bottling plants were scattered around the world and that during the war they served ten billion bottles of Coke to our GI's at home and abroad. Overseas this was about ninety-five percent of all soft drinks sold at post exchanges. To supervise this huge operation, one hundred sixty-three employees of The Coca-Cola Export Corporation put on military uniforms and traveled throughout the world, checking on quality. They became known among our armed services as "Coca-Cola colonels."

Coke, however, was not always that plentiful. In the far outposts, the product was often hard to come by. All sorts of stories are told about how it was valued. In some of the remote regions when an inadequate shipment of Coke came in, the chaplain of the outfit might be asked to exercise his Solomon's judgment so that the men could share and share alike. Soldiers might shoot craps to see who would get a bottle or portion of a bottle. Where it was an extremely scarce commodity, it was sometimes kept in a safe, where safes were available. It was valued along with letters and pictures from home. Kahn reports that "in the Solomons, a single bottle of Coca-Cola sold for five dollars (in New Guinea, an offer of six and a half was rejected out of hand); in Casablanca, for ten; in an Alaskan outpost, for forty. A field-artillery sergeant in Italy who got two bottles in 1944, drank one and raffled off the other among the men in his battalion, the proceeds going to swell a fund for children of members of the unit who died in action. Four thousand dollars was collected from soldiers vying for the bottle, and the man who won it was too overcome with emotion to drink it."

Through Ernie Pyle, Woodruff heard about this incident and from his company sent two thousand to the fund, but did it in such a discreet manner—to keep the company from being deluged with such requests—that few of his top officials even knew about it.

There is no way to estimate the tremendous impact the act of supplying Coca-Cola to all the troops had on the drink throughout the world. Our own ten million service men brought home a built-in thirst, and consumption on the home front went up sharply. Literally millions of people with whom our uniformed men came in contact on all continents were introduced to Coke. The world market, which had been brought along at a satisfactorily fast clip during the almost two decades since Woodruff organized The Coca-Cola Export Corporation, simply exploded. The complaint of the other soft drink companies that the expansion of the Coca-Cola empire had been done at government expense was legitimate enough, but they couldn't make too much noise about it. Woodruff had established the whole operation as a patriotic gesture, and anyone making a public issue of the product's gain on that basis would even further advertise the drink and its prestigious niche built into the mind of mankind.

After a thorough survey, Woodruff had his Export Corporation assign the sixty-four plants which had followed the armed forces around the world to permanent homes. These were strategically located to cover many blank spaces on the map where Coca-Cola was in demand but too far from a reliable source of supply.

Many of the plants, especially those in our enemy countries, which had been closed down during the war, were reopened. Coca-Cola representatives, who were citizens of those countries, having played a star role in establishing Coke in their homeland before the war and keeping the plants in operation during it, welcomed the end of the war. It meant that they could again be active members of The Coca-Cola Company organization without fear of being shot as spies.

One of the dramatic examples of Coca-Cola employee dedication to Woodruff and to the product he represented is the story of Max Keith. Woodruff met Max in 1933, and the two men were immediately attracted to one another. The president of Coca-Cola, always in a search for good men who could step into positions of responsibility with the company, quickly recognized in the German the kind of employee who could make things happen in his country. Coca-Cola G.m.b.H., a wholly owned German Coca-Cola subsidiary, had been set up in 1929, and Woodruff persuaded Keith to get into the business. At that time, the output from the bottling plants in Germany was small in comparison with other regions.

Woodruff's selection of the man was more than justified. In less than six years, Keith was supervising all production in Germany, and the production had risen to astronomical figures compared to its humble beginning.

After World War II broke out, Coca-Cola concentrate was no longer available in Germany. Keith had a supply of concentrate on hand. This he rationed carefully to his plants and even managed to smuggle in a modest amount of concentrate from neutral Switzerland, which fortunately made some Coca-Cola available in Germany for a little while longer.

To keep his bottling plants in operation, Keith developed an alternate drink from fruits, carbonated water and other ingredients available in Germany. Called "Fanta," it was accepted enthusiastically where Coke was not available. More important, it helped Keith keep his organization intact.

Max Keith was never a member of the Nazi party, but with his personality, salesmanship, and a limited supply of Coca-Cola, remained on good terms with the German high command. With a Woodruff touch, he made a contribution to the German war effort by bottling water in Coca-Cola bottles and storing it in bomb shelters and in farm buildings as a source of uncontaminated emergency water should the city supply be destroyed by bombs. This helped to keep his plants working with official approval. Better still, the high command put him in uniform, gave him a staff car and appointed him as an officer in charge of all soft drink operations in the country, its allied and occupied territories. He was free to travel. This he did, covering Italy, France, Belgium and all countries under German jurisdiction. He visited with bottlers wherever he could find them, with encouragement and suggestions that would help keep the business going. Most followed and profited by his advice. Coca-Cola plants on enemy soil were not intentionally flattened by our bombers, but where they were casualties, the unlucky bottler salvaged what equipment had been left whole or was repairable and put it aside for future use.

Max Keith, more than any one person, was responsible for keeping Coca-Cola alive in German-occupied countries. One of his plants at Essen continued untouched through the war, surviving on Fanta. Although most of Essen, with its high military potential, was one of the principal target areas for our bombs, the Coca-Cola plant was spared. With much relish, Woodruff likes to tell why. The bottling plant was located near one of the largest and most active houses of prostitution in the city. Allied intelligence suggested that these be passed up as target areas, since both might later prove invaluable to the needs of the conquering troops.

Coca-Cola G.m.b.H. continued to bottle and market Fanta until 1949, when the supply lines to unlimited quantities of Coca-Cola concentrate again opened up and the plants were able to get back into full production. The next year The Coca-Cola Company acquired the Fanta trademark from Coca-Cola G.m.b.H. and spread worldwide the drink with which Max Keith had possibly saved the central European market for Coca-Cola.

Because company rules specified a retirement age, Robert W. Woodruff officially retired from The Coca-Cola Company on January 1, 1955, less than a month after he had passed his sixty-fifth birthday. Theoretically this meant giving up any authority he might have over the control of the company and its operations. He remained on the board of directors, but the only title he kept was chairman of the finance committee.

"The finance committee has no authority whatsoever," he pointed out.

Technically this may have been true and no doubt would have applied to a man of lesser stature stepping down as an official of almost any company. Not Woodruff. He gave up his salary and presumably his authority, yet one of his first acts after retirement was to move into a suite of offices much larger and more elaborate than those he had occupied when he had been officially the Boss during the creation of his empire.

The Coca-Cola Company was his baby. While he had not been present at its birth or even through its toddling years, he had adopted it as a weakling, unsteady on its feet, and had fathered and mothered it into a giant. One of the basic concepts of parenthood is that no matter how old or large a child becomes, to those who reared it, it still remains a baby.

Perhaps he was no longer Boss of The Coca-Cola Company in name, but Woodruff remained the Boss in performance and spirit. He continued to operate as before. No shifts in the higher echelon of personnel, no policies or major decisions involving the present or future of the company were made without his approval. Many of his old associates had retired and gone into other fields or had moved on to their rewards in some celestial bottling plant. He keenly felt that his obligation was to keep his company virile and growing with young, competent officials. He had brought many of them up through the ranks, where they gained experience and were taught all phases of the business.

"There is no way," he said, "that any organization or individual, at any stage of its life, can sit back, rest on its laurels, and be content to collect the rewards already won. You continue to grow or you deteriorate."

Woodruff's friends, among them company employees with whom he was closely associated day by day, could detect little, if any, change in the pattern of the life he had established over half a century. He continued to run his company down to the details where they mattered. He kept himself informed on the progress at Emory University Hospital and Clinic which, with both his money and guidance, fast developed into one of the finest institutions of its kind in the country.

In retirement Woodruff remained closely involved in the affairs of his home town of Atlanta. The city fathers made few decisions concerning its progress or its future without first talking them over with the man at 310 North Avenue. Though he never ran for or held any public office, Woodruff's influence on civic matters, from local to national, was strong. Under several presidents, he carried the number one guest card of the White House.

His myriad interests included the state and national Safety Councils, Boys' Clubs, Boy Scouts and many, many others to whom he gave a helping hand, financially and otherwise.

He followed his life-long pattern of remembering the birthdays, anniversaries and special events of friends all over the nation and continued his practice of inviting to Atlanta and meeting with the boards of directors of numerous large corporations (which incidentally resulted in many of these establishing plants or branch offices in the South). He took the time to discuss the problems of and give advice when he was asked to many of his friends in other lines of business.

He could have been one of the princes of Serendip, for he practiced the rare art of making good things come true for people who deserved but least expected them. Many of these he did anonymously and this gave him some of the most enjoyable moments of his life.

With all of this, he found time to play. One of his pleasures was golf, and when he was at home in Atlanta, he spent many an afternoon at the Peachtree Club or East Lake or Capital City with a foursome of friends.

Often he would fly to California or New York or Washington, D. C. for a few games of golf at clubs in which he held memberships. His foursomes in those places often included presidents, screen stars and other personalities whose names were household words in America.

Woodruff, however, spent most of his playtime outdoors with horses and dogs, fishing gear and guns. The Wyoming high country was a favorite playground. Each year he and Mrs. Woodruff relaxed for weeks in late summer and early fall at their TE Ranch west of Cody, where they rode the cattle and game trails with their guests and where he visited with rancher friends and others who took pride in introducing him as one of their Cody citizens. In later years he gave up the more rugged hunting life he had followed as a younger man, far back in the Thorofare and high mountain country, and spent his vacation periods closer to the ranch and town of Cody.

Since he had been old enough to hunt with his Uncle Joel Hurt and Grandfather Winship, Woodruff's first love of the outdoors had been bobwhite quail hunting. All of the days he felt he could spare away from the office in the fall and winter seasons were spent at Ichauway Plantation, where his hunting teams were always ready to go. After retirement he followed approximately the same schedule at Ichauway that had been his way of life since he and Mrs. Woodruff first opened their doors to guests early in 1930. Each year he entertained shooting partners and friends through most of the season.

For Woodruff, Ichauway holds happy and unhappy memories. Two of his intimate friends and several of his farm employees who were also close friends passed away at the plantation while he was there, and it was here that Miss Nell suffered the stroke from which she never recovered.

Woodruff was at the plantation when he, too, experienced a much lighter stroke. At the time he didn't realize it, but when he returned the next day to Atlanta, he went to his home on Tuxedo Road and upstairs to his room. Dr. Herndon, who dropped by for one of his regular visits, found him there, sitting quietly in a chair. At first glance he seemed in his usual state of health, except that he was too quiet and noticeably unresponsive for Woodruff. When he finally spoke, there was a slight slur in his speech.

Herndon immediately recognized the symptoms. He wanted to make a more thorough examination, but Woodruff would have none of it. "I'm all right," he said. The doctor remained with him until bedtime and returned early the next morning. Woodruff shrugged off any suggestion that he might be in difficulty.

"I'm all right," he repeated. "Tomorrow I'm going back to the farm."

"If that's the way it is," Herndon replied, "I'd better go with you."

The next day he flew to Ichauway with his doctor and two other friends close to him. Mrs. Martha Ellis, his niece who had served as his unofficial hostess in Atlanta, New York and Ichauway since the death of her husband, went along, as did Luther Cain, his personal friend and valet. There were no other guests. They had planned to be at the plantation for only a brief period of complete rest.

After a few days at Ichauway, Woodruff got out of bed in the middle of the night. When he stood up, his leg gave away and he almost fell. He braced himself against a bedside chair and touched the buzzer that connected his room with Luther's. In a matter of minutes both Luther and the doctor were there. This was definitely a stroke. His right arm and leg had no strength and little use. His speech was noticeably slurred. Luther and the doctor got him back in bed and Herndon immediately called Dr. Herbert R. Karp, chief neurologist on the Emory Clinic staff.

Dr. Karp flew to Ichauway and made his diagnosis there. He assured both Herndon and Woodruff that the stroke was a light one, in that part of the brain that controlled the nerves and muscles on the right side of the body. He also suggested that instead of carrying Mr. Woodruff to Emory Hospital for treatment, his best therapy was to remain at the plantation until he recovered, which should be within a few weeks.

Dr. Herndon had a diagnosis of his own. "With his determination and doggedness, Mr. Woodruff will get over it. He's the only man I've ever known who can overpower a sleeping pill."

Herndon and Mrs. Ellis cancelled all of their other business dates and they and Luther remained at Ichauway for about a month. It was one of the longest periods Woodruff had been at the plantation during the hunting season without having an endless round of guests to enjoy the quail coveys and the rides through the fields and woods.

As Dr. Karp had predicted, Woodruff's speech cleared up rather quickly. He was longer gaining full use of his right arm, hand and leg, but with the courage with which he had met all unsavory situations throughout his life, he made himself use his arm and hand and walk without a cane or other support. As Herndon had suggested, he simply overpowered his affliction, and after about a month at Ichauway he came back to Atlanta.

His doctors had diagnosed that alcohol, which lowered instead of raising Woodruff's blood pressure, had been the cause of his trouble. After he recovered, Herndon recommended that he could still have a drink or two, but should confine his intake to no more than two ounces before lunch and two ounces before dinner. "I tried that a day or two," Woodruff smiled, "and figured that if this was all I could have, to hell with it."

So he voluntarily gave up the pleasure of his cocktails, martinis and such, but continued to keep a supply of alcoholic beverages for any of his guests who wanted a drink at any time.

The most disappointing aftereffect of Woodruff's stroke was his decision at the beginning of the next season to pass up quail shooting. During several of the opening days he went out with a couple of his hunting partners before he concluded that his balance was not as good as he thought it should be for walking through the rough woods. He didn't give the hunt up entirely. Though he no longer attempted to handle a gun, he continued to go afield with his parties. Sometimes he rode the hunting wagon. Many times he rode his horse along with the hunt, but never got out of the saddle to shoot.

"Only trouble," he quipped, "is that it takes two people to put me on a horse and three to get me off."

Woodruff spends as much of his year as possible at Ichauway Plantation, which he calls the "farm." And indeed it is, for a large part of the activity there centers around the cattle and the crops. Here he finds more peace and relaxation than anywhere else, even while he remains deeply involved in its operation. Always a restless spirit, he follows the pattern established over a lifetime and moves frequently between his home and office in Atlanta, his apartment in New York and such places as south Florida and southern California, where he visits friends. Every few years he makes a foreign tour to visit with his organization men and his bottlers in other parts of the world and to see old friends in the company who have kept the overseas business thriving.

When he's at home in Atlanta, he goes daily to his office. There he keeps abreast of what is happening in his Coca-Cola empire throughout the world; with the directors of his several foundations he makes decisions of where the income from those foundations may be used to make the world a better place in which to live; he reads his mail and studies reports from every source in which his office staff knows he might have an interest; he meets with friends around the luncheon table in his office suite and discusses everything from football to foreign affairs.

"Having lunch with the Boss," one of his friends said, "is always a delightful occasion. And the price is right."

All during the year, Woodruff makes a trip for a few days at a time to Ichauway. He must go back to the farm now and then—as he says—"to readjust my sense of values." He's there at the planting of the crops, in the growing season, when the crops are being harvested. He finds much pleasure in driving for hours along the woods roads that wind through the heart of the plantation, watching for quail coveys that jump up beside the road and for other wild creatures so abundant in the open pine woods or around the oak thickets. He spends most of the hunting season at his plantation, leaving only to attend board meetings or business sessions which grow less numerous each year, or for other special occasions. Ichauway is his contact with the good earth and the people there who are the salt of that earth— which represent the basic values of life.

The tranquility and even tenor of Ichauway seem to restore his soul. The qualities there are a far cry from the almost unbelievable forces which were marshalled to spread the religion of Coca-Cola throughout the world, and which for so many years occupied a major portion of his existence. The plantation seems like a barrier between the more dynamic years with their critical decisions, myriads of board meetings, conventions, seething cocktail parties and formal dinners which were an integral part of Woodruff's life for so many years. Now, large gatherings are more of an irritation than a challenge. He avoids them when he can. He wears a hearing aid and can understand little in the cacophony of conversation and laughter. Much more to his tastes are the quiet talks at the famous round table in his gun room or at the dinner table, and the reflective pipe of tobacco with some friend at the fireside in his bedroom at retiring time. He rarely speaks of his own accomplishments and, however proud he may be, is more than likely to simplify the great successes of his company and the details of how they came about.

His humble summation is, "I've been lucky."

Woodruff continues to occupy himself with business and personal affairs. He's kept informed of every move made by The Coca-Cola Company and often adds his own deft touch to some project proposed or underway. He keeps in touch with both the problems and accomplishments of his friends, helping where he can when one is in difficulty and feeling a sincere sense of pride in the honors and successes of another. Joe Jones, one of Woodruff's strong right arms and close associates over several decades, often remains days at a time with him at Ichauway and the two carry on a volume of business and personal matters from the farm.

In his retirement, Robert W. Woodruff has remained as interested and active as he has been throughout his life, from the day he took off his college clothes and put on a pair of overalls to go to work.

Woodruff was well into his eighth decade before he began to let the world take off his wraps and discover him. It is paradoxical that the man responsible for making Coca-Cola a household word in every spoken language should himself remain so far behind the scenes that many of the people working for him were more widely known than he was. One of the stories biographer E. J. Kahn, Jr., tells illustrates how this happened in New York. Woodruff was traveling with one of his employees, Turner Jones, who routinely took care of all expenses when the two men traveled together.

Jones was settling up with the hotel cashier (says Kahn) who knew and respected Mr. Jones of The Coca-Cola Company, when Woodruff decided he wanted to cash a personal check and appeared at his employee's side. The cashier asked Jones if Woodruff's check was all right, and the astonished Jones vouched for it. As the two men were walking away from the cashier's window, Woodruff said quietly, "What man can want more than to identify another that he in turn may identify him?"

That was the way Woodruff wanted it during the greater part of his life. It went against his nature to be "loudly thanked" or to occupy any part of the stage where others were involved, and usually they were. He felt that he could accomplish more in business and get more out of his personal life by letting others take the credit.

In everything he did, Woodruff tried to live a life of anonymity. Men of letters who wrote about his fabulous plantation or ranch respected his wishes and never used his name or even the name and location of those places, except in general terms. The little favors he did his friends were usually in such a roundabout way that his friends never knew. His gifts to benefit mankind were almost always by an "anonymous donor." He refused to accept literally hundreds of honors which would have put the spotlight on him. With all of his other traits of aggressiveness and drive and often stubbornness, he was basically a very humble person and never sought or encouraged glory or fame. Had he promoted himself, he certainly could have been as well known as Will Rogers, Dwight D. Eisenhower and other such famous men of his time.

Woodruff was well into his eighties before he began to allow this barrier to be broken down and to accept some of the awards so long over-due. Those closest to him were a bit surprised when he agreed to accept the "Shining Light" award, and with it an eternal light to burn in the little park in front of the new Coca-Cola office building. Once a year one of these lights, placed in an appropriate location, is dedicated by the Atlanta Gas Light Company and WSB radio and television station to Atlantans who had contributed magnanimously to their fellow citizens in the state and to the welfare of mankind. The question in the minds of many who did not know Woodruff very well was why this recognition had not come years before it did.

There was a saying among his colleagues that the best way not to get help from one of Woodruff's foundations was to approach him and suggest that if he'd help, they'd name a building or something else for him. But he consented to allow Emory University to name one of its new buildings the Robert W. Woodruff Library for Advanced Studies, even though he had given no financial help toward its establishment; subsequently one of his foundations made a grant for the purpose of acquiring additional volumes to help fill its shelves. Although he had at first objected, he later acquiesced in naming the medical complex the Woodruff Medical Center, which consists largely of buildings erected with donations from Robert W. Woodruff or one of his foundations.

When it became known that Woodruff had become more lenient toward being recognized, honors began to pour in from colleges, institutions, associations and organizations from all over America, most of whom had one way or another felt his influence. Graciously he accepted them and allowed them to become public knowledge.

All of this acclaim, though so richly deserved, was long overdue.

ICHAUWAY
PLANTATION

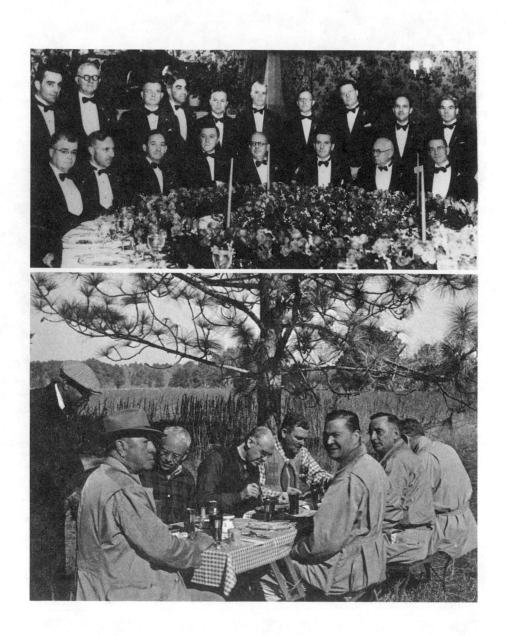

HEADQUARTERS OF THE COCA-COLA COMPANY

Chapter 6
Friends and Associates

It is true that no man can be an island. Many have tried to hide themselves away from the world, or to position themselves above human association and the challenges of living. These lead barren and unrewarding lives. They leave behind them fruitless voids.

Both the tradition and destiny of the human race is that man was not born to live alone. The days of his years are made richer and more complete by his association with others. Our lives are inextricably woven into the patterns of other lives. How intricate often depends on the individual, his ambitions, his goals and more important, what he hopes to give back to the divine powers who gave him life.

Friends are the most necessary segment of any man's existence. Without them life is meaningless. Without friendship there can be no satisfaction in what we accomplish, no sympathy in what we fail to do, no closeness in either triumphant or bitter moments, no love. Friends are the backlog of whatever wealth we may possess.

Robert W. Woodruff's friends over the span of a long lifetime would make up one of the most interesting and assorted groups ever assembled in this or any other generation. They have ranged the echelons almost from the unbelievable to the sublime, and the variety has been endless. A great majority of these were his business associates, and many of those were very close to him.

No one will ever know whom he considered his most intimate friend, unless it were his mother or his wife. Rumor once had it that he considered it might be the one Woodruff was talking with at the particular moment, but only while he was talking with him. This, of course, was not in the proper perspective, for every friend counts with him, and there is little variance in degree. The closeness of his association and friendship does not end when the conversation is over.

Since he himself has made no evaluation, how could anyone possibly evaluate for him? The worldwide list of people with whom he did business, played or enjoyed social activities would itself fill a volume, and the stories of these associations might fill a shelf of books. Of all these, what biographer would have the temerity to make a choice of this one or that one? Even The Man himself would never make such an attempt.

Except for the risk of incurring tremendous displeasure from the many hundreds of friends and associates whose names might not appear here, what would be a better way to delineate such of Woodruff's traits as forcefulness, humor, astuteness and judgment than stories of his business and personal relations with a number of the people in his life? The sum of these add up to both the complex and simple personality of The Man.

Many of these men whose lives were influenced by Woodruff, or his life by them, go back to the years before I became acquainted with Woodruff. Many others I have known through my association with him. One of the things which has never ceased to impress and often to amaze me was his attraction to such a variety of individuals that ranged from peasants to poets and kings. All had certain qualifications that drew him to them. Essentially these were honesty, dignity in their stations in life, ambition, imagination and color. Dull, drab people seldom attracted him.

Woodruff was as much at home with Phonograph Jones and Max Wilde in a Wyoming hunting camp as he was at a state dinner in the White House. In his earlier days he shared campfires and tents with these men in the big Thorofare country between the massive Absaroka Range and Continental Divide. All men appealed to him and he was especially intrigued by those whom he considered were doing a good job, no matter what their profession or line of business.

Woodruff welcomed new acquaintances that he found charming and with those qualities he admired, but he always placed a special value on those who had gone with him along the trail for many years. This was indicated in a birthday note that went with a gift to one he had cherished over long seasons.

"Although I value newer friends
They don't replace the old.

The new ones are like silver;
The old ones pure as gold..."

One of those for whom he had an abiding affection was Walter Teagle. When they first met in 1920, Teagle was president of the Standard Oil Company of New Jersey, and Woodruff, as a salesman for White Motor Company, had sold him on adding White trucks when he replaced his equipment at Standard Oil. Later, in the early 1920's, he and Woodruff were members of a group that purchased a fifty-four-hundred-acre plantation on the Georgia-Florida line below Thomasville. Woodruff said he was the "poor man" in that group of industrialists, and that it strained his resources somewhat, but he felt that his association with the other successful men would help him in many ways. They named the plantation Norias, after a section of King Ranch in Texas, where all of the members had hunted in the past.

Because of their interest in quail and dogs and the outdoors, he and Teagle became fast friends. At that time there was little real scientific knowledge of the bobwhite quail. This group of men, along with other plantation owners in the region and in collaboration with the federal game authorities, commissioned Herbert Stoddard, a well-known scientist and ornithologist, to make a study of the bobwhite. The result, now well-known, was the most complete and authoritative work on this game bird, with recommended management practices that would bring the quail population to the carrying capacity of the land.

Some years later Walter White and Woodruff sold their interest in Norias to establish their own plantation on Ichauway Creek in Baker County, Georgia. They and the other members persuaded Mr. Teagle to buy all shares so that he would be the sole owner.

"I've forgotten what he paid per acre," Woodruff now says with a chuckle. "He didn't ask for our advice or have an appraisal made. He made his own and sent each of us a check. Whatever it was, no one complained."

After Ichauway was established, Woodruff and Teagle had many visits together when they were either hunting, training dogs or breeding them in a search for championship stock. No national champion ever came out of this collaboration, but their dogs did win many lesser field trials.

When the two men did not have a chance to visit, they exchanged letters on a variety of subjects, but usually about either business or hunting dogs. Teagle's only enthusiasm that Woodruff did not share to the same degree was fishing. Teagle was an artist with a fly rod, and perhaps his favorite game fish was the Atlantic salmon. He owned memberships in clubs on a couple of Canada's noted salmon rivers and spent much time there in season. He was determined to introduce Woodruff to a salmon on the end of a line.

One of the stories told often by Woodruff and recounted by his biographers involved an invitation by Teagle to meet him at Kedgwick Lodge and spend a week fishing for salmon in the famous Ristigouche River. Woodruff accepted the invitation, but not on Teagle's terms. He said in his telegram that he would arrive at Kedgwick Lodge on Friday night, fish Saturday, and return home Sunday. Teagle's wire came right back, "Don't bother."

The two men remained close friends as long as Teagle lived. After Teagle's death, Woodruff was heard to remark that he and Walter White were two men who had the greatest influence on his life.

Another man very close to Woodruff in his hunting and other outdoor activities was Roy Rogers. They had become acquainted in the days before Ichauway and hunted quail together whenever one of Woodruff's business trips brought him close to Baxley, where Roy worked for the U. S. Department of Agriculture. Their mutual interest in bobwhite quail and hunting dogs ripened into a deep friendship.

"He was one of the most knowledgeable outdoorsmen I ever knew," Woodruff said. "He knew and loved dogs and they loved him, and for that reason he was an excellent trainer. He could see the qualities in a dog even while it was a puppy. He raised and trained Lloyd George, the finest four-legged hunting companion I ever knew."

Part of the story of Roy Rogers and Lloyd George has been told in the saga of Ichauway Plantation and is worth repeating here. It emphasizes one strong facet of Robert W. Woodruff's character and personality.

Lloyd George was sired out of royal blood. His ancestors reached back to the Count Noble-Gladstone strain of Lewellyn setters that made field history in America. Roy became intrigued with the puppy when it was only a few weeks old; it was the only one in the litter with the persistence and determination to continually climb over the side of the wooden box in which the puppies were housed.

Roy lavished both affection and discipline on Lloyd George from his puppy days and developed him into one of the best hunting dogs anywhere. The setter's fame was not limited to the countryside around Baxley. Quail hunters came from all over the country to hunt with Roy and his dog, and fabulous sums were offered by wealthy sportsmen who tried to buy the setter. All offers were turned down as positively as if they had been made for a member of the Rogers family.

Mr. Woodruff was the exception. The evidence of how devoted he and Roy Rogers were to one another was proven when Lloyd George went to Ichauway as a member of the plantation team. A short time later Roy followed the dog to Ichauway and took over the job as trainer and master of the kennels, and later as manager of the plantation.

The morning Lloyd George died, in his fourteenth year, the plantation went into mourning and the concensus was that he should have a proper funeral. This decision climaxed in one of the most unusual ceremonies ever to take place in the land of Thronoteeska, which was the Creek Indian name for the Flint River.

Most of the plantation personnel had jobs that needed being done during the daylight hours, so the funeral was held at night. The gathering included more than a hundred people and all the dogs at Ichauway. The funeral procession started on one of the winding plantation roads several hundred yards from a high bluff overlooking the Flint River. With the casket on a wheelbarrow, the group wound single file through the woods, its way lighted by the weird flame of torches made from pine knots and resin-soaked wood. To the Negro spirituals hummed softly by the group, one of the coon or fox hounds, also on leash in the procession, occasionally raised its head and bayed, adding to the mournfulness and mystery of the night.

The high wooded point was a proper setting for Lloyd George's first resting place. This was a part of the plantation the old dog loved to hunt.

The bluff overlooked a big bend of the Flint River and on the knoll stood century-old live oaks, festooned with long streamers of Spanish moss. As the dog's casket was lowered into its grave, the plantation hands sang "Swing Low, Sweet Chariot" as only an Ichauway choir could sing it.

Later Lloyd George's remains were moved to a small plot just outside the plantation "circle." He was the first to be placed in Ichauway's dog cemetery. Over the years this nook of hallowed ground became the burial place of other greats of Ichauway dogdom, a field of bygone champions, every one illustrious in its way. Of the hundreds of dogs which have run on the plantation, these are the elite, the nobility, the kings and queens and princes of generations of fine bird dogs.

Roy Rogers followed Lloyd George to the Happy Quail Lands some five years later. The man who took his place was Guy Touchtone. Guy was a farmer and carpenter who had helped put up the buildings around the circle, and who, through his association with the man who preceded him and the knowledge he had gained of the schedules and programs on the farm, seemed a logical successor.

"I never did have anything but a temporary job," Guy once told me. "The day after Roy's funeral, the Boss said, 'You'd better take over and run this show until I can find somebody else.' I've been here ever since."

He held this temporary job almost a quarter of a century until the Boss retired him, gave him a thousand-acre farm adjoining the plantation and built a house there for his erstwhile employee.

Bill Etchells followed Touchtone. Bill was a Canadian by birth out of Broomhill, Manitoba. With the exception of a period in World War II, he had been in the dog business all of his life. He came to Texas in 1938 to work for G. A. Story and left in 1941 to serve four years with the Canadian Airforce. After a medical discharge in 1945, he came south again, this time to work in Lee County, Georgia, with John Gates, one of the noted trainers of bird dogs.

Woodruff knew of Etchells and invited him to Ichauway to talk about a possible connection there.

"If you can get that job, take it," Gates advised him. "That's the best plantation in the South."

Ichauway's Boss and Bill Etchells liked one another, and in the spring of 1955, Etchells went to work on the plantation as trainer and supervisor of the kennels. He also initiated a program of raising the quail population by putting into operation such sound management practices as controlled burning and the planting of feed patches in wooded areas.

His first year at Ichauway, the total take of bobwhites for the season was about three hundred birds. Within a few years he had raised this to around three thousand birds for the season, and this could have been doubled had his Boss desired. But Woodruff remembered the lean days of hunting and preferred to keep the season's bag well within limits.

When Touchtone retired, Bill Etchells took over as plantation manager. With his able assistant, Bill Adkins, they have not only supervised all farming, but have built up the quail population almost to the carrying capacity of the land. These two men have become important cogs in the wheels of Woodruff's life, for he retreats to Ichauway Plantation all during the year to find peacefulness and relaxation from the turbulent world outside.

Woodruff was a very serious student of public affairs. He not only contributed more than his share through two world wars, he kept himself informed at all times on matters of national interest. This was good business for his company, which was international in scope, but it was more than that. One of his great prides was in his country. Because of his vast comprehension of business, civic and social patterns and how they were interrelated, he became an advisor of U. S. Presidents from the days of Herbert Hoover. Although a staunch Democrat, party lines did not bind him and he served where he was asked and needed, though it might sometimes be inconvenient for him. Over the years he dedicated his time and counsel to many developments of national import. These were often so varied in scope that they bordered on the incredible, but they had one thing in common. All were toward making his nation and his community a better, safer place in which to live.

Over half a century or more the list is long; National Citizens Committee for Welfare and Relief Mobilization of 1932; Business Advisory Council, Department of Commerce; Franklin D. Roosevelt's Inner Council of Businessmen; National Industrial Committee, Metropolitan Opera Fund; National (F. D.) Roosevelt Memorial Committee; trustee, National Safety Council (In 1949 he organized and was on the executive committee of the Atlanta chapter, National Safety Council); appointed by Secretary of Commerce Charles Sawyer to Advisory Committee on Highway Safety; board member, National Mobilization of Resources for the United Negro Colleges; member of advisory committee of Ford Foundation to recommend distribution of ninety million dollars for medical schools.

E. J. Kahn, Jr., in his biography *RWW,* tells a typical Woodruff story in connection with this gift from the Ford Foundation.

In the allocation of these funds, the most controversial question (says Kahn) was whether comparatively small funds should go to a large number of schools, or a very few schools should get large bequests. The then dean of the Harvard Medical School had been arguing the latter case quite eloquently; it made sense, he said, for the bulk of the money to go to Harvard and two or three other "peaks of excellence," because these places trained men who in turn went out and improved other places. Woodruff thought this plan was discriminating unfairly and unwisely against the smaller schools, like Emory, but he held his tongue until well into the second day.

Then he spoke up. He said firmly that if the "peaks of excellence" plan was adopted rather than the broader distribution plan he favored, he would personally hire a public relations firm to tell the entire country how the distribution was being carried out, and that he didn't think the country would like it. He realized, he continued, that he was known as a friend and proponent of Emory, but that was irrelevant.

"I'm not talking about Emory," he said. "Don't worry about Emory. I can take care of Emory myself." Woodruff carried the day.

Other national interests to which Woodruff gave his time for the betterment of his country were the National Manpower Council; Council for Financial Aid to Education, Inc.; Boys' Clubs of America; Federal City Council; President Kennedy's Task Force of Foreign Economic Assistance; and many others of lesser stature.

With his business and other interests, The Man seemed to have an unlimited capacity.

Since Hoover, all of the U. S. Presidents have in one way or another availed themselves of his wealth of judgment and perception. Over many years he had a pass to the White House, but never used it except by invitation. He attended many formal and informal dinners there. He was close to Roosevelt, Truman, Kennedy, Nixon and Ford, and closer to Johnson who had often asked his advice back in the years when he was on his way up the political ladder to the presidency.

Eisenhower and Woodruff had much in common before they met for the first time at Cason Callaway's Blue Springs home on the southern slope of Pine Mountain. During the war, the general, realizing what a morale booster Coca-Cola was to the troops, had put a priority of Coca-Cola bottling plants and ordered them along with his arms and ammunition. To the men in service, Coca-Cola was a symbol of America and the things there worth fighting for. Woodruff was the general behind Coca-Cola on the home front. They recognized in each other the qualities of sincerity, integrity and leadership. Both loved hunting and golf, and their friendship developed from the very beginning. It was natural that Ike should hunt at Ichauway with Woodruff, and that they should have many golf games together at the Augusta National Golf Club and other courses. The American Assembly, one of Eisenhower's projects to bring together businessmen, labor, the professions, the government and members of all political parties in an effort to solve major national problems, received Woodruff's full support, financially and otherwise.

Their friendship continued to ripen over the years. Woodruff was one of those who urged Eisenhower to run for President and did his share to help his friend win by a large majority of the votes. Before and after Ike's terms in the White House, Woodruff's files contain many personal notes from Eisenhower expressing appreciation for their friendship and what it meant to the Eisenhower family.

During his years as the nation's chief executive, Eisenhower devoted as many days to hunting, fishing and golf as his official duties would allow. Wherever it were possible, Woodruff was included. When Ike visited George Humphrey's Horseshoe Plantation between Tallahassee and Thomasville, he often found a boy-like delight in slipping through the cordon of

Secret Service men assigned to protect him and have a visit with the Woodruffs at Ichauway.

Woodruff was always one of the most welcome guests at the White House. The President felt that Woodruff's presence gave charm and dignity to those occasions when other empire builders or world dignitaries as Prince Philip and Queen Elizabeth or Winston Churchill were present. Woodruff found a quiet delight in swapping cigars with Churchill and bringing the Churchill brand to some of his cigar-smoking friends.

Woodruff's patriotism was by no means limited to national affairs. He was recognized as one of the most avid boosters of his state and of Atlanta, his home town. Georgia's governors over the span of more than half a century called on him for his support and advice. They worked with him when he made a move, as he often did, to have the boards of directors of national corporations hold their meetings in the state, with a view toward the establishment of a manufacturing unit or branch plant and offices.

Many of the governors had lunch regularly with him in his office. If they were hunters, they went as guests to Ichauway. A number of these whose friendships he especially valued sent him pictures to hang in his vast gallery of photographs in his office, in his home and on the walls of his plantation house. Over the years he was on governors' staffs, not only from his own, but other states as well. Carl Sanders outdid the other governors by making Woodruff a general—instead of colonel—on his staff.

"This is as it should be. You outrank us all," said Sanders.

Most of all, Woodruff was proud of his city and for many years had a big hand in its destiny.

Most of Atlanta's mayors talked over their civic problems with him. The two mayors who looked upon Woodruff as a sort of oracle and depended on him for advice in many of their decisions which affected the city were William B. Hartsfield and Ivan Allen, Jr.

Hartsfield was one year younger than Woodruff. They had grown up as boys together in Inman Park. When Robert Woodruff was in one of the early jobs of his career as purchasing agent for his father's Atlantic Ice and Coal Company, Hartsfield was also employed there as a part-time secretary and stenographer. Hartsfield studied law at night to prepare himself for better things ahead. Both left the ice and coal company and followed their various pathways, and while they remained friends, it was not until Hartsfield was elected mayor of Atlanta, in 1937, that the closest association of their lives began. Fourteen years before that—the same year that Woodruff had taken over as president of The Coca-Cola Company—Hartsfield had won his first political election as alderman from the third ward.

Hartsfield often boasted, when he was in other parts of the country, that he was mayor of "The Coca-Cola City," and at home he proved it by serving Coca-Cola to all of his guests and posing for pictures on any special occasion under the picture of Woodruff that hung prominently in his office. There was hardly a problem of any consequence that he did not discuss with the Boss of Coca-Cola, and often when he found himself in the throes of a problem that needed the support of the city's civic and business leaders, Woodruff would invite the key men to his office dining room for lunch and, with his diplomacy and sound reasoning, help get support that the mayor needed.

One of those troubled times was in the early days of integration. Many of the other cities around the country were battling through those early stages of integrating the lunchrooms and the buses and there was much conflict between the races, some of which developed into near riots. At Hartsfield's suggestion, Woodruff called a luncheon meeting of the city's most influential citizens ("I could never have gotten all of them together on my own," Hartsfield once said.) and the plan was worked out so that the city could be gradually and peacefully integrated in spite of all the background noise by white supremacists and Negro agitators. In this respect, Atlanta was recognized as one of the foremost cities in the nation.

When Hartsfield retired as mayor, Woodruff arranged to have a portrait of Hartsfield painted by the artist Malcolm Rae to hang in the Atlanta airport passenger terminal which had been named the Hartsfield International Airport in honor of the six terms of service that this distinguished citizen had given to his city. Woodruff also connived, without Hartsfield's knowledge, for a job that would keep his friend in comfortable circumstances for the remainder of his life.

Hartsfield was succeeded as mayor by Ivan Allen, Jr. Allen was a generation behind Woodruff, who had been friends over many decades with Ivan Allen, Sr., a businessman and civic leader.

The personable younger Allen walked heavily in his predecessor's footsteps, in that he found Woodruff one of his most valuable allies and confidants in running the city. He called on Woodruff just as Hartsfield had done and received the same quiet advice and cooperation.

Ivan Allen, Jr. has many stories that are sounding boards of Woodruff's influence and personality. Two of these concern John O. Chiles, an Atlanta realtor and one of the leaders in the affairs of the city.

Chiles was one of the men who seemed to have no respect for the affluence and dignity of the city's most influential citizen. Woodruff enjoyed and was immensely fond of him, and there was often good natured banter between them.

Once when guests were having drinks before dinner, one of them was asked if he'd like to have another drink.

"Just give me a child's portion," the guest said.

Woodruff glanced at the realtor who sat close by and said, "Make it a big one. What he means is a John O. Chiles portion."

When a group of railroad officials considered selling air space above their tracks in Atlanta they conferred with Mayor Allen. "Could you recommend a realtor," one of them asked, "with whom we might discuss this?"

The mayor named a few, among them John O. Chiles.

"Who is John O. Chiles?" the man asked.

Mayor Allen thought quickly. Instead of going through a summary of Chiles' accomplishments in business and in his community standing, he said simply, "He's the only man in Atlanta who calls Mr. Robert W. Woodruff 'Buster.'"

"That's a good enough recommendation for us," the executive replied. "How can we get in touch with him?"

The racial crisis for Atlanta fell even more heavily on Allen's shoulders than it had on Hartsfield's. The more sober minds knew that given time, it might work itself out peacefully, but the strife baiters would not let it lie. Stirred up by opportunists, it almost arrived at a boiling point several times. It reached an explosive stage in 1966 when both sides gathered in the streets and there was real danger of a race riot. Ivan Allen, with his raw courage, went into the middle of the crowd and climbed on the roof of his automobile. Before he could calm the mob, someone toppled him from the car with a thrown object. When he climbed again to the same place, the crowd was silent.

"I've tried to reason with you," he said. "I hope we won't have to take other measures."

In the face of this threat of widespread violence, Governor Carl Sanders had an inclination to call out the National Guard, but he too was one of the men who relied heavily on the judgment of Woodruff and went to see him. Woodruff explained gently that force was seldom the answer to such problems and that it should be used only as a last resort.

His prediction was fulfilled, the potential riot quieted down, and the processes of integration went on—not always smoothly, but steadily and without serious incidents. There was a stir of feeling in the white community when Martin Luther King, Jr., one of the leaders in the conflict to place his brethren on an equal basis of all citizens, was awarded the Nobel Peace Prize. Woodruff voiced the opinion that any citizen so greatly honored worldwide should also be honored at home, and the mayor proposed that King be given a testimonial banquet.

The announcement wasn't too well received. Few of the businessmen took the time to even acknowledge the invitation and former Mayor Hartsfield, one of the promoters of the event, went to see Woodruff.

"Looks like we'll have to call it off," he said.

"Go on through with your plan," Woodruff told him. "If nobody else comes, I'll be there."

Hartsfield passed this word down the channels of the business community, and the banquet was a tremendous success with most of Atlanta's dignitaries attending.

Probably the largest crisis in the city's efforts at integration came when Martin Luther King, Jr. was assassinated in Memphis. Woodruff and Governor Sanders were at the White House, talking with President Johnson when the news came. The President passed the message that had been handed to him by an aide on to Sanders and Woodruff.

"I'm sorry," he said, "that I have to be the bearer of this news."

In Atlanta Mayor Allen stayed at his office, preparing for what might be the worst ordeal the city had faced since Sherman. He had ordered every member of the police force back on duty. He had called the heads of all the Negro colleges in Atlanta, asking them to use their persuasion and powers to keep their student bodies calm, and had talked to other civic and business leaders of his city, asking them to do what they could to help keep the city quiet.

It was well after midnight when his office phone rang. The call was from Woodruff who had left the White House and was back in his hotel. The mayor explained what he had done and was doing to keep his city calm. Then, according to Allen, Woodruff said quietly, "Mr. Mayor, our city will be the focal point of the nation in the next few days. Anything can happen. Thousands of people will attend Dr. King's funeral. To take care of them and of the funeral costs, you will probably have a large number of expenses you might not be able to legally pay. What I want you to understand is that you are to do whatever is necessary in Atlanta to keep the city peaceful and orderly, regardless of what it costs. You are to do this and it will be paid for. Do you understand?"

"It was the finest gesture and the biggest boost that could have been given to the job we had ahead," Allen said later. "I had been given a blank check to keep our city on an even keel. As Mr. Woodruff had foreseen, more than two hundred thousand people came from all over the country to attend Dr. King's funeral. The way we were able to handle it, there was no extra expense, and the funeral was conducted quietly and under the most dignified circumstances."

Another of Ivan Allen's stories that he enjoys telling about Woodruff's influence in the community with only a nod of his head, a grunt, or a word or two happened at a meeting of the directors of The Commerce Club, a downtown luncheon club to which most of the affluent men of the city belong. It is a refined and dignified place which the members enjoy and to which they are proud to bring their out-of-town guests.

"Back in the turtleneck sweater days," Allen said, "there was some agitation to relax the formality of the club and allow turtlenecks to be worn there. This had been heartily endorsed by a couple of the town's leading merchants who were doing a landslide business in the sweaters.

"The matter was discussed by the board of directors. The merchants argued strongly for the change and the board, with the exception of Woodruff, voted unanimously to revise the rules and permit the male members and their guests to wear turtleneck sweaters in the dining room.

"Mr. Woodruff, who was sitting next to me, turned and asked, 'What are they talking about?'

"'Turtleneck sweaters,' I said.

"'Don't like 'em,' he replied.

"There was silence for a moment, then one of the board members suggested tentatively that another vote be taken on the sweater question.

"It was and again went unanimously, but this time in favor of keeping the rules as they were."

Another city official that Woodruff admired was Herbert T. Jenkins, who served Atlanta as its police chief for a quarter of a century and who was prominent in helping both Hartsfield and Allen keep Atlanta a good place in which to live. The chief often visited Woodruff at his office and in his home and gave him a miniature gold police badge to carry in his pocket.

"Often," Chief Jenkins said, "he would ask if he could help in any way. Only two or three times I would say tentatively, 'We're having a bit of trouble with so-and-so. If someone could just speak to him...' I have no idea who would speak, but after that this troublesome fellow would be the most cooperative you ever saw."

With Woodruff's encouragement, Jenkins wrote several fascinating books about his experiences on the Atlanta police force, and when he retired as chief of police in 1972 after forty years on the force, Woodruff maneuvered to have him assigned a research job at Emory University.

Literary people have always held a fascination for Robert Woodruff. A man able to express himself well in words intrigues him, yet his own ability at this is far beyond some of those he admires. Some of his letters to friends and acquaintances are literary gems. Once he had written for publication in a national magazine, "Without that instinct of workmanship, that homely urge to do a job, we are lost. With it, we are invincible. It has been our guide in times past. It is, I think, our sure foundation now and a promise of power and glory in days to come."

Mrs. Lucille Huffman, Woodruff's secretary for fifty years, keeps a special set of volumes into which has gone stories and clippings about him, unusual pictures and letters that had a special appeal to her boss. Many of these are masterpieces and of rare expression that makes them worthy of such a file. Included are the sermons written only for Woodruff by the Reverend Richard C. Gresham, who had forsaken a naval career for the ministry and assigned himself as Woodruff's personal pastor even before they graduated together as boys at Georgia Military Academy. Woodruff affectionately called him "my preacher." Once Dick Gresham, commenting on his friend's abiding concern for his fellow man and the helping hand he perennially extended to those in need, wrote to him in almost biblical language: "You are not only a well-cleaner; you have dug a well so deep within yourself that you have tapped the crystal-clear water of the river of life. And constantly you are giving out of yourself that which helps ailing folk, steadies wavering people, encourages those a-wearying, rouses drooping hopes, and aids many a one to climb higher the hills of achievement. Through you, whether you know it or not, our Father in Heaven is continuously pouring this stream that makes glad all that it touches."

One of Woodruff's graphic friends and a Coca-Cola associate was Ralph Hayes. The files carry many of the Hayes letters, speeches and comments. High in the list of those that Woodruff likes were the notes given at his seventieth birthday party relating to the day of his birth, December 6, 1889. Said Hayes, "I must report that on this day in 1889, public order took it on the chin everywhere. What the press termed a Saturnalia of lawlessness spread across the country. Diphtheria broke out in Illinois. A horse kicked a man to death in West Virginia. A foundry exploded in Maryland. A train wrecked in Pennsylvania. There were difficulties with the Mormons. The Indians were reported restive. Gales swept the Great Lakes, a cold wave hit the South, and the cashier of the House of Representatives absconded with ninety-three thousand dollars belonging to the members and a blonde belonging to a non-member. There were strange happenings everywhere. The earth seemed in torment. The universe was on a binge.

"Then came Woodruff, his frame reinforced with steel, his torso wired for sound, a built-in loudspeaker installed and operating. Some say he was blowing midget rings from a small seegar, but for that I cannot vouch. For this, however, I do vouch: from then till now, he has been a potent influence to prevent anything from sinking into a state of settlement, or anybody into a condition of composure."

Another man of letters Woodruff greatly admired was Grantland Rice, the noted writer of sports. Grantland Rice turned out reams of colorful copy on golfer Bobby Jones and on Ty Cobb, the "Georgia Peach" of baseball. Both these men were intimate friends of Woodruff, and Rice became a regular visitor at Ichauway Plantation. "Granny," as Rice was known to his friends, wrote many delightful columns about Ichauway, several touching on a philosophic note that he no doubt gathered from his host:

"A great hunting dog is one of the kings of sport, and watching him work is a beauty beyond words...He goes out at a wild gallop—keen and eager to do his job. Suddenly he whirls in mid-air and comes to a full point. He had just passed a covey of quail and the dashing, quivering, animated animal of five seconds before is now a living statue—a frozen masterpiece of black and white—a picture beyond the conception of any artist or the imaginative words of any poet...The killing is only a small part of the game—the field work of the dogs is one of the epics of the sport."

Granny Rice killed one of the largest turkeys ever taken at Ichauway. He wrote a graphic description of this hunt in his autobiography, *The Tumult and the Shouting:*

"On this hunt at Ichauway my guide, Roy Rogers, and I had hidden in a deep swamp near a turkey feeding ground. We were there at 3:30 a.m. in the pitch dark and fifteen minutes later it began to pour rain. We waited two hours more for dawn, hardly breathing. It was around 6:00 when the turkeys came in. My target glided to perhaps twenty yards from me. I blasted 'neck high' at him. He went into the air like a rodeo bronco. Then with a great thrashing he was gone.

"I foundered up to catch sight of his tail feathers disappearing behind a clump. I dived. It was like jumping into a threshing machine. He all but beat me to death with his wings. Finally I came out of there dragging my prize by his well-wrung neck. I felt like Dempsey after he had finished off Firpo."

Rice considered that the gobbler was too magnificent a bird to be desecrated by roasting for the table, so he sent it off to be mounted as a keepsake of his great hunt. Woodruff's biographer Harold Martin tells the rest of the story:

When the mounted gobbler (says Martin) was delivered to his New York apartment—a gobbler standing some three feet high with a beard eight inches long—Mrs. Rice took one startled look at it.

"What's that thing?" she asked.

Rice explained that it was a turkey he had conquered at Ichauway by winning a wrestling match with it, two falls out of three.

"Get it out of here and send it back where it belongs," Mrs. Rice ordered.

The gobbler was returned to Woodruff and now stands in all of its dignity beside the fireplace in Woodruff's dining room at Ichauway.

In 1951, three years before Rice's death, Woodruff established the Grantland Rice Fellowship Fund at Columbia University to provide scholarships for young writers, as well as to recognize "those qualities of heart and mind and character that have made Grantland Rice a beloved figure to his contemporaries..."

When Woodruff was complimented for this fine gesture to his old friend, he shrugged it off by saying, "Let's just say that Granny himself did it."

Ralph McGill was another journalist friend for whom Woodruff had a long association and deep affection. Although McGill wrote often over a period of many years of Ichauway, the TE Ranch and The Coca-Cola Company, he respected his friend's wish to remain anonymous and in the background and seldom identified his host, the plantation or the ranch when he wrote stories of those places.

One of the few differences Woodruff and McGill experienced was in politics. Both were staunch Democrats and supported the Democratic party until Eisenhower. As close as he was to the general, it was natural that Woodruff should transcend party lines and support his friend. McGill hung tenaciously to tradition and threw all of his support to Adlai Stevenson. Woodruff tried to win McGill's backing by having him with Eisenhower at Ichauway, but the journalist had already made his promises to Stevenson and made every journalistic effort in behalf of his candidate. What did annoy Woodruff was that after Eisenhower became President, McGill wrote a column or two critical of him and some of the appointments within his administration. But the friendship of the two men was above even power politics, and the admiration and respect each had for the other grew even stronger as the years went on. McGill visited him at the plantation and ranch and they were together much in Atlanta. Woodruff's file of letters is full of communications that he prized from his highly regarded friend.

One of the stories told of their relationship is that back in the days when McGill was a struggling columnist on *The Atlanta Constitution,* and often found himself rather financially strapped, Woodruff would call the editor of *The Red Barrel* and have him give the writer an assignment.

One of the embarrassing (on McGill's part) events that happened between the two men was in 1951 when *The Saturday Evening Post* asked McGill to do a story on Woodruff. The scribe turned out some of his best writing in describing one of the most successful men in American business, but one who had ever remained behind the scenes and as anonymous as possible, both in his operation of The Coca-Cola Company and his tremendous philanthropies.

The story on Woodruff was an excellent one. The *Post* editors spoiled it for both McGill and his subject by changing the title to "The Multimillionaire Nobody Knows." This meant that Woodruff would get a bushel of letters, abusing him for being wealthy or asking for an incredible variety of donations with which he would be unable to comply. Some would be even threatening letters if he did not come across with the cash. This was usually the result of any article or story about Woodruff's wealth.

B. C. Forbes, editor of the *Forbes Magazine,* was a great admirer of Woodruff and often wrote about him and The Coca-Cola Company in the pages of his magazine. One of the highlights of his association with Forbes was on the thirtieth anniversary of that magazine when it promoted the selection of the fifty foremost business leaders in America. These were chosen by the businessmen themselves out of some seven hundred recommendations by newspapers and chambers of commerce over the country. Woodruff was one of the fifty. A brief sketch of each was carried in the next issue of the magazine. Of Robert W. Woodruff, it said:

"His superb salesmanship and broad business principles have made his product known and in demand all over the world. Generous sharer with all handling it. His innate modesty and kindly understanding have won him many devoted friends. His benefactions in the field of medicine are further evidence of his wide human sympathy."

Jack Tarver was another friend who followed in McGill's footsteps as editor of *The Atlanta Constitution,* and who went on to the presidency of Cox Enterprises, which include the Atlanta newspapers. Tarver was often a luncheon guest at The Coca-Cola Company office and in Woodruff's home, and occasionally he was invited to Ichauway to hunt quail. Though he was not an enthusiastic hunter, he and Woodruff had many other things in common.

Other men whom Woodruff lifted out of the newspaper field and brought into the Coca-Cola complex were such highly talented people as Archie Lee and Hunter Bell.

Woodruff knew Archie Lee both as a reporter for the old *Atlanta Georgian,* which he left in 1919 to get into the advertising field with D'Arcy Advertising Company. After Woodruff went in as president of The Coca-Cola Company in 1923, he and Lee worked many years together. D'Arcy handled the Coca-Cola advertising and through Archie Lee came up with brilliant campaigns based on both Woodruff's and Lee's ideas to increase sales. Much emphasis was devoted to the bottled product. Together they built up this phase of the business, selling Coca-Cola to the world through billboards, magazine ads and radio. Through the depression of the early 1930's, when most businesses were struggling, Coca-Cola continued to show a remarkable growth. The advertising campaigns had much to do with this.

Another newspaper man that Woodruff brought into his organization and who made invaluable contributions to it was Hunter Bell. The Boss of Coca-Cola always kept one eye open for promising young men, and he had followed Bell's career from his graduation at Emory in 1921 to reporter for

The Atlanta Journal. In four years there he had become city editor, one of the youngest ever to serve a metropolitan newspaper in this capacity.

Hunter Bell was employed by The Coca-Cola Company in 1930, assigned to the company's advertising department and to public relations which had to do with the news releases. He became the chief contact man between the company and a large segment of its locally owned and operated bottling plants. He served as editor of *The Red Barrel,* a company publication, and later as supervisor of two additional company magazines, *The Refresher* and *The Coca-Cola Bottler.* He was vice president and advertising manager of The Coca-Cola Company between 1959 and 1963.

Bell wrote one of the most detailed accounts of the history of The Coca-Cola Company and was instrumental in helping with the preparation of many phases on this biography of Woodruff.

Because he led a vigorous outdoor life at hunting, horseback riding and golf much of the time, Woodruff has remained the picture of rugged health. With the exception of his two small strokes in the early 1970's that partially immobilized him for a few months, he has never slacked his full schedule of passing much of the hunting season at Ichauway and visiting the plantation frequently during other seasons of the year and of making regular trips to New York, the West Coast and other parts of the country and of making an occasional visit abroad.

In spite of his perennial good health, many of his activities have been closely tied in with doctors and people of the medical profession. Much of this was due to his development of the Woodruff Medical Center and having there representatives who could keep him reliably informed as to its needs. His personal physicians who served a dual role of administering both to him and to the hospital and clinic complex have also been among his cherished companions.

It wasn't that Woodruff often needed his personal physician for medical reasons; he just liked to have him close by. Historian Kahn tells a story of Dr. J. Elliott Scarborough, Jr., who was an important cog in the early development of what was later to be the Woodruff Medical Center. The Woodruffs and Scarboroughs were close friends and often dined together at one of their houses.

On any night (relates Kahn) that he felt lonely, Woodruff was apt to drive over to the Scarboroughs', or to call up the doctor and ask him to stop by. Such summonses had nothing to do with the state of Woodruff's health; he simply liked to have Scarborough around. One evening the doctor, feeling out of sorts himself, retired early. Woodruff phoned and asked him, in a tone of seeming emergency, to come right over. Dr. Scarborough sighed, arose, dressed and drove to Woodruff's, returned home an hour or so later, undressed, went back to bed and sighed again. His wife then asked him what Woodruff wanted. "I don't know," the doctor said before dozing off. "He never told me."

Scarborough was Woodruff's close associate and confidant for almost thirty years. He was a farm boy from Mount Willing, Alabama, who had attended Harvard Medical School and specialized in cancer. The beginning of their association came about as a result of a tragedy in Woodruff's life. In 1937, it was discovered that Miss Emily, his mother, had cancer. Around Atlanta there were no private facilities for treatment of this dread disease. Woodruff began to look around for the best doctor available in this field that he could bring to Atlanta. His investigations revealed that one of the most likely candidates was J. Elliott Scarborough, Jr., who was working in New York. Both his background and training appealed to Woodruff. Accompanied by Robert Mizell, Emory's director of development, Woodruff went to New York to interview Scarborough. In spite of his training and background, they found the young doctor living in meager circumstances with his new wife. He was in further training under a Rockefeller scholarship, but ready for a change.

Woodruff and Scarborough liked one another immediately, and over breakfast at the Amabassador Hotel the young doctor accepted the challenging assignment in Atlanta.

It was a move which was to prove profitable for both Woodruff and Emory University. Under Scarborough's direction and with Woodruff's backing, the clinic, created for the diagnosis and treatment of neo-plastic disease, developed into one of the finest in the country. Woodruff gave the clinic whatever equipment and construction he thought was justified. A typical story is that not long before Elliott Scarborough himself died with cancer in 1966, he told the clinic's benefactor that it badly needed a beta-tron, necessary for a certain type of cancer therapy. The machine cost two hundred fifty thousand dollars. Woodruff told him to go ahead. After Elliott's death, two Emory officials informed Woodruff that there was no suitable building in which to house the betatron. He again gave his permission, but I heard him say later, "It cost me a million dollars extra to build a place to put the damn thing."

Dr. Scarborough was one of those in Woodruff's tight inner circle of friends. They not only spent much of the time together when Woodruff was in Atlanta, but Scarborough was included on some of the business and pleasure trips taken by the Woodruffs to New York, to the West Coast, TE Ranch and Ichauway. Scarborough hunted because it was expected of him, but his two main interests at the plantation lay in fishing the beautiful Ichauway Creek that wound for miles through the plantation, and in making the acquaintance of all the owls around the place. He could hoot so realistically that he'd have owls following us from tree to tree as he and I fished down the creek, or he could gather them into the circle at night.

"Cut that out," Woodruff told him once. "These critters are eating up all my guineas."

Shortly before Scarborough's death, Woodruff went to see him in the hospital.

"I thought you had planned to go to Ichauway," the doctor said.

"I cancelled the trip."

"If it was on account of me," Scarborough replied, "you go ahead. And don't worry. I'll be all right."

When Dr. Scarborough finally lost his bout with cancer, Woodruff said through glistening eyes, "He was the greatest man I've ever known."

Later when all of the buildings housing the hospital and the schools of medicine, nursing, dentistry and health sciences were renamed the Woodruff Medical Center by the Emory trustees, they also named that property housing the Emory University Clinic the J. Elliott Scarborough Memorial Building.

Dr. E. Garland Herndon, Jr. succeeded Scarborough as Woodruff's personal physician. He had come to Emory in 1958 from Walter Reed Hospital where he had served as a kidney specialist. He was stockily built and physically strong and had been a football star at Wake Forest University. He was personable and had Woodruff's genius for getting people to do things and get along together. He was skilled in his profession and worked long hours at it. All of these things Woodruff saw and liked.

Herndon went through the stages of medical professor, medical director of Emory University Hospital, director of the Clinical Research Facility at Emory Hospital, associate dean of the School of Medicine, and vice president for health affairs at Emory University. He was responsible for much of the growth and improvement of the Woodruff Medical Center. He was largely responsible for the correlation and efficient operation of all medical units of the Woodruff complex.

Herndon's pride in stepping into Scarborough's shoes as Woodruff's doctor was aptly expressed in a letter to his eminent patient: "To serve as your personal physician is a privilege I shall cherish always."

This meant, of course, that his long hours at the Emory job would be even longer. Added to them were his visits to the Woodruff home on Tuxedo Road, where he often remains until his patient is ready to go to bed, and when there are any suspected irregularities in Woodruff's health, he might also check again the next morning before his long day at the office.

Herndon turned his official duties over to his staff and accompanied Woodruff on many of his trips. At Ichauway he again took up quail shooting, something he'd had no time for while he so closely followed his medical career, and in a few seasons became a very good shot, something that pleased Woodruff immensely. He was at Ichauway when the Boss had his second stroke. He cancelled all of his appointments and remained with Woodruff for a month until he was well enough to return to Atlanta.

"Dr. Herndon is one of the best things that ever happened to us," said Luther Cain, Jr., who was also at his Boss's side during those critical days.

To be nearer his patient, Herndon bought a house on Tuxedo Road close by the Woodruff home, where he can be on call or check his patient as frequently as desirable or necessary.

Another physician whom Woodruff admired and to whom he felt

close was Dr. M. W. Williams, who ran the Mitchell County Hospital at Camilla, not too many miles from the plantation. "Buck" Williams, who had landed at Camilla after his graduation from Emory Medical School in the early 1930's, had helped establish a nursing home, clinic and hospital, so badly needed in the immediate region. Many of his patients were tenants or sharecroppers with hardly enough money to supplement what they grew on the land, and Dr. Williams and his associates did much charity work in Mitchell, Baker, and adjoining counties.

Woodruff, always with a quick ear to hear about people who gave of their time, their substance and themselves with little or no hope of reward, invited Dr. Williams over to the plantation for a dove shoot and was immediately attracted to him. His knowledge of medicine, as well as his dry, sharp sense of humor, appealed to the Boss of Ichauway, and he became the plantation doctor. Anyone with a fracture, cut or "inside ailment" was sent to the Camilla hospital, and Doc Williams would meet him there at any hour. If the patient was too hurt or sick to make the drive, then Dr. Williams would pay a house call to Ichauway.

He was a frequent visitor to Ichauway when Woodruff was there and participated in the quail and turkey hunts, dove shoots and barbecues given on special occasions. He always had a quip for the Boss. Once when he downed a bobwhite after missing three in a row, he said, "Even my old blind hog occasionally picks up an acorn." After he attended Woodruff's seventieth birthday dinner at which close to one hundred forty guests were present, the Boss asked him how he liked it.

"It's the only party I've ever been to with so many men present," he said, "that somebody didn't start a fight."

He often wrote to Woodruff in Atlanta, giving humorous accounts of doctoring country style, and with their serious moments too, extolling the beauties of the southern Georgia countryside, and giving bits of news of what was happening on and around the plantation.

After Buck Williams had administered to the ills of the plantation folk for three decades, Woodruff and Lee Talley, discussing what an asset he had been to Ichauway, conceived the idea of sending him a thirty-year service pin. While he had never been employed by either The Coca-Cola

Company or Woodruff except on a fee basis at Ichauway, they decided on a Coca-Cola service pin. His acknowledgment of this and the telegram that came with it are in the Woodruff special file. Doc Williams' letter said in part, "The only telegrams we ever received were the minimal words stating an aunt or uncle had passed, or once a year from papa (who was a preacher) at annual conference, stating whether we had to move or not. When we did move we children generally cried and that was the only time he would buy us a Coca-Cola. And who can ever forget how train water tasted."

Buck Williams suffered a stroke about a year after he received his service pin. It left him depressed, with trembling hands where they had been so sure and steady in the operating room, and with a dismal outlook on the future. Not long after that he took his own life.

Dr. A. A. McNeill, Jr. followed Doc Williams in the Camilla hospital and as Ichauway doctor. Capable, efficient, charitable to many unable to afford a doctor, he has followed admirably the tradition left by Dr. Williams. He is on call for Woodruff, his guests and the plantation personnel.

Other men in the medical and dental profession for whom Woodruff has a high regard were Dr. F. Phinizy Calhoun, the famous eye specialist who had treated Woodruff, and R. Turner Simpson and Dr. Thomas Conner, who in later years had done his dental work. He frequently invited them to Ichauway to shoot quail and tremendously enjoyed their visits. He never quite forgot his first experience with dentists and the braces, and it was a tribute to these two men that he put all of his dental problems in their hands. For Doctor Calhoun, he helped establish an endowed chair of opthamology at the Emory Medical School in the doctor's honor.

The list of guests who dined with Woodruff in his New York clubs, his Atlanta home and office, who rode and fished with him at his TE Ranch and who regularly came in season to Ichauway Plantation was both long and notable. It included people from all brackets of life. One stratum of friends in whom he seemed to find special pleasure were those associated with the entertainment world. Many of the stars of stage, screen and radio appealed to him, but in some he recognized interests and traits of character similar to his own. Out of this group were a few who shared with him innumerable, pleasant hours.

Not only that, but he used their talents too, in his job of selling Coca-Cola. His company sponsored many nationwide programs with such top stars as Morton Downey, Leah Ray, Edgar Bergen, Eddie Fisher, Anita Bryant and others.

Morton Downey was one of those whom Woodruff has known over the span of many decades. Although younger than Woodruff by some twelve years, he is one whom the Boss of Coca-Cola includes among those he calls "one of my chillun." Downey had been successful as a singer in Paul Whiteman's band, in concerts, plays and motion pictures before he went on a program sponsored by The Coca-Cola Company in the early 1930's and immediately became a favorite of the Boss.

One proof of Woodruff's affection for anyone is that he never misses an opportunity to tease that person or to scold him for one negligible reason or another. Sometimes this is done to bring a friend out of the clouds and back to earth, as he did to Downey, where Woodruff had served as the groom's best man when he married Peggy Boyce Hohenloe.

"Look at Morton," he said. "He's the world's oldest choir boy. He earned his first five-cent piece by singing when he was nine years old. His mother gave him a nickel to shut up. With that nickel he bought a Coke, and he's been in the business ever since."

Indeed Downey has been. Over the years his investments in Coca-Cola stock and bottling plants escalated into several million dollars.

Morton Downey and his wife were usually on hand at most of the highlights in Woodruff's life—his birthday and anniversary celebrations and on other special occasions. The two often dined together in New York or Atlanta and Downey was a regular visitor at TE Ranch and Ichauway.

Several Christmases after both friends had lost their wives, Woodruff called Downey from Atlanta. "Why don't you come down and spend Christmas with me," he suggested. "I've got two charming widow friends who'd like to come over and have dinner and spend Christmas Eve with us."

"What're we gonna do?" Downey asked. "Take pictures?"

It was a quip that delighted Woodruff and he didn't forget it. The next year when Downey got married again, Woodruff sent him a camera.

Two other friends in the entertainment and communications field are

David (Sonny) Werblin and his wife, Leah Ray, who in past years had been a singer on the Morton Downey Coca-Cola show. Woodruff was always attracted to men who accomplished things, and Sonny Werblin is one of those. He also has a humorous way of looking at whatever transpires and rarely takes them or himself seriously. Once Woodruff sent him, along with a few more friends, a thing I'd written on how to prepare wild game meat for the table. From most he received thank-you notes and a modest amount of praise. Sonny's comment, after looking at all the gory photographs was, "I'll never eat meat again!"

Werblin has a flair for spotting talent and promotion. As director of the talent division of the Music Corporation of America, he had developed a number of promising young actors, actresses and singers into stars. In 1963 he went out of his element and with other partners bought a defunct football club known as the New York Titans.

With his ability to recognize talent of all kinds and his promotional genius he renamed his club the New York Jets and with Joe Namath, his star quarterback, developed it into the top team in the American Football League. Everyone knows the story of how, against all odds, the Jets won the National Football Championship by beating the Baltimore Colts to put the American Football League on par with the National Football League, which is one of the great single feats in professional football.

Few people know the rest of that story that Woodruff told to a few friends. Werblin's partners were not content to let Werblin run the show. Sonny resented their interference and became disenchanted with the partnership. His partners said they would sell for six million dollars or buy his share. Werblin called his friend Woodruff. "I've gotta raise six million dollars," he said. He explained his situation.

"You had a good investment at the two hundred fifty thousand you put in that team," Woodruff said. "You did a good job and made it pay. Six million dollars pulls your percentage down a long way. If you sell out your share at two million you've got a handsome profit."

Werblin thanked him and hung up. Although Woodruff said later that Sonny had wrestled mightily with the decision, he did sell his share in the club and moved on to other accomplishments. He was ever the aggressive winner, and that was something else the Boss liked. Sonny and Leah Ray visited with Woodruff often, either in Atlanta or New York, or he with the Werblins in New Jersey or Florida.

One of the reasons Ichauway Plantation means so much to him is that it gives Woodruff an opportunity to visit with many friends that he seldom sees during other parts of the year. Plantations were bought and sold and some of his neighbors who owned plantations between Newton and Albany over the years were John Olin, William C. Potter, Richard K. Mellon, W. Alton (Pete) Jones, Hal Price Headley, John Grant, Richard Tift and Bobby Jones. Jones liked the winter living style of Woodruff, so decided he'd like a plantation of his own.

"I owned it for one year," he said. "It cost me more to operate it for one year than I paid for it, so I sold it."

To the plantation set, the winter season in south Georgia was a special part of the year. Much as other plantation owners had done in another era, they visited together for turkey hunts, dove shoots, drinks or dinners or just to pass the time of day. Most of the plantation owners were or had been men prominent and successful in the world of finance or business and all had much in common.

When only one or two bird-shooter guests were at Ichauway, Woodruff sometimes enjoyed carrying them up to see his friend Price Headley. Headley always brought out a bottle of rare old bourbon that he called "Old Joe," as an honor to Woodruff. Often Jim Hanes, who owned a plantation above Albany he called "Senah" (Hanes spelled backward), came down to join the fun. He was hearty and robust until well into his eighties. Many of these men Woodruff had been associated with over a lifetime of business.

Over many years some of his greatest pleasure was in the winter season, when he entertained what might be termed a cross section of America. They were people he liked and enjoyed having around him. The list reads down from the pages of *Who's Who* to such lower strata of society in which this humble biographer abides.

Certain guests came back year after year and if they gave any thought to this at all, they knew they were accepted. Most went through the ritual of shooting quail. Some liked it better than others. But all fit themselves snugly into the plantation style of living—a fire on the hearth in the morning when the room was cold, coffee brought at getting-up time, breakfast, then the morning hunt. There was usually coffee, Coke, hot bouillon or cocktails at the round table in the gun room before lunch, a nap after lunch and back to the quail woods again. Cocktail time after the day's hunt—generally known as "milking time" around the plantation—was again at the round table, where events of the day were discussed and plans made by Woodruff for the next day. After dinner hour there might be a fox hunt if the Boss wished some special entertainment for his guests, but often the evening meal was followed by a card game—poker in the older days, gin rummy later on. This might go on into the later hours, depending on who was the loser.

Bernard Gimbel was one guest who seemed to enjoy the after-dinner sessions as much or more than the hunting. He and Woodruff were old friends, belonged to a number of New York clubs together, and usually had long visits when Woodruff was in New York. Bernie loved gin rummy, and Woodruff said he was one of the worst players he knew. "When he'd get behind," Ichauway's Boss said, "he'd start doubling the stakes, and that's not any way to beat the game when both luck and cards are running against you."

Another friend who was a regular shooting partner of Woodruff's over a long period of years was Ty Cobb, who broke many records as a major league baseball player. Cobb was a good shot and made no bones about it. He and Woodruff were imbued with the same kind of competitive drive. When they hunted together, they usually made a bet on the number of birds each was able to bring in during the course of a hunting day. Woodruff frequently beat him, and this made Ty so mad that sometimes he wouldn't speak to his host for the remainder of the trip.

The baseball player was rough, aggressive and often even rude, but Woodruff admired any man for his ability, spirit and endeavor. Ty Cobb regarded him in the same light and had enough faith in his friend to invest heavily in Coca-Cola stock when Woodruff took over the company. Because of it, he became a wealthy man.

One of the incidents Woodruff tells happened after Ty Cobb's baseball playing days were over. He had ambitions to take over the Detroit Tigers, for whom he had played, as manager, and asked his hunting partner for advice.

"If you do," said Woodruff, "I'll have to lay odds that you wouldn't last out the season."

"Why do you say that?"

"You're too damn mean," Woodruff said.

Over the years the continuing parade of guests went on at Ichauway. One favorite was John A. Sibley. A couple of years older than Woodruff, Sibley had been closely associated with him since 1923, and with Coca-Cola interests even before that. He had represented the bottlers in their suit against the parent company to keep Coca-Cola syrup at the price specified in their original contracts and in other matters; had given the company a shellacking all the way through the Supreme Court. This was before Woodruff's venture into the business, but he was familiar with the case and with the brilliant work of this young lawyer.

When the state tax problem arose in 1934 and The Coca-Cola Company moved its offices to Wilmington, Delaware, Harold Hirsch, company attorney who was in declining health, decided to retire and keep his home in Atlanta. Remembering Sibley's performance in the bottler suit, Woodruff persuaded him to go to Wilmington as the company's general counsel.

From Wilmington, Sibley put on his suit of armor and went into a six-year battle to establish The Coca-Cola Company's exclusive right to the names "Cola" and "Coke." He won his cases through most of the lower courts, then suddenly the judgments seemed to go against him. One case was reversed in the Fourth Circuit Court of Appeals, another in Canada's Supreme Court and still another in England's House of Lords.

Sibley was a fighter. He tightened his belt to go ahead, but Woodruff's vision told him this was not the right thing to do. He suggested to his attorney that with such precedent, even though in a way "foreign," that perhaps going ahead might be bad judgment. Sibley, feeling that his day of usefulness to the company might be waning, resigned and came back to Atlanta to take over a position as lawyer-banker for the Trust Company of Georgia, an institution in which Robert Woodruff's influence was strong.

Someone asked John Sibley, "Did you talk with Mr. Woodruff before you accepted this job?"

"No," said Sibley, "Mr. Woodruff knows I am here. I wouldn't be here without his approval."

Each fall to Ichauway came a number of Wyoming friends for a few days of quail shooting. These were the people with whom he visited at the TE Ranch and in Cody when he made a trip to the northwestern state. All were old friends—Glenn Nielson, head of the Husky Oil Company, Lloyd Taggart, rancher on a large scale, Milward Simpson, former governor and U. S. Senator, Bud Webster, who owned an automobile business in Cody and a Coca-Cola franchise, Tom Molesworth, a craftsman in the business of making unusual furniture out of native woods and who had created the masterpieces that graced the large ranch house in the Woodruff's western home and who had also made furniture for Woodruff's bedrooms at Ichauway, and Max Wilde, the old western guide.

Once at Tom Molesworth's home in Cody, Woodruff had shown a very strong facet of his character. We were there for drinks before we went out to dinner—the Woodruffs, Molesworths, Wildes and this reporter. When we started talking about a place to eat, Max and Alice Wilde were in another room.

"Go see if Max will eat with us," Woodruff suggested to me.

I found the Wildes and passed on Woodruff's words. Max, with perhaps a bourbon too many under his belt, looked at me and said, "If the sonofabitch wants me to eat with him, he'll have to ask me himself." He and his wife went out a side door.

I relayed the message to Woodruff. Instead of being angry, he was distressed.

"Where did he say they were going?"

They hadn't left that information. Molesworth and I spent half an hour on the telephone, calling their home, the Elks Club and other places Max was known to frequent before we found them. I handed the phone to Woodruff.

"I'm really sorry you left," he said. "We won't have near as pleasant a meal without you and Alice. I was counting on it. Come back and join us."

The Wildes did and the incident was not mentioned again.

At the ranch, the Woodruffs entertained as generously as they did at Ichauway. The season was different, for some of the most pleasant days in the high country of Wyoming are in August and September, after the heat of summer and before the cold sets in. Woodruff said the TE was Miss Nell's place and while there he was under her orders. She enjoyed it as a vacation place for sisters, nieces and nephews and their families. Woodruff spent a part of the summer there, usually a week or so at a time. He brought along his own friends or business associates and gave those not accustomed to it a taste of the West with long horseback rides into the TE Hills or fishing for the huge brown and cutthroat trout in the South Fork of the Shoshone River that ran through the ranch.

Sometimes he made unexpected plans for a guest. On my first visit to the ranch, when I said I had never killed an elk but would like to, he sent me with Max Wilde on a two-day saddle trip over hazardous trails into the high country of the roadless, wilderness Thorofare, many miles from the TE. The guide and I were in the saddle for long hours. We covered some of the most rugged country under the shadow of the continental divide, saw an abundance of elk and brought out a trophy rack.

When we got back to the ranch, my eyes still shone from the excitement of the experience, but I was walking bowlegged when I could walk at all.

Woodruff divided his time at the TE between squiring his guests by saddle around the country and visiting with his friends in Cody or at other ranches in the vicinity, or dropping into Cody's exclusive Director's Club, of which he was a member, for a few hands of poker or gin rummy.

Before he was off again to the West Coast, New York or his office in Atlanta, he always found time to visit with Milward Simpson, another old friend whose home was in town but who owned an attractive summer cabin on the South Fork above the TE Ranch. Simpson had been both governor of his state and one of its United States Senators, and the two friends shared many delightful moments together at dinner in the Simpson cabin or at the ranch.

The TE was well equipped for guests with a huge, rambling ranch house and a number of guest cabins between the home and Buffalo Bill Cody's original cabin and outbuildings that the Woodruffs maintained in their original, primitive charm. Dick Loftsgarden had been his foreman almost since he had acquired the property and remained with him until Woodruff sold the old Buffalo Bill ranch to Charles W. Duncan, Jr., who at the time was president of The Coca-Cola Company.

Duncan had often been to the TE as his guest; now Woodruff went as Duncan's guest and was very pleased that his fellow worker in The Coca-Cola Company maintained and used the TE as he himself had done, in the best traditions of the old West.

The people who have passed through Woodruff's private dining room in his office suite represent as awesome an array of talent as one could imagine anywhere. With his infinite capacity for planning, he might have two or more persons who should get together on some common cause, or simply because he knows they are friends. Sometimes these luncheons may be for a purpose, to get needed information, to get opinions, to propose some project in which an associate is interested. Usually though, they consist of only a few of his friends breaking bread and making small talk. His luncheon guests may be invited a day ahead of time, or an hour, or a few minutes. Before he's ready to walk from his desk for a tomato juice cocktail before lunch, he may call Mrs. Huffman, his secretary, and say, "If Bo Jones is around, ask him to come in and eat with us," or "See if Luke Smith is free for lunch," or "See if you can find Fred Perrin." These men, and any others he asks, are likely to be there, whatever else they may have planned.

Over a few decades I have been privileged to become acquainted with some of Woodruff's friends in many walks of life. I have never met one who was not tremendously individualistic, regardless of how successful he might be by the accepted standards. These were the kind of people the Boss liked to have around. I never ceased to be amazed that most of those men I have known through Woodruff are very much like him in one respect. No matter how prominent one is or has been, or how many honors have come his way, he's likely to be a common, down-to-earth person, easy to talk with, very modest and with a lot of enthusiasm.

James V. Carmichael was one of those who often sought Woodruff's counsel when he served in the state legislature, ran for governor and took over as head of Lockheed's Marietta plant which originally had been established by plane designer and manufacturer Larry Bell and was known among some of the Woodruff crowd as the Bell "Boomer" Plant for the prosperity it would bring to the region. Jimmy Carmichael turned down a job in top management at Coca-Cola, electing to retain his position as president of Scripto, whose basic products were ball-point pens, pencils and cigarette lighters. Jimmy's charming personality and quick wit made him a desirable part of any gathering.

A constant companion in the Woodruff circle is Raymond W. Bowling. Ray first became connected with the Woodruffs in 1938, his first job as Mr. Ernest Woodruff's secretary.

"That was back in the years," he says, "when jobs were hard to get and I really needed one. Mr. Ernest helped me in many ways. I made up my mind then that I'd spend the rest of my life doing whatever I could to make things easier for the Woodruffs."

Bowling spent most of his adult business life associated with Coca-Cola and since he has retired from the company has taken on the unofficial job of keeping up with the financial news so that he can keep his friend and former Boss informed on what is happening in the world of business. Items of unusual interest are condensed so that Woodruff can save much time out of an active schedule and yet get the full impact of a lengthy item. Woodruff depends on him for news of mergers, financial deals and such barometers of business.

Ray is a constant companion at the luncheon table, an occasional guest at Ichauway, and many nights he and his wife Esther dine in Woodruff's home, or Woodruff has dinner with them. This is a companionship which has endured at work and play over many years.

Many consider that over a lifetime of friendships and associations one of the men closest to Woodruff was C. B. (Abie) Cowan. These two were attracted to one another before the 1920's, when Abie worked under him as a salesman for White Motor Company and later succeeded him as manager of White's southeastern division, a job he held until his retirement.

The roulette wheels and other casino games had an equal attraction for both and they often traveled together to Cuba or to Nevada to try their skills with the experts. If Abie found himself strapped, as he sometimes did after a run of bad luck, Woodruff always came to the rescue. His spontaneous wit, his dry humor on every occasion, was often the bright spot. Once when Joseph P. Kennedy, father of senators and of a president, was a guest at Ichauway, he was introduced to Abie as the American Ambassador to the Court of St. James.

Abie shook hands and then turned to his host. "You gotta be kiddin'. This fellow doesn't look that important."

Abie Cowan always had a comment or a new story that left his audience rocking with merriment. In preaching his funeral, Reverend Richard Gresham said of him that "perhaps he had already rocked St. Peter with gales of laughter about the train announcer in the Birmingham station, calling the trains for so many stations with unpronounceable names." Everyone who knew Abie understood.

He went with Woodruff on a large percentage of his trips—to Ichauway, the TE Ranch, Europe, almost anywhere his friend suggested they visit. He shot turkeys, quail and doves at the plantation, but was never too impressed with the duck shooting at Bottoms Up, the large houseboat that Woodruff and some of his associates maintained in Cheshowitska Bay, on Florida's west coast. After a round of drinks, a sumptuous dinner and a poker game at night, Abie was often in no mood to face a frigid dawn in a duck blind. Once when all the boats, guides and hunters had left the houseboat before daylight in a frozen wind, Abie bribed his guide to wait around the corner until all the other boats were out of sight, then bring him back to the boat to finish his morning nap.

That was, of course, where Woodruff, with his usual penchant for turning up at unexpected times, caught him and Abie had no choice but to again face the bitter pre-dawn wind. Such escapades over the years gave Woodruff much pleasure.

Other prominent men and women whose lives had touched Woodruff's many times along the way and of whom he was very fond both in business and in a personal way were Tom Glenn, who was nearer the age of his father and who had successfully conducted the affairs of the Trust Company of Georgia; Sherman Billingsley, who owned and ran the Stock Club in New York; Steve Hannagan, a noted press agent that some said Woodruff had hired to keep his name out of the papers; James D. Robinson who had headed the First National Bank in Atlanta; and Oveta Culp Hobby. President Eisenhower had once tried to persuade Woodruff to take a post in his cabinet. Woodruff refused, but talked the President into appointing Mrs. Hobby in his place as Secretary of Health, Education and Welfare.

There was Jack McDonough, who rose from a job of salesman with the Georgia Power Company to chairman of its board of directors, and who was often a guest at Woodruff's luncheon table and a frequent guest at the plantation; and Cason Callaway, who with his brother Fuller ran the Callaway Mills in LaGrange until Cason built his home at Blue Springs and created the world-famous Callaway Gardens on Pine Mountain. Woodruff once smilingly said that "Cason never makes any little plans," after the developer had told him that he intended to use one of his lakes at Callaway Gardens to select-breed bass as one breeds cattle and have that lake stocked with bass, "every one of world record size."

There were Jack and Marisa Adair, constant companions at dinner and at Ichauway, where Woodruff took delight in pointing out that at quail hunting, "Marisa could outshoot her husband three to one." Jack was president of Adair Realty Company, a firm founded by his father and which contributed immensely to the building of Atlanta as the Southeast's most important city. Jack often praised his friend as "a warm and wise counselor, a builder of industry, a builder of the South, and most of all a builder of men."

The list of people who had an influence on Woodruff's life, or he on theirs, seems endless. It goes on and on, and with innumerable little anecdotes of sharing happy as well as sometimes frustrating moments. Woodruff had a great admiration for Benjamin F. Fairless, president of U. S. Steel. Two things they had in common were hunting and a fascination for traveling by train. Woodruff likes to tell about the time they leased a private car for a hunting trip into southern Canada. When they settled up with the railroad, Woodruff said, "I thought we'd bought the damn thing."

One of Woodruff's favorite clubs was the Capital City, in Atlanta. He found pleasure in having drinks there with friends, sharing lunch or dinner in one of the private dining rooms and getting into an occasional round of poker with people he liked. Once, in the middle of the depression, this Atlanta club, with a backwash of receivable accounts that could not be paid, almost went under. It was deeply in debt and had no operating capital. Woodruff, with James D. Robinson, Sr., a fellow member, worked out a schedule that would provide a cash flow adequate to pay off the debt.

William P. Timmie, manager of the club for several decades, depended on these men for advice and for help when any problem arose. When the Capital City Club was in more healthy financial circumstances, Timmie came up with a plan to build a hundred-thousand-dollar night club and showed how it might pay for itself and make a profit. The directors couldn't see much sense in such an expenditure, but Woodruff could, and he helped the manager put his idea across.

Timmie followed Woodruff's advice on his personal investments and before he died was a millionaire. Because of Woodruff's interest in Emory University, Timmie left a sizeable portion of his estate to the Emory medical complex.

There could hardly be any way to determine which group of people — outside his family — knows or has known more about Robert W. Woodruff than anyone else. A vote might go to his doctors, another to his valets, chauffeurs, cooks and other household help. Possibly, however, if one had any way of compiling the information from both those here and departed, the concensus might lean slightly to that group who has served him over the last two-thirds of a century, in some such intimate capacity as a personal associate in one way or another.

When you live with a person day and night, you are likely not only to share many of his innermost thoughts and feelings, but to know his likes, dislikes and disposition in many matters. If he is displeased and it's on his mind, he may talk about it at night over a pipeful of tobacco in front of the fire, especially if he knows that what he says is confidential and will go no farther than the confines of a tiny room.

Among these were James Roseberry, his valet, and Lawrence Calhoun, his chauffeur, who you will remember began to save their money and put it in a bank account. When he found out about it, as he does most of what goes on around him, and asked the purpose of their effort, they told him that the way he spent his money, they knew he would need someone to take care of him in his old age. Naturally the thought touched him deeply.

There is Luther Cain, Jr., who followed James Roseberry as Woodruff's valet and who, as his master grew older and had lost Miss Nell, lived with him almost twenty-four hours a day, except during periods when his Boss was off to Europe or on some other distant trip—or when someone relieved Luther in Atlanta. When Luther's stamina began to fade and his eyesight grew dim, he did not relinquish his job, but Calvin Bailey moved in to give him a hand. Cal got his Woodruff training with the Boss at Ichauway and he and Luther made a perfect team, in later years one or the other often spending the night in Woodruff's office that adjoins his bedroom. Following Luther's retirement Cal came to Atlanta to take over the home duties there, and in both places is assisted by Eugene Wilborn. At Ichauway also was Dan Redding, who took care of the gun room, kept guns and boots clean, and always had an apt observation about goings-on around the plantation. When Dan was felled by a heart attack, Buddy Lee Johnson, who had helped around the plantation house, moved easily into his spot. There is Saul Brown, whose job it is to see that the wood pile remains larger than is necessary and to keep the fires going in the living room and bedrooms when temperatures plummet.

Mattie Heard was cook at Ichauway for many years. When the Woodruffs discovered Mattie she was a caterer in Atlanta and had helped them put on several parties in their Atlanta home. They liked her personally and were charmed by the way she handled food.

Woodruff at first employed her for the season, then on a year-round basis as the sole boss of his kitchen at Ichauway. Each year she moved south for the winter season, lived on the plantation, and kept the big table in the dining room heaping with meals that only she could prepare.

She was a sweet, thoughtful person with an abounding faith, devoting herself to God and to the Woodruffs. These sentiments were expressed in a poem she once sent to her Boss.

I've never seen God, but I know how I feel.
It's people like you who make him so real.
He's the stars in the heaven, a smile on some face,
A leaf on a tree, or a rose in a vase.
He's winter in autumn, and summer in spring . . .
In short, God is every real, wonderful thing.
I wish I might meet Him, much more than I do.
I would if there were more people like you.

When Mattie went on to the reward she surely had earned, her place in the kitchen and in the big plantation home was filled by Rosa Mae Bailey, Cal's wife, Elvonia Brown, Saul's wife, Gertrude Jackson and Corinne Mills, who keep the house spotless and whose meals and attention are the delight of every visitor.

Since it came into existence, the earth and all on it have been in a constant state of change. Continents shift and change shape. Mountains rise and are ground down again. Edens turn into deserts and deserts into Edens. The oldest living things cannot live forever. Nothing on earth is completely permanent, or impervious to change.

This is as true of organizations as it is of continents and mountains and Edens. The processes of growth and disintegration may not be as ageless, but the formula is the same.

For almost a century, from its beginning with an iron pot and boat paddle in a man's back yard, the empire of Coca-Cola has spread throughout the world. Much of this conquest is attributable to the plans, direction and vision of one general, but it was accomplished by the almost fanatic zeal and devotion of his troops.

This army, like all else, has gone through continuous change. Lieutenants and captains have fallen and others came out of the ranks to take their places. The Commander-in-Chief, often suffering inside because of the loss of some stalwart, had to make adjustments and keep his ship on course.

Woodruff looks back to literally hundreds of men and women who made contributions and often sacrifices that the Coca-Cola empire might flourish. Most of those who started with him in early days with the company have gone on now; a few continue to march proudly with him.

He recalls Mr. W. C. Bradley of Columbus with affection. Bradley had been in school with his father, had built an industrial empire of his own in Columbus, and was one of those in the syndicate formed by Ernest Woodruff to purchase The Coca-Cola Company from the Candler family. He served as chairman of the board of directors for years.

Robert Woodruff often looked to his older friend for advice and for support in his planning and actions. He recalls that in his early days there was a question of changing the formula by reducing the amount of some of the ingredients which were scarce or had become too costly. By doing this the company would make more money. To Woodruff, this was dishonest.

He didn't need any moral support to back his decision, but he wanted Mr. Bradley to know what might happen.

"I told him," Woodruff said, "that the way prices were, we might lose a million dollars that year if we stuck by our formula."

"What's your thought?" Mr. Bradley asked him.

"To cheat on the formula would be to cheat our customers," young Woodruff said. "I want to follow it to the letter."

"Do what you think is right," Bradley told him.

Woodruff was able to report to him later that their decision had showed a profit instead of a loss.

Mr. Bradley's son-in-law, D. Abbott Turner, was another of Woodruff's Columbus friends. He valued Turner's business judgment. Turner and Woodruff were elected to the board of directors of The Coca-Cola Company at the same time. This was in February, 1923, and as this is written, these two men are the only members left of that board of directors.

Both are outdoorsmen and over half a century spent many days together in the field—big game hunting in Wyoming, bird hunting in the Canadian provinces, and of course turkeys, quail and doves at Ichauway, as well as on Abbott Turner's farm near Columbus.

Many men have ridden out the years while Woodruff, officially and unofficially, remained and directed the activities of The Coca-Cola Company. The anecdotes revolving around some of those with whom he worked are indicative of his personality and character.

There was Harrison Jones, who came to The Coca-Cola Company as an attorney three years before Woodruff took over as president. Whether it was Jones' seniority or his knowledge that his Boss seemed to make all the right moves, there was always a friendly tension between the two men. Both were fierce competitors, though much different in nature. Woodruff for the most part was rather quiet and retiring; Jones an aggressive and often blustery fellow, never at a loss for words. At the drop of a suggestion he could make an extemporaneous, eloquent speech that swept an audience off its feet. Woodruff was content to let him do most of the speechmaking. Harrison Jones became one of his most successful sales managers for the company.

Perhaps his personality was best summed up in a speech the eloquent Ralph Hayes made on the occasion of Woodruff's sixtieth birthday, in which he charmed his audience with his accounts of various members of the organization.

It seemed that in talking to Jones, he had understood Harrison to admit that on a certain matter he had been mistaken. For Jones to ever admit error was unthinkable—completely out of character. He asked Harrison to repeat his admission that he had been mistaken.

"Good God, no," Harrison Jones thundered. "I never said such a thing. **I said that what I might say could have been mis-taken.** 'Mis-taken' means 'taken amiss,' you goddam dumb-bell."

Harrison Jones, who became known as "the voice of Coca-Cola," retired as chairman of the board in 1952, after a third of a century of service.

Woodruff went through a long succession of presidents of The Coca-Cola Company. Officially they were named by the board, but Woodruff himself selected them, usually from men he had brought up through the ranks, and whom he had watched develop into top-rate company men. Naturally, some performed much better than others, but through all of the periods, under his guidance his company continued to expand and prosper.

One of whom he was always exceptionally fond was Lee Talley. Lee came from the very bottom up through the ranks. He came into the organization the same year that Woodruff took over as president, but at the other end of the pecking order. Harrison Jones, as sales manager, hired him as a route salesman in Wisconsin and Minnesota. To Talley, an Alabama lad by birth, this was forbidden land, but he showed his mettle and stuck it out, greatly improving the company's profits and image in the territory assigned to him.

Woodruff, who always kept an eye on his most promising younger men in the company, arranged to have him transferred into the Canadian territory under Eugene Kelly. The idea was to give him as wide a variety of experience as possible and a better chance for advancement. Lee had a delightful story about this. After he had been in Canada for a while, he asked Kelly, who was his boss, for a promotion and raise in salary. Kelly told him that he would take the matter under advisement.

"He was a man of his word," Talley said once. "He did take the matter under advisement and kept it there during the whole of my twenty years in his service."

Lee often quipped that the difference between his station in life and Woodruff's was that he remained at Emory until he graduated and that the Boss had gotten the jump on him by not wasting his time at Emory, but getting out after one school term and going to work.

It has been said that the Boss had a number of ways in which to express his affection for a friend. If he quipped or fussed at him about some trivial matter, that was one way of showing his regard. If he doubled his fist and hit the fellow in the chest or belly, that was even more personal. If he did all these and then pinched the guy's cheek, that was love. Talley's cheek was one of the few he ever pinched.

He loved to tease Lee Talley. Once, after we had finished dinner at my home and while we were still at the table, Woodruff caught my eye, winked and then turned to Talley.

"I never thought," he said, "that you'd do a thing like that."

For a moment Lee was appalled.

"Like what, Boss?"

"If you don't know, that makes me more ashamed of you."

"My lord," Talley said, looking at me, "what'd I do?"

"Well," I said, getting in on the act, "I guess it was a little unusual."

Talley was baffled, but only until it began to dawn on him that he was being had. Then he entered into the spirit of the thing, begged to be informed about his misdeed, and gave his Boss a wonderful evening of apparently being exasperated with him.

They had their differences. As president of the company, Talley occasionally made moves of which Woodruff did not approve, as the promotion of Fanta—which Max Keith had created in Germany in World War II to keep his bottlers in business—from a local product into the worldwide market. But Woodruff growled his acquiescence, and Talley made it into a profitable line for the company.

The series of presidents Woodruff had selected up until the time he elevated Talley from head of the Export Corporation was almost as varied as the other friends in Woodruff's life. He was careful always never to have them leave the company with any degree of humiliation, dissatisfaction or at a financial loss to themselves.

There was Arthur A. Acklin, who had worked in the Internal Revenue Service before he came with Coca-Cola. As vice president and treasurer of the company, he installed a system to help improve the tax status of The Coca-Cola Company. Acklin's mind was sharp, mathematical and analytical, and he installed other measures to keep the financial affairs of Coca-Cola in order. Being a Georgia country boy, he was also an outdoorsman and spent many pleasant days with his Boss at Ichauway and at Bottom's Up, the fishing and duck-hunting hideaway on the Cheshowitska River. He was the first president to succeed Woodruff who, in 1939, moved up to chairman of the board and of the executive committee.

H. B. Nicholson was another who worked up to the presidency. He too had come through the ranks, both in this country and abroad, to president of the Export Corporation and treasurer of The Coca-Cola Company. He had once put on paper a list of progressive moves by which he thought the company—even though it was doing very well—could be improved to keep up with the changing times, and this had greatly impressed his Boss. So he moved "Nick" up to the top spot to let him put his ideas into effect.

Nicholson, originally from south Georgia, was also an outdoorsman, a bird hunter and a very fine shot. Woodruff liked having him around. He spent many days out of each season at Ichauway.

A number of other presidents went through the mills—William J.

Hobbs and William E. Robinson—with Woodruff very much at the helm.

When Talley was moved up to chairmanship of the board, he was succeeded as president by another Georgian, J. Paul Austin, who had followed Lee Talley as president of the Export Corporation and then gone on to executive vice president of The Coca-Cola Company. Paul had also been through the mill, working in a number of branches of the organization. Woodruff recognized in his education and training a tough, capable administrator. Austin had graduated from Harvard Law School, had been a ranking officer in the U. S. Navy. Woodruff had seen to it that he was familiar with the major Coca-Cola activities at home and abroad. The Boss had much to do with the assignment of those in whom he recognized the qualities of leadership, watching them through all the processes.

An associate once said of Woodruff, "He worked hard at trying to create into his own image every likely young man who might some day head The Coca-Cola Company."

He came close to accomplishing this with Paul Austin. Paul's business judgment was sound; he could see ahead and was quick to take action to avert any possible disaster or take advantage of favorable breaks. He talked easily with heads of governments and established friendships for himself and his company all over the world. He was honest, straightforward and zealous about the integrity of his product. Under him the business expanded and prospered.

Woodruff found only one flaw in this image of himself. Austin sometimes trod on toes. He dominated, but without the subtle humility every man recognized in Woodruff. In his charm and persuasiveness he lacked the soft approach that made men go beyond the call of duty and then beyond that for the Boss.

Knowing how effective this spark could be in all leadership, Woodruff brought along other men who were themselves of sound business judgment but who possessed a different quality of approach to problems which might need smoothing over. One of those on the way to the top, but who was felled by an untimely heart attack, was Lee Price, a personable young man who was a Woodruff favorite and who was rising to a top executive job. His loss was a blow in many ways to Woodruff.

Later on he lost another close friend, whose business judgment and personality had brought him to the threshold of a brilliant banking career at the Trust Company of Georgia, another Woodruff interest. Charles E. Thwaite, Jr., died of a heart attack while hunting with Woodruff at Ichauway.

Other men did make the top brackets. One was Charles W. Duncan, Jr., who did not come up through the ranks, but rather was "inherited" through the purchase of Duncan Foods Company, a Texas company with an expansive operation.

The stock transaction made Duncan one of the largest shareholders in Coca-Cola, and he came on the board of directors. A little later, Woodruff's friendship and persuasion brought him in as president, but for what he classified as "personal and business reasons," he finally resigned. He consented to remain as a member of the board. This was the Duncan to whom Woodruff sold his Wyoming ranch, for he knew it would be maintained and operated in the best of traditions.

Although incorporated in Delaware, The Coca-Cola Company was originally and continues to be considered as essentially a southern corporation. Over the years it has been run largely by southerners. As this is written, in Woodruff's eighty-ninth year, the company's president is J. Lucian Smith, who was reared in southern Mississippi and like so many before him came up through the ranks.

"He's one of the best troubleshooters we've had," the Boss says of him. "When things are going wrong anywhere, he is able to smooth them over without any fuss or fanfare. I count on him in any such unusual circumstances."

Luke Smith keeps up with every important detail of the company's business, and during those lunch periods with the Boss that he frequently has is able to give a report or answer a question right off the tip of his mind. Woodruff likes that ability, for he's had it himself through all of his years with the company.

The Boss finds much pleasure in having Luke Smith at the plantation, usually in the company of someone else closely associated with The Coca-Cola Company or a friend to whom he wishes to give a special treat. He knows that his president was brought up in the quail fields and woods and he is intrigued with high-class bird dogs and enjoys a day's shooting.

Through the years all of these presidents have been supported by a wealth of talent down through the ranks, men usually selected by the Boss and whom he considered to have played a prominent role in establishing Coca-Cola as a universal establishment. There were the stalwarts such as John Talley who, like his brother Lee, had been president and chairman of the Export Corporation; Charles W. Adams, Donald R. Keough, Benjamin H. Oehlert, Jr., Fillmore B. Eisenberg, Delony Sledge, Carl Thompson, Holland Judkins, Pope Brock, and Fred Perrin, who spent long years in the service of the Woodruffs, was always there when the Boss needed him, and reached the rank of corporate secretary of The Coca-Cola Company. All of these were men on whom Woodruff relied heavily in business and often in personal matters—all men he enjoyed having around him when he worked and when he played. They were an integral part of his life. He often had a story that he liked to tell about some experience with one of these favorite people.

A few of these choice bits included such people as Eugene Kelly, the only employee Woodruff carried with him when he came to Coca-Cola from White Motor Company. Kelly spent most of his Coca-Cola years in Canada as head of the company's Canadian organization and retired a wealthy man, as did many who worked for Woodruff.

Kelly never married. Woodruff, who liked to tease his tall, debonaire friend, told him he was too stingy to support a wife.

"It ain't that," Kelly said. "When I wake up now with a hangover, I have only one hangover. If I was a married man, I'd wake up with two headaches."

"Kelly was always telling me," Woodruff smiled, "that since I'd been responsible for his success, he was going to do something for me in return. The occasion came once when we were in London together. Kelly excused himself momentarily and went into a gun shop. When he came out, he was beaming."

"I've just ordered a Purdy gun for you," he said to Woodruff.

"That's a pretty expensive piece of metal," his Boss replied.

"The man said it would cost me five hundred," Kelly reported.

"Five hundred what?" Woodruff asked.

"Five hundred dollars, I guess," Gene said.

"You'd better check again," his Boss chuckled.

Kelly came out of the store a second time, a bit pale around the gills and not quite as enthusiastic as he had been on his first trip.

"You're right," he said. "It wasn't five hundred dollars. It was five hundred pounds." (At that time a pound was worth about five dollars.) Kelly gulped and said, "but I told him to get it anyway."

Woodruff prized that gun as a magnanimous gesture from his close-fisted friend.

"That was almost as bad as something Red Deupree did," he said.

Richard R. (Red) Deupree and Woodruff were associates and friends for many years. Deupree was known as "Mr. Procter and Gamble." He started with the firm as an office boy, and long before his seventy-five years of service ended had worked his way through the ranks to chairman of the board. He was an astute businessman and he and Woodruff served together on many boards of national and international corporations, among them The Coca-Cola Company.

Red Deupree was a horseman (when at home he rode for an hour every morning before breakfast), an outdoorsman and hunter, and Woodruff had him as a guest at Ichauway for several days each season, usually around the sixth of December, on Woodruff's birthday. In his late eighties he continued to ride and hunt six or seven hours a day.

He and Woodruff seemed to get a lot of pleasure out of chiding one another.

"You're always giving people things," Deupree would say. "Why don't you ever give me something?"

"Because," Woodruff would reply, "you never give me anything."

"What about that gold cigarette lighter I gave you?"

"Then look at it another way," Woodruff replied. "You're the only other man who ever gave me a gift and then told me how much it cost."

Often Red Deupree came to Ichauway from his duck club in Utah, and sometimes he hunted there under severe weather conditions of snow or sleet or in subfreezing temperatures.

"You're a fool," Woodruff would say.

He did chuckle over one story Deupree told on himself. After two days in a frozen duck blind, Deupree went to see a doctor for something to help a developing congestion in his head. The doc prescribed pills. The next day Deupree was back in the doctor's office.

"The pills have helped my cold," he said, "but they're tearing up my stomach. How long will I have to take them?"

"How old are you, Mr. Deupree?" the doctor asked.

"Eighty-nine."

"You won't have to take them long," the doctor replied.

Woodruff always said that one of the most vital assets to selling Coca-Cola, as well as keeping his organization out of difficulty of one kind or another, lay in public relations—with his customers, his bottlers, the news media and with the politicians. Governors, state legislators, senators, congressmen and even local electees often were empowered with the authority to clip the wings of The Coca-Cola Company in one way or another.

In the early years with the company, he handled much of the political contact himself. Later he developed an arm of his organization as a liaison between the company and the lawmakers. The men he selected to run it were highly skilled in creating and keeping the goodwill of enough men in power to help head off any annoying or harmful legislation.

One of the early men in this field was "Uncle" John Edmondson, who devoted much of his attention to the Georgia legislature, most of whose members knew and admired him. He was helpful in keeping down a much talked about one-cent state tax on Coca-Cola and other soft drinks and knowing how to deal with those unethical legislators who planned to introduce such a tax in an attempt to be bribed or bought off by the company.

Edgar J. Forio and Ovid R. Davis, who followed Uncle John Edmondson some years later, went on to more national contacts. Both men, highly respected officials in the company, had a wide range of friends on the higher-up political circles and did much to keep the company's goodwill, not only among the lawmakers but in certain governmental departments that together exercised a wide range of controls over the larger business organizations in the United States. All of these men were favorites around Woodruff's luncheon table.

225

One political contact that the Boss himself had for long years was Senator Walter F. George. But he was much more than that. The Woodruffs often stopped by the senator's home in Vienna for a meal or to pay their respects to Senator and Mrs. George, and the senator was a regular visitor to the plantation. Raised a country boy, he was intrigued with every phase of life at Ichauway. Most of all he loved his association with everyone on the place, and one of his delights was the plantation choir, which collected on the stairway and sang Negro spirituals.

The senator cared little about the quail and other hunting. He was a fisherman, and with one of the plantation hands, who was an excellent fishing guide, made many trips down the creek with a fishing rod in his hand. He was of the old school and did not believe in fishing on the Sabbath Day. He would not compromise that principle, though sometimes admitted he was sorely tempted by the picturesque creek.

The venerable statesman in his late seventies decided that he would not run for reelection, which would have meant carrying on a rugged campaign against Herman E. Talmadge, an ex-governor, so he stepped out of the political arena. Woodruff, having an idea of the senator's financial condition, arranged to set up the Walter F. George School of Law Foundation at Mercer University, which would in effect provide a comfortable salary for Senator George the rest of his life.

Although the gift was a great boon for the Mercer Law School, the senator never taught there. When he left office, he was appointed by President Eisenhower as Ambassador to NATO, where he served for several months until his death.

Another man prominent in political circles who was a longtime friend of Robert Woodruff was James A. Farley, who was generally conceded to be "the man who had elected Franklin D. Roosevelt to his first term as President." Both master salesmen, although in different fields of operation, it was only natural that Woodruff and Farley should be thrown together. Under Roosevelt, Farley had served as Postmaster General, and Woodruff was impressed with the manner in which he handled that job while helping keep the Democratic party effectively intact as chairman of the Democratic National Committee.

Farley had differences with Roosevelt over the third-term issue, which meant that eventually he would give up his cabinet post under the President and his strong voice in the Democratic party. Most of the top businessmen in America knew this as well as Farley did, and he could have taken a high-salaried job with almost any industrial giant in the nation. He had innumerable offers, but he suspected that what the companies and other organizations were really trying to buy was his influence in high political places. In spite of his shaky financial situation, Farley had no intention of being used where he considered he was not accomplishing something worthwhile.

Woodruff, with his ear always tuned in to the business grapevine, watched these developments with more than passing interest. He knew the throes that Farley was in, and it was Woodruff who, as he often did, came up with a perfect solution for his friend's problem.

"Why don't you," he suggested, "come with The Coca-Cola Company?"

"What would I do?" Farley asked.

"In a sense," Woodruff said, "we can get you completely away from the American scene. You won't be expected to spend your time applying political pressure anywhere. You'll have a job that requires all of your time dealing with affairs outside the United States. I think you'd be the perfect man to fill the job as chairman of The Coca-Cola Export Corporation."

"Thank you," Farley said. "Let me think it over."

A few days later he came to see Woodruff. "We've talked it over and you've made yourself a sale," he said.

"Who'd you talk to?" Woodruff asked.

"My wife."

"I always knew she was a damned sight smarter than you," Woodruff said.

As Woodruff had known he would be, Farley was an excellent choice to head the Export Corporation. His connections extended far beyond the borders of the United States, and he added immeasurably both to the prestige and profit of the worldwide market.

During his lifetime every man is lucky to have one good right arm—someone to work effectively with him at whatever he undertakes—who is completely honest and reliable, who is there when he is needed, who is devoted and loyal, and who is qualified to do the hundreds or the thousands of jobs which need being done.

Two such associates whose records of service reach back into the fourth decade or longer, and who are very much a part of Woodruff's business and in many ways his personal life, are Mrs. Lucille Huffman and Joseph W. Jones.

Arthur Acklin, by whom Mrs. Huffman was employed as secretary, "loaned" her to his Boss for some extra work that needed getting out. That was in 1928, and she has been with Woodruff as his secretary since that time, in a little office just outside his door, always there when he needs her.

She has been an integral part of his business life and looks after a prodigious amount of his personal affairs. Over the last half century one of her numerous jobs has been to maintain a running account of Woodruff's business, social, personal and philanthropic activities. She has collected them in some thirty-two volumes of scrapbooks containing magazine stories, newspaper accounts, letters that he prizes highly and many of his graphic replies, along with records of his many honors and awards. These are the real biography of Woodruff's life.

Her chores are endless. On file in other scrapbooks are also literally thousands of pictures taken at dinners, social affairs, meetings of many kinds and special events. Each year she wraps hundreds of Christmas presents for Woodruff's friends, including all of his employees at Ichauway Plantation.

When Woodruff "retired" to his new offices in 1955, Mrs. Huffman went with him in the same capacity she had held for so many years. When her time for retirement came, the Boss asked her to stay on a while longer. She graciously obliged, but it required a special vote of the board of directors to keep her on the regular payroll. It still does, and becomes almost a ritual each year when that special occasion rolls around. As Kahn tells it, there is usually no difficulty in bringing this to pass. D. Abbott Turner, chairman of the employees retirement committee, merely says, "Mr. Woodruff wants another extension for Mrs. Huffman. All in favor say 'Aye' and don't anybody say 'No.'"

The other person who has dedicated most of his life to the Boss and who perhaps knows more about him than anyone else is Joseph W. Jones, who holds a high position of trust and is looked upon by Woodruff more as a member of the family than as an employee.

This Jones—and there have been many Joneses in Woodruff's life—is a living encyclopedia of information of people, events, transactions and dates that have in any way concerned his Boss since 1935. That was when he came to work as an employee with the company.

For a brief period of years he was secretary to Colonel Hamilton Horsey, president of The Coca-Cola Export Corporation, during which his devotion to the company, his willingness and capability brought upon him all manner of jobs in the office. From doing secretarial work for a number of executives in the parent company, he graduated to office manager and when World War II began to take help out of the organization, Joe ran the place, down to the last details.

"I even had to keep the typewriters, adding machines and other equipment in repair," he said. "There was nobody else to do it."

In those early days of the war, Woodruff, with so much going on in his business and his participation in the war, did a lot of traveling by train between his various offices. Peter Brown, his secretary, traveled with him and kept up with his correspondence and other affairs on the road.

When Peter Brown went into the armed services, Joe Jones inherited that job too, of making business trips with the Boss. This was the beginning of his close association with Woodruff.

Through the 1950's and 1960's, Joe went through a number of changes in his official connections with The Coca-Cola Company. Involved in these shifts and advancements were such high echelon officials as George Adams, John Goodloe and Lee Talley—and, of course, Woodruff.

Woodruff would have preferred Joe Jones as his personal aide and not connected with The Coca-Cola Company, but Joe wanted to be thusly identified. Those running the company also wanted to keep him as an employee. The result of all the maneuvering between the top people was that in 1956, Joe Jones was made assistant secretary of the company; in 1959, assistant treasurer; and in 1961, secretary and assistant treasurer of The Coca-Cola Company.

These two positions, with several more full-time jobs of handling much of Woodruff's business and personal affairs, running the company airline, the basic supervision of Ichauway Plantation and taking care of much of Woodruff's foundation work became a load that no one man could handle. Joe suggested that he should step down as secretary of the company and that those duties be turned over to Fred Perrin, assistant secretary, who had been with The Coca-Cola Company for many years and was conversant with the duties.

Management finally agreed, and in 1972 Joe was made a staff vice president but also kept his assignment as assistant treasurer. This move put him closer than ever to the Boss. One of his duties was as treasurer of the Trebor Foundation, and he practically ran that organization since Arthur Acklin, its president, was in failing health. When Acklin retired, Joe Jones became president of Trebor, and later was elected chairman of the Joseph B. Whitehead and Lettie Pate Evans foundations, both former responsibilities of Woodruff. Still later he was elected a trustee of the Woodruff Fund.

Woodruff made few trips that did not include his personal aide and confidant. Joe was always there when and wherever the Boss needed him. There were, however, a few exceptions to this.

Joe Jones remembers the year when his wife Lee was expecting her first baby. Woodruff had made plans to spend Christmas at Ichauway and asked Joe to go along.

Joe explained about the baby and said that he wanted to be with his wife. He would make arrangements for another secretary to accompany the Woodruffs to their south Georgia farm.

"I don't want anyone else," Woodruff insisted.

"I'm sorry," Joe said, "but I can't go."

Woodruff rather grumpily accepted this and went off to Ichauway without him.

Lee's baby wasn't due until around the first of the year, but it made a surprise advent two days before Christmas. Elated, Joe called his Boss to report on a safe arrival.

"Good!" said Woodruff. "Now you can come on down."

Since Woodruff had never gone through the experience of fatherhood, it was difficult for him to evaluate Lee's need of her husband at such a time, or Joe's desire to be with her and the baby. Joe stood firm in his decision and Woodruff, as much as he would have preferred Joe, agreed to having a different aide with him at the plantation through Christmas of that year.

If ever there was an indispensable man, Joe Jones comes as close as anyone could. He has to read an extraordinary amount of material to keep up with markets, business reports and news — everything which might apply to, or in any way affect, The Coca-Cola Company. When he finds a long item in which Woodruff might be interested, he condenses it to a few sentences or paragraphs for his Boss to read. He must help supervise the operations of the company's three planes. He must answer a tremendous amount of correspondence, a good percentage of which is from people asking for donations or for help of one kind or another. Some are worthy of consideration; most are not. All get a gracious reply over Woodruff's signature.

Joe Jones' genius for a multiplicity of chores comes out of a background of finding some way to accomplish whatever the Boss wants done. Whether it's finding a special taxidermist to mount an albino quail taken at Ichauway and framing it under special glass, or getting some special piece of equipment for the plantation, or any one of dozens of other odd chores, he seems to know the right people to contact. He is a very fine writer and excellent editor, very precise about details and takes it upon himself to edit all manuscripts in which Woodruff is in any way involved.

His tasks and chores in taking care of his Boss are never-ending.

One of the author's regrets is the impossibility of including all of the people who have been a part of Robert W. Woodruff's life. We have mentioned only a few whom he's known under unusual circumstances or who have been closest to him in one way or another, who have shared immeasureably in his personal life or his business ventures. The stories told about them were for the purpose of making you know more about the man himself and the immeasurable influence for good he's had during those years in which he has lived.

MRS. ROBERT WINSHIP WOODRUFF

Chapter 7
"Miss Nell"

On her golden wedding anniversary someone asked "Miss" Nell, wife of Robert W. Woodruff, to make a toast that would be appropriate for the occasion. She did. She stood, raised her glass and said, "To my Bob, whose companionship makes life one glorious adventure."

Years later, Robert W. Woodruff was asked, "What was the most satisfying moment of your life?" Without an instant's hesitation, he said, "When I married Nell Hodgson."

This is only an indication of the kind of life they had together.

Woodruff, always an exceptionally active man, was likely to have a dozen or more projects underway at any given time. Often it was possible for Mrs. Woodruff — Miss Nell — to travel with him. Many times it wasn't, and then she was always there in the background, a bulwark of strength upon which he relied, sometimes more heavily than he realized.

Miss Nell shared with her man his love of horses, dogs and the outdoors. For years they kept horses at their Atlanta home, and both were prominent in local and national horse shows. In 1929 Woodruff was director and chairman of the executive committee of the Atlanta Horse Show Association and in 1929 and 1930 was a director of the National Horse Show Association. In spite of his eternally busy schedule, he and Mrs. Woodruff took time to follow the bridle paths around the city and always found much pleasure in riding together over the back roads and trails at Ichauway. They looked forward to the months of late summer and early fall when they and their guests at TE Ranch might spend hours in the saddle, riding the TE Hills or making the long trek to the "Cow Camp," where they had lunch before again taking the trail that brought them back to the ranch house.

Woodruff thinks the highlight of all their early equestrian experiences together was a four-day horseback ride they made between Atlanta and Asheville, North Carolina. Much of the way was along secondary roads — most roads, including the main highways, were unpaved in those days —

and they went a part of the way through semi-wilderness country, having to find lodging at night at wayside inns and other places which had accommodations for their horses.

"It was almost like we were pioneers of another age," Woodruff said.

Miss Nell looked forward to spending a part of each summer at the TE Ranch. It was a treat when she could have some of her family, such as her nephews and nieces be there with her—and they usually could—to enjoy ranch life. With riding, fishing and trips into Cody there was always something to do at the ranch. Because of business pressure, Woodruff was unable to remain with her at the ranch during the entire couple or more months she was there, but he came—often with friends or business guests—several times during that part of the year.

After Wyoming, they spent most of the winter season together at Ichauway. Except for an occasional stag affair, Miss Nell was always at the plantation, though she smilingly claimed it was only as a "guest."

"You're the boss at the ranch and at home in Atlanta and in New York," he'd tease her, "and you can't be the boss everywhere, so I'll take over that job down here."

She affably agreed and took him at his word. Usually when anyone approached her about a decision to be made, she'd smile and say, "You'd better ask Mr. Woodruff. I'm just a visitor here."

Everyone knew this was not the way of it, for unless a stag party was in progress, Miss Nell ran the housekeeping at the plantation just as she did in her other homes. Mattie Heard had done some catering for them in Atlanta, so the Woodruffs carried her with them to run the kitchen at Ichauway. She was with them at the plantation for almost four decades, until Mattie was no longer able to supervise the kitchen and housework.

Mrs. Woodruff taught Mattie some of the recipes for which the old cook was famous, among them Mattie's dove pie, as toothsome a dish as ever came out of anybody's kitchen. Miss Nell was responsible, too, for the country-style menu that called for a dinner of vegetables in the middle of the day and "supper" at night with a main meat course, a procedure that has lasted through the years under the skillful supervision of Rosa Mae Bailey, who followed Mattie as "chef" in the kitchen.

Not all of the noonday meals at the plantation were served in the main dining room of the big house. When Miss Nell was there, lunch was often carried from the kitchen to meet the hunting parties in the field, where it was served piping hot on special tables hauled out and set up in the woods. Sometimes the hunting parties met at the skeet club where they had lunch in front of an open fire.

When hunting season at Ichauway came on in the fall until it closed at winter's end, Miss Nell divided her time between the plantation and her homes in Atlanta and New York. She was always at Ichauway when the parties were mixed and wives were along with their sportsmen husbands. When the wives participated in the hunt, she went along. She never tried to shoot, but cared more for the riding and found almost as much pleasure as her husband in watching the well-trained dogs. She would ride all day with a hunting party.

When the Woodruffs were at the plantation—no matter what the season—they found pleasure in riding together over the place. If it were by car, the Boss took the back plantation roads and they would spend an entire morning or afternoon meandering through some portion of Ichauway to look at the condition of the crops or inspect cattle and other livestock or look for wild turkeys in the hidden corners.

The favorite horseback ride, which usually lasted two or more hours, was up the creek from the plantation house. This was over a woods road from which a part of the stream is visible. The road winds through the pine forest and drops into little swales choked with hardwoods. It goes through the turkey woods to the high bluffs overlooking the Alligator Bend and Orange Hole sections of the creek. From there the trails fork, most leading generally back by the skeet range to the plantation house.

The back side of the range slopes off into a sizeable grazing area, and one of Miss Nell's favorite stories concerned this meadow and Bobby Jones, the renowned golfer. He had just won what golfdom called the "grand slam" by winning both the British and American amateur and open championships in one year—possibly the only time this will ever be done by one man, since most top golfers graduate quickly from amateur to professional.

Over many years Bob Jones was often a guest at Ichauway, and on this occasion he agreed to bring along his golf clubs and put on exhibit some of his miraculous golf shots. The meadow had been staked off to indicate various distances up to three hundred yards.

From the top of the mound overlooking the meadow, Jones hit his "Sunday" shot with a driver. The ball sailed high and long and came to rest beside the one-hundred-seventy-five-yard marker. His drives normally were from seventy-five to one hundred yards farther. He put down another ball and drove it to approximately the same place. He looked back at the Woodruffs, standing behind him.

"Either call an engineer," he said, "or get me a doctor."

The course was resurveyed and they learned that the distances indicated on the stakes had been measured from the bottom of the slope into the meadow instead of from the actual spot where Bob Jones had hit the ball.

In many of those years between Woodruff's birthday on December 6 and Christmas, Miss Nell was away from the plantation and in Atlanta or New York to buy Christmas presents for the plantation hands and friends. In later years she and Woodruff often spent Christmas at Ichauway and had as their guests persons who might otherwise be alone and lonely at this season of the year. Many business friends of the Boss owned plantations in the Albany-Thomasville area, and these were often a part of the Christmas plan when the Woodruffs were at Ichuaway.

Miss Nell recognized the plantation as a place of retreat and seclusion where her husband could find strength and reassurance in times of grief or trouble. There he could readjust his sense of values and often find compensating qualities for those he might have lost. Often after the funeral of someone close to him, or when he was in deep sorrow, she would say, "Bob, why don't you take so-and-so and go down to Ichauway for a few days?"

Always she suggested a companion who was close to the Boss, knew his way of thinking, and who should go along simply as an understanding companion while he recovered from the shock of his loss. There was no planned program of readjustment. Ichauway itself was the healer. Miss Nell was not only deeply devoted to him; she understood her man.

As a very young girl, Nell Kendall Hodgson was interested in nursing. She often said, "I never had a well doll." Hardly in her teens—age fourteen

—she took a correspondence course in nursing and a little later persuaded her parents to let her train at a private hospital in Athens.

She had every intention of entering the nursing profession when she met Robert Woodruff, a cadet at Georgia Military Academy. In spite of the limited time they had together, their romance blossomed, even while Nell was headed for a nursing career.

Woodruff once said, "At one point, I began to believe I was too healthy to attract her."

After he went to work in Atlanta, Robert continued to court his Athens sweetheart, but not until 1912 was he able to persuade her that she should shed her nurse's uniform and devote the remainder of her life to him as a housewife and companion.

The wedding was said to be one of the most brilliant social events ever held in Athens, with reams of accounts of the nuptials in the newspapers, but neither Robert nor his young bride could have cared less; they faced a lifetime together.

Miss Nell never gave up her interest in nursing. Six years after their marriage, when Woodruff became involved in the war effort as a civilian and later in the Ordnance Department as a captain and then as a major and moved to the Rochambeau Apartments in Washington, his wife went with him and again put on her nurse's uniform, this time as a Red Cross volunteer, to help organize training courses for nurses. To better equip herself for this work, she took eighty hours of special training. She received a permission accorded only a few—that of serving as a nurse's aide in any military hospital in the United States.

In 1946 she was one of the first persons awarded honorary membership on the faculty of Emory's nursing school.

In 1948 she originated the idea of granting an award to the outstanding senior student who was graduating as a nurse. The school designated this the Nell Woodruff Award.

In 1954 she was the only woman in the seven-member delegation to the World Health Organization meeting in Geneva, and in 1955 she attended the eighth assembly of the World Health Organization in Mexico—both upon the invitation of President Eisenhower.

Miss Nell was dedicated to her husband. She gave him strength when he needed it most, and many times the viewpoint of a practical woman on matters of business. She adored him and he was a man who needed that adoration in times of stress. Once she said of her Bob, with a wry touch of humor, "He has the beauty of Adonis, the strength of Hercules, the daring of Lindbergh, the quickness of Mercury, the lure of John Gilbert and the touch of Midas—just enough of the boy, just enough of the caveman; in fact, just right—except when he's all wrong."

Her life was Woodruff's, but in the background she was always the nurse; capable, sympathetic, and like her husband, dedicated to those in trouble.

When she was at the plantation, any sickness or trouble there naturally gravitated to her. She took complete charge. Through four decades, the plantation personnel knew they could depend on her in any emergency.

"You just watch Miss Nell," one of them said, "when somebody at Ichauway gets hurt. No matter how bad they are broken up, or how bloody, she knows exactly what to do. And they know she knows, so they generally begin to get better right away."

Never did a person on the place get sick or hurt that she did not have them brought to the big house where she could treat them; or if they were unable to get to headquarters, she went to them.

Woodruff thinks that Miss Nell's finest hour of her unofficial nursing career came on January 18, 1968. Because of her interest and devotion to the Emory School of Nursing and her help to many of its students, the Emory Board of Trustees decreed that the nursing school there would be named the Nell Hodgson Woodruff School of Nursing. At the ground-breaking ceremonies for the school's new building, Miss Nell removed the first shovelful of dirt on the site of the structure. A platform had been built for these ceremonies, and all the dignitaries were on the platform. All except Robert W. Woodruff. He refused to take a place on the stand, but remained down in the crowd, characteristically not wanting to detract in any way from this day that belonged to his Nell. The speakers pointed out that when Mrs. Woodruff, because of her nursing activities in two wars and her interest and assistance to the nursing profession over many years, had been given an honorary life membership in the Georgia State Nurses' Association, the citation had emphasized that her marriage to Robert W. Woodruff did not take her away from nursing, but rather, through her, he gave nursing to humanity." Those words had made her very proud and meant so much to her that they were repeated at the ceremony. All of the speakers praised her dedication to the science and art of nursing. Though he refused to participate directly, anyone watching Woodruff would have known how proud he was of his wife and the honor being paid to her that day.

Across the years the Woodruffs maintained a number of homes in widely separated locations. It made no sense to his frugal father that Woodruff should own an apartment in New York and homes in Atlanta, Baker County and Wyoming.

"It's conspicuous extravagance to have so many homes to keep up. You ought to settle down somewhere," Ernest Woodruff told his son.

"But Pa," the younger Woodruff replied, "have you ever heard of a man with four houses and the same wife in all of them?"

The home that Miss Nell enjoyed most was the fifth they owned in the Atlanta area since their marriage. She found it in the Charles King mansion on Tuxedo Road in Atlanta's northwest section. They had many friends in the neighborhood. The spacious mansion, located on twenty acres of rolling, forested land, with two swimming pools, large rooms and an enormous downstairs playroom, had been built by Charles King a dozen years before Mrs. Woodruff found and fell in love with it. It was a magnificent setting in which to entertain their friends from all over the world, and expansive enough inside and out as a playground for her growing host of young nephews and nieces to whom she gave the run of the place, sometimes to the dismay of their parents. But Nell wanted it a lived-in place as well as a showplace.

To Miss Nell, life was indeed a glorious adventure. It seemed that she was brought into the world especially gifted to be the helpmate and to complement the varied activities of her remarkable husband. The days moved by in a fascinating panorama of travel, different homes and new friends who quickly came to recognize the Woodruffs for the genuine folks they were. She walked hand in hand with a man whose competitive drive for accomplishment was matched and mellowed by his deep concern for others.

Mixed in Nell Woodruff's personality was a bit of the pixie. She liked to tease the people of whom she was very fond. One of these was Gene Kelly, who was often a guest of the Woodruffs wherever they were.

At Ichauway, Nell observed that Kelly, whenever he saw signs that hot cakes would be served for breakfast, would pass up the first serving of eggs and bacon or sausage and wait to gorge himself on the hot cakes. The sign of cakes to come was syrup pitchers placed on the table.

One morning Miss Nell foxed him. She did not plan for hot cakes, but put the syrup pitchers on anyway. Kelly passed up eggs, bacon and biscuits and waited. Breakfast over, he was still there, waiting.

"Go get your boots on," Woodruff said. "You're going quail-hunting."

"Where are the hot cakes?" wailed Gene.

"Breakfast is over," barked Woodruff. "Get going."

Kelly wasn't to be outdone. He detoured through the kitchen and filled his pockets with biscuits to munch on during the hunt.

Woodruff told me of a field trial his wife once attended with him. He entered a dog named Mattie, which some months before had been run over and almost killed. One hip was broken, and the plantation handlers worked with her for months before she was able to even put that foot on the ground. But she had a remarkable nose, and the Boss decided to enter her in the Georgia-Florida field trials.

Woodruff, his wife and Bill Etchells went down to see Mattie compete in the trials. With Etchells handling her, she won handily.

In accepting the trophy, Woodruff could not resist the temptation to needle the owners of competing dogs. He probably wouldn't have, except that all of those men on the plantation circuit were intimate friends.

"All of you boys," he said, "had better start upgrading your kennels. They can't be very good dogs when they lose to a three-legged bitch."

When he sat down, Nell said, "Bob! you shouldn't have said 'three-legged bitch'!"

Later Bill Etchells commented, "I'm sure she was right. We didn't ever win another trial down there."

One of the best evaluations of Miss Nell's character and personality came from Mrs. T. Erwin (Virginia) Schneider, who was a longtime friend and traveling companion. Mrs. Schneider said:

To me, one of the most outstanding things about Nell was that, although as Bob's wife she had almost unlimited wealth and power, she never lost her intensely human touch. She was a beautiful, charming, irresistible woman. In spite of all this, she remained with the same steadfast sense of values that she had when she was a girl in Athens. This may have been one of her greatest achievements, because if power corrupts, it certainly did not corrupt Miss Nellie. She kept the same fundamental strength and a deep religious belief —a very sustaining one. With this she had a marvelous sense of humor that put everything in perspective.

I think this will illustrate her sense of values as far as power is concerned. Years ago we rode the train to get to their ranch in Wyoming. We were on the train two nights between Chicago and where the car from the ranch was supposed to meet us. It was a long trip before the days of air conditioning.

Had we known in advance that the train made one stop to take on water, we could have arranged for someone to meet us there, saving half a day of tiresome train ride. We didn't, but before we got to the water stop we were in the dining car discussing it, when the conductor came through and asked for Mrs. Woodruff. She acknowledged his call and he came to our table.

"The president of the railroad," he said, "has telegraphed to order a special stop, where a car from your ranch will meet you."

Nell thanked him graciously, and when he left, she asked me, "Virginia, have you ever had a train stopped for you before?"

"I can't recall anything like this ever happening for me," I admitted.

With a twinkle and a wry smile, she said, "Isn't it wonderful what a little five-cent drink can do!"

As always, her sense of values was in the proper place and her feet were on the ground.

Nell loved all the beautiful things that life gave her. She loved beauty, loved going into hotels with gorgeous flowers in the room. She was aware of them at a secondary level; they never took primary importance over the things that really mattered. She loved jewelry too. She was the only woman I knew who, when dressing for the evening, had a choice between emeralds, sapphires, pearls and diamonds. Yes, she enjoyed them and at the same time she never forgot how fortunate she was to have them. This enabled her to keep her values and always be in good taste.

One of her favorite stories had to do with a prized string of pearls. It involved a trip to Europe by boat. When she traveled by boat she always became seasick—and I did too. Anyone who gets seasick is infuriated with people who say that it's "all in the mind." But Nell had suffered through her share of seasickness.

Then came a time when Bob was making an important trip and he wanted her to be the delightful hostess that she could be, and not in her room suffering from *mal de mer*. He promised to give her any gift she selected if she could remain well on that particular crossing. Nell said, "All right. I'll take a string of pearls."

He accepted the challenge. She had tried everything, it seemed, and in desperation turned to Mother Sills seasick pills. They did the job and upon their return, the Woodruffs went by Tiffany's in New York to select the pearls. Later in telling the story, as she often did at informal dinners, Ada Healey, her hostess on this occasion, remarked, "This is the first time in my life I ever heard of a woman earning a string of pearls by staying out of bed."

So Nell had to add that to her seasick story.

As the richest woman I ever knew, she was most meticulous in everything she did. I do not believe she realized this trait of her character. She was never late in her life. She was the best organized person in the world. She could have run a hospital to perfection; oh, those nurses would have stepped lively under her gentle but firm discipline. She had all things planned and superbly organized.

Once I said, "Nellie, I bet you know how many linens and

what kind you have in every one of your homes." Although she ran four homes at the time, she knew everything that was in them.

If she had stayed in Athens, she would have been active in and probably the head of everything for the good of that community. I cannot imagine a man having a wife who was a better help to her husband than Nell Hodgson Woodruff.

On the other hand, she could have earned a living on the stage. She was a perfectly marvelous mimic and a born storyteller.

When we were going to the World Health Organization in Geneva—Nell having been appointed by President Eisenhower— we debated on whether to fly or take a ship. Nell suggested that since we were going into a "rarefied atmosphere," we should take it slowly, board a ship and have time to discuss her role as a delegate and do some planning.

We went over on the *America*. Never have I seen a stateroom so filled with bon voyage gifts of fruit, flowers and other tokens of friendship. Nell went over the gifts carefully until she found one from her Bob, which was the highlight of the trip. In fact, I'm not sure she really saw all the others until she began making a list for her thank-you notes.

We were in Geneva the night the 1954 desegregation decision was handed down by the Supreme Court. One man at our dinner table was very anxious to know how she felt about the decision. Nell calmly replied that it could not have been otherwise.

Over the years there were many nice things said about her, but she thought one of the nicest came at Geneva. Here she was a citizen delegate in glamorous surroundings. This was something over and above any of the many fantastic experiences she had enjoyed. She worked at her job. We went out to the Palais at eight o'clock in the morning. We attended every meeting. No one could have been more conscientious. We were there the greater part of a month.

At the end of the meeting, one of the delegates remarked that Mrs. Woodruff had done something very outstanding, very unique.

He said she represented "the wealthy American woman to the world in an entirely different fashion from the way in which they had become accustomed to viewing wealthy American women."

I asked him to expand that thought.

He said that to the majority of people the American woman was a part of the Riviera, the jet set, very sophisticated, very worldly in airs and speech. In Mrs. Woodruff they found an American woman to whom they themselves could relate.

Nell appeared totally unaware of what she had accomplished. Of course she stood out conspicuously among all the other delegates who were in a sense professionals as part of the governments of their respective countries.

In spite of her insulation from many of the problems common to most of us, Nell had an amazing empathy and sensitivity to the lives of others with whom she came in contact, whoever they might be and whatever they might be experiencing.

Miss Nell loved music and had a lovely voice. One of her delights was joining in with the plantation choir, composed of field hands, dog trainers, the kitchen personnel and all who wished to join in. Most Saturday nights during the winter season they assembled at the big house—dressed for the occasion in their "Sunday best"—and gathered on the steps leading to the upstairs hallway to sing old plantation spirituals. There were no strings or other music—all harmony and Negro spirituals which never have been more beautifully sung. Nell was one of that choir, as were other such singers as Morton Downey whenever they were visitors at the plantation.

Miss Nell was with her husband at Ichauway in January, 1968, when she had a stroke from which she never recovered. Her passing was mourned by friends from all over the world, but by none so much as those on the sprawling plantation where she and her husband had spent so many happy hours and years together.

Two special guests the Woodruffs always enjoyed having at Ichauway, as well as at the TE Ranch, were Mr. and Mrs. Rutherford L. Ellis. They were often together in Atlanta and were included on many of the Woodruff trips and in the birthdays and anniversaries the Woodruffs held each year in such places as New York's Stork Club and at the Greenbrier in West Virginia. This couple was more family than guests. Martha Ellis was Miss Nell's niece, and the two were always very close. Ruddy was almost like a son. He was highly regarded in business circles as president of Lipscomb-Ellis, a successful insurance firm, and he served as trustee of Woodruff's Trebor Foundation, on the Lettie Pate Evans Foundation and the Egleston Hospital board. He was the first president of the Atlanta Safety Council, founded by Woodruff. One of the few laymen to be selected for such an honor, he received the American Cancer Society Award, given for distinguished service in cancer work. He gave much of his time to the cancer organization for fourteen years.

After Miss Nell's death, Ruddy and Martha Ellis were constant companions of Woodruff, visiting with him often, having him over to their home for dinner, being with him on many occasions when they thought he might be lonely or discouraged. Both meant a great deal to him during this period of trial.

Little more than a year after Woodruff had lost his Nell, Ruddy Ellis was felled by fatal heart disease in his sixty-fifth year.

Woodruff, following his devout philosophy that "Life is mostly froth and bubble. Two things stand like stone. Sympathy in another's trouble, courage in your own," helped in every way he could to get Mrs. Ellis through this tragic period of her life. Her children and other family occupied much of her time, but not all. Woodruff saw to it that she was given minor assignments here and there to help her fill out those extra hours. He often had her over to dinner, with other friends, as he and Miss Nell had done when Ruddy was there. He was someone with whom she could discuss her problems, and to whom she could make suggestions about running his household with a woman's touch. When he had a dinner party at his home, he often asked her to join it, and when he invited a mixed group to Ichauway, he asked her to go along to be with the other ladies as a sort of unofficial hostess.

Gradually, through sympathy, friendship and companionship, they grew into one another's lives. She serves as his hostess in Atlanta, at Ichauway, and in the New York River House when he is with other friends in

247

those places. He has found in Martha an avid outdoorswoman. This he admires. As Miss Nell before her, she does not care for shooting, but she likes to ride and has her own special horse at the plantation, and with Woodruff often goes along with the hunting parties.

Woodruff finds pleasure that his and Nell's niece is fascinated by all living, growing things. She pores through books to learn the name of every flower, shrub and plant that grows in the soil at Ichauway. She knows the names of the songbirds, and Woodruff listens to her suggestions for Christmas card paintings by Menaboni, just as he had listened to Miss Nell, and then, just as he has always done, makes up his own mind.

A large part of my association with Martha Ellis has been at the plantation. She is interested in everything that goes on there. I noted that Woodruff was pleased with her enthusiasm at the new calves when we inspected the beef cattle, at the bird dog puppies bred on the place, and at the horses when we inspected them in their winter stalls or in the summer pasture, at the planting and cultivation of the crops and in the harvesting. Anything unusual about the operation fascinates her, as does a quail covey at any season of the year.

For exercise she takes walks around the circle and up the creek road, or along the roads or trails around the skeet club. She always brings back some exciting news about what she has seen or encountered. Woodruff enjoys all this, and she knows him well enough to know that he does.

The Boss likes originality and Martha Ellis is very clever with both her ideas and her hands. Who would think of making color photographs of all the shelters, where the hunting wagons stop at noon for rest and water and often at night under certain conditions, and putting them into a picture album identified by name? Mrs. Ellis did and Mr. Woodruff keeps it on top of his office desk at the plantation. She has so many such little unique touches that add pleasure to his days. She always has a delightful bit of verse about Ichauway of some happening there.

She has the same deft touch that Nell had in arranging flowers, in redecorating where it is needed and in little ideas for the household help to make Woodruff's several places of residence more enjoyable for him.

Mrs. Ellis in no way tries to take up where her aunt had left off. Her only thought is to make Woodruff's declining years as comfortable and pleasant as possible. It is something Miss Nell herself probably inspired from the Great Beyond and would certainly have approved.

Luther Cain, Woodruff's personal valet and close friend who had dedicated himself to making his Boss as comfortable and happy as possible, put it succinctly: "Without Mrs. Ellis, I don't know what we'd have done."

Another favorite niece of the Woodruffs was Nell Hodgson Watt, named for Miss Nell and always known as "Little Nell." As a child, she was practically adopted as one of theirs. Having no children of their own, they lavished affection on this Nell Hodgson. Her Uncle Bimpa (Woodruff) taught her to ride and to shoot and gave her an expensive initialed shotgun for her treks afield with him at Ichauway. She spent many happy days with her second parents, as she called them, at the TE Ranch in Wyoming and at Ichauway. She says the first ride she ever remembered having with him at the ranch was unforgettable. He put her on a horse and they rode the TE Hills for five hours in the rain. As she recalls the experience, she says, "I don't believe I've ever been happier."

Woodruff put her through school just as he would have a daughter of his own, and when she married Robert Gilkerson Watt, he gave her a party that not only Little Nell but everyone attending it will never forget. Her own favorite orchestra leader, Freddie Martin, was there with his band, and the famous screen stars included Morton Downey and Edgar Bergen with his satellite Charlie McCarthy. Downey participated in the program and Edgar Bergen and Charlie McCarthy put on a show. It is reported that Edgar said to Charlie, "We have here the cream of southern society," and that Charlie glancing slowly around at the crowd, which indeed did include some of the most prominent people in the state, replied, "Well, they look curdled to me."

When a daughter came along, Nell Watt passed the name on to her and she became known as Nell, Jr. Historian Kahn says that some years later when baby Nell was a growing young lady and all three Nells were in the house, Woodruff wanted something and yelled, "Nell!"

"Which one do you want?" his wife called.

"When I yell 'Nell,' all of you come," he said.

Nell Watt was a constant companion and a comfort to him after he'd lost Miss Nell. In spite of the demands of her growing family, she made herself available whenever he needed her. When he was away from home, she wrote letters imploring him to take care of himself and telling him how much he meant to so many people. She helped him get over one of the most difficult periods of his life.

There was no way Miss Nell could have chosen her nieces, but she would have been immensely proud of them and pleased with their attention to the man who had been her life mate.

The Trust Company of Georgia Building fronts upon the park at Five Points in downtown Atlanta which Mr. Woodruff presented to the city.

ATLANTA MEMORIAL ARTS CENTER

THE WOODRUFF MILLIONS HAVE ENRICHED EMORY UNIVERSITY

Chapter 8
Good Samaritan

Some of those who feel that they are well acquainted with Robert W. Woodruff say that the beginning of his interest in helping people who are sick or in need began soon after he bought Ichauway Plantation and met the old Negro with malaria.

Not so, say others; he was born with this special star in his crown. He has always been drawn to people in need.

The malaria epidemic, however, could have been one of the highlights and the beginning of his interest in the Emory University School of Medicine, for in a way it was his first collaboration with the medical school on a rather extensive scale. The story is now well known how a malaria control program was established on the plantation through the medical school and the U. S. Public Health Service, and in a few years the trained staff had eliminated this and other crippling diseases in Baker and surrounding counties.

Throughout his life any person in distress and even in need appealed to him, and the pattern of his existence included a perennial crusade to ease the suffering or burdens of others. Had he been a small-town merchant, his principles of dedicating himself to other people would have followed the same inclination, for this has been one of the basics of his character. The large fortune he accumulated by his own efforts only allowed him to expand those horizons. The Reverend Gresham spelled this out when he said, "Through you, whether you know it or not, our Father in Heaven is continually pouring the stream that makes glad all that it touches."

The malaria episode may have started it, but what really triggered the gigantic development through which Emory went over the next decades under the tall shadow of Woodruff were two tragedies in his life. His maternal grandfather Robert Winship, to whom he had been very close in his earliest years, had died of cancer at the age of sixty-five.

In 1937, Woodruff's mother was sick. It was diagnosed as cancer. There was no place in the Southeast that specialized in cancer except the Steiner Clinic at Grady Hospital, which had been established for charity patients. This was woefully inadequate.

Woodruff had already put the wheels in motion for the establishment of the Robert Winship Memorial Clinic in Emory University Hospital as a part of the medical school operation. The new format called for specialty treatment and for a research and teaching center, specializing in cancer and benign tumors. The objective of the clinic was then, and still is, to treat patients, and in the process to educate young medical graduates as well as undergraduates in the latest techniques of cancer diagnosis and treatment, so that professional service could be available wherever these young doctors established practice.

Woodruff always felt that if these facilities had been available soon enough, his mother's affliction might have been properly diagnosed in time.

With the Robert Winship Memorial Clinic underway, Woodruff and Bob Mizell went to Memorial Hospital in New York and employed J. Elliott Scarborough, Jr., who had just completed his advance training in cancer at the hospital there.

Those were the opening guns of a long campaign which created Woodruff Medical Center — its eventual name — as one of the finest establishments of its kind in the nation.

Woodruff passes most of the credit for this on to others. Among these key men were doctors, administrators and businessmen, and they worked long hours to accomplish remarkable results. Woodruff was always in the background. Few important moves were made without his approval. In a sense he was the power behind the growth of Emory's medical excellence, just as he was the power behind the expanding empire of Coca-Cola. In both, his lieutenants were prominent wheels in the machinery.

When, in 1935, Woodruff was elected to the board of trustees of Emory University, one of the university representatives who impressed him greatly was Robert C. Mizell, development officer at Emory, where his main duties also included raising funds for the expansion of the Emory complex. Mizell quickly became Woodruff's main contact with Emory. Woodruff recognized the depth and quality of his business judgment and discussed with him many of his personal business affairs. Mizell was the man who had helped organize the battle against malaria in Baker County and had brought in the resources of both Emory University and the U. S. Public Health Service. Close personal friends as well as business associates, Woodruff and Mizell spent many pleasant hours together planning ahead for the future of Emory.

Woodruff relied on him when, in 1944, Emory University was asked to assume responsibility for the Atlanta Southern Dental College and to make it Emory's school of dentistry, along with the existing school of medicine and school of nursing. It was reported that considerable indecision existed in the board of trustees, until Woodruff, who had given much study to the facts gathered for him by Mizell, gave a nod of approval. The vote was unanimous to establish the school of dentistry.

The school of medicine was having its problems. It had depended largely on practicing doctors who volunteered their services for lectures and teaching. The time had come for a full-time, paid faculty, especially for the basic sciences, instead of having to rely solely on volunteer teachers. Three trustees, one of them Woodruff, agreed to underwrite the anticipated deficit. The report is that after a year or two, the other trustees dropped out of this arrangement, leaving on Woodruff's shoulders the burden of making up this deficit, which ranged annually from one hundred fifty thousand dollars to four hundred thousand dollars.

This was unsatisfactory to both Woodruff, who felt obligated to meet this deficit, and the school of medicine, which was never quite sure that the deficit would or could be met. In 1952, Woodruff advised Dr. Goodrich C. White, president of Emory, and Robert Mizell that they should draw a blueprint for Emory's future plans that would put its schools of medicine, dentistry and nursing, its hospitals and its other related services on a firm business foundation. Should the plan commend itself, he said, the Emily and Ernest Woodruff Foundation would consider underwriting it.

Dr. White turned the memorandum from Woodruff over to Boisfeuillet Jones, who had received both his undergraduate and law degrees from Emory and had considerable experience as dean of administration for the university. After several months of consultation with the respective deans and key faculty members, Boisfeuillet Jones came up with a plan for organization and development which would provide for balanced budgets in the health services while supporting needed faculty and staff and related expenses. The plan would require five million dollars of capital from the Emily and Ernest Woodruff Foundation, four million for endowment to offset the continuing deficit anticipated and one million for construction of an office building to house a projected Emory University Clinic.

The key to the plan for financing the school of medicine was organization of the full-time clinical faculty into a partnership for the private group practice of medicine and a contract between the partnership and the university. The partnership would pay reasonable costs for facilities provided by the university, and the physicians would support themselves, pay all costs of their private practice, teach in the medical school program directly for about one-fourth of their time, and make reasonable contributions to the general teaching and research budgets of the medical school.

The partnership was designated as the Emory University Clinic and, as of this writing, has had twenty-five years of highly successful operation and growth. It has some two hundred sixty physicians participating and contributes substantially each year to the operating budget of the school of medicine in addition to direct contribution of physician services as faculty members. Woodruff takes special pride in the Emory Clinic and in his essentail role in its conception and development.

Emory trustees approved the plan for development of the health services in late 1952, and the university put it into effect in January, 1953, under direction of Boisfeuillet Jones, who was later named vice president and administrator of health services. The plan was presented to Woodruff for consideration of the foundation support requested immediately after approval by Emory. Dr. Philip Weltner was asked, as a consultant to the foundation, to study the plan in detail and make recommendations. After several months of intensive consideration, Woodruff advised Emory that the foundation would provide the five million dollars requested.

Subsequent gifts to Emory, made or influenced by Woodruff, have exceeded one hundred million dollars and, with the Woodruff Medical Center as its hub, the university has expanded in directions and in ways possibly not even dreamed of in the beginning by its principal benefactor.

Major capital improvements made possible through Woodruff's leadership and support include the Woodruff Memorial Building for Medical Research, additions to the Anatomy and Physiology Buildings, major expansion and renovations to Emory University Hospital, major additions to the Emory University Clinic building, a rehabilitation training and research center, an administration building for the medical center, a dental school building, a building for the Nell Hodgson Woodruff School of Nursing, named for Mrs. Woodruff, a new patient wing at Crawford W. Long Memorial Hospital, and improvement of teaching and research facilities at Grady Memorial Hospital. In addition, a number of independent health agencies became affiliated with the Woodruff Medical Center, again with support made possible by Woodruff, including the Center for Disease Control (formerly the Communicable Disease Center) of the U. S. Public Health Service, Wesley Woods geriatric center, Henrietta Egleston Hospital for Children, and the Atlanta Veterans Hospital. Improvements were also made in contractual relations and operations between Grady Memorial Hospital and the Emory School of Medicine.

Jones did such an outstanding job that he was appointed to many national health advisory groups. President Kennedy appointed him in 1961 as Special Assistant to the Secretary for Health and Medical Affairs, Department of Health, Education and Welfare—the nation's top health policy position—where he served for nearly four years. Woodruff brought him back to Atlanta in 1964 as president of the Emily and Ernest Woodruff Foundation, which had grown into one of the largest foundations in the nation.

Dr. Philip Weltner was already with the foundation as a consultant on the flood of requests that continuously poured in from all sources, and to make suggestions where money was needed for a worthy cause. Dr. Weltner's background fitted him admirably for Woodruff's good right arm in the appraisal of human needs ranging the spectrum from individual to community needs. Raised in Augusta, he had received his college training at the University of Georgia and Columbia University.

He could understand Woodruff's sympathy for the underprivileged, for he himself had that same depth of feeling. His career in these matters was varied. He had been an officer in juvenile court, had spent much of his time helping to get wayward boys and girls back on the right track, had campaigned for the reorganization of the Fulton County juvenile court system, and continuously worked for reform in the Atlanta city courts. He waged a battle against the Atlanta loan sharks who preyed on unfortunate people.

Weltner's achievements in education were his most notable and recognized works. He drew up the legislation that created the board of regents of the University System of Georgia, and had been appointed its first chancellor. He resigned from this post in a few years and went into government work as regional director of the old Resettlement Administration. He later became executive director of the Atlanta Housing Authority, and then in World War II went into the Office of Price Administration.

In 1944, he came to Oglethorpe University as president. After more than a century this grand old school, founded in 1835, was in difficulty and in dire need of an administrator who was experienced in working with young people and whose background was broad enough to handle administrative and financial affairs. Weltner was admirably suited in all of these categories. He held the college together over a period of nine years, sometimes on precarious ground. He strived for and got excellence in education rather than devoting his energies to building enrollment, which he said was the misguided ambition of most modern colleges.

In 1953, when he retired from Oglethorpe University, Dr. Weltner devoted much of his time to work with Woodruff in his philanthropies.

When Woodruff was inspired by an idea, any action he took usually went through several stages. During one of these stages it might be considered impractical and discarded. If no flaws developed, he would drive it through, even though the odds might be against him.

The development of Atlanta's Memorial Arts Center is an example of one such vision and the course it followed.

As he often did, Woodruff ruminated over this for many hours, while he sat quietly smoking in front of a fire or had other moments alone, to consider the angles with which he was familiar and work out the basics in his own mind.

Although not particularly fascinated by music or overwhelmed by the other fine arts, many of his friends were, and he realized that one of the attractions his city lacked was a focal point for the many organizations and persons whose activities and lives did revolve around art, music, drama, and other expressions of the soul.

Another plus factor of such an arts center was as an attraction for many big business organizations which considered themselves in the growing economy of the South. Atlanta was the recognized hub of southeastern traffic, communications and business, and Woodruff's idea was to make it even more attractive to them from a cultural standpoint.

After much deliberation and study from all angles, he proposed his idea to a number of people who, in one way or another, were involved in arts and the promotion of them. The enthusiastic response convinced him that his idea was sound. But he didn't stop there. He wanted to be certain how badly it was needed. He talked with Dr. Philip Weltner, who had given him wise advice on many philanthropic matters.

Dr. Weltner proposed a study to determine what should be done.

"You've just named yourself chairman of that committee," Woodruff smiled.

Dr. Weltner found there were sixteen Atlanta organizations devoted to the arts. They ranged from the annual Grand Opera and the Atlanta Symphony to civic theatres and music clubs.

All of the facts brought to him by Dr. Weltner convinced Woodruff that Atlanta did need a suitable home for the arts. After much consideration the site selected was Piedmont Park, an expansive public playground in northeast Atlanta, with a lake, golf course and large expanse of playgrounds and open space. Located near it was the Piedmont Driving Club which dated back to the carriage days. Its members were the aristocrats of Atlanta, and in itself it was a cultural asset to the city.

Woodruff's proposition was that if the city would raise one and a half million dollars to help build the center, he would donate four and a half million dollars.

Mayor Ivan Allen, Jr., anxious for other improvements the city badly needed, included the one and a half million dollars in an eighty-million-dollar bond issue. Many of his projects, including the cultural center in a predominately white population in the northeast section, portended for many a further mixing of the races. In Atlanta at the time, although integration was being gradually accepted, it still was a big issue, and the bond proposal was voted down.

Woodruff said, "The hell with it." The cultural center seemed a lost cause.

The Man, however, is not one easily discouraged. As soon as he recovered from his first disappointment of the bond issue, he had at his luncheon table several men who were interested in the proposed arts center and whose judgments he valued. He told them that if they would raise two million dollars from private sources for a cultural center somewhere in north Atlanta, he would provide four million dollars of the cost.

Fund raisers for this purpose were well on their way to the goal he had set for them when Atlanta suffered one of its most tragic losses in history. On June 3, 1962, an air tragedy at Orly Airfield near Paris took the lives of one hundred thirty members of the Atlanta Art Association—men and women foremost in the cultural life of Atlanta, many of whom were directly or indirectly involved in the establishment of the center proposed by Woodruff.

What before the Paris crash had been considered a needed community project now was a consecration to friends who had helped to start and were so much a part of it. Completed plans called for more money than the six million dollars originally estimated, and Woodruff promised half of the proposed twelve-million-dollar cost. He later bought for the arts center additional adjacent land for about two million dollars and gave an endowment fund to the Arts Alliance of ten million dollars.

When, in 1967, the new Memorial Arts Center at 1280 Peachtree Street was dedicated with impressive ceremonies, Woodruff was not even there. He had seen and approved the complex days before, and with a nod and grunt expressed his satisfaction for this fitting memorial to those friends in whose honor he had helped to build it.

He was not mentioned at the ceremonies, and his name does not appear on the plaque of donors. Mrs. R. W. Woodruff is listed instead. That's the way he wanted it.

Most of the large Woodruff philanthropies have come out of one or another of the several sizeable foundations that as a trustee he helps to direct. One of these, now the Emily and Ernest Woodruff Fund, Inc., of which he is chairman, was created to receive the estates of his mother and father. Trebor Foundation, Inc. is his own. Two others, the Lettie Pate Evans and Joseph B. Whitehead foundations, have had for more than three decades the benefit of his guidance and influence.

He has been a faithful steward, always recognizing his responsibility to see that the millions of dollars of income produced each year by these four foundations are passed along through his efficient team of administrators for purposes that will serve the greatest needs and largest numbers.

The quality of judgment of The Man in these matters is reflected in one of the reports brought to him by someone outside his immediate organization. Those on the inside, knowing their boss, would have passed it off without comment and never mentioned it to him.

"You shouldn't give any more money to that group," his informant said. "There's a power struggle going on there, and a lot of bickering and dissension among the top brass."

Woodruff thought that over for a few minutes while he appeared interested in some object on his desk.

"We are not concerned about personalities," he finally said when he looked up. "Time will take care of the personalities. A worthy institution is always bigger than any of the individuals running it."

Much of his foundation money went, of course, to Emory and to a number of other colleges and to institutions dedicated to the relief of human suffering, but he reached far beyond the sick and those who might otherwise be deprived of an educational opportunity. He made contributions to the welfare of people in all strata of society. An example is the creation of beauty spots that shine like gems in an expanding sea of office buildings in his city.

One of these which became known as Central City Park is in the heart of downtown Atlanta, at Five Points. He simply arranged for the purchase of more than a block of stores, office buildings and other such establishments and provided funds for those buildings to be eliminated and the land under them transformed into a beautiful park to be owned and operated by the city. It immediately became a daily haven for hundreds of nearby office workers.

This gift to the city was made in the name of "an anonymous donor," and while many guessed, for a long time only a few were aware of the identity of the man who made this fabulous and gracious gesture to his fellow citizens.

He didn't stop there. He gave the city money to match a federal grant for the creation of the Martin Luther King, Jr. Community Center, including a block of recreation and park facilities opposite the King entombment and Ebenezer Baptist Church where Martin Luther King, Jr. and his father served as pastors.

Through his foundations or personally, Woodruff provided funds for the establishment of three other parks where they were sorely needed in the wilderness of commercial structures surrounding them. One of these was a triangular area at Peachtree, West Peachtree and Baker streets in downtown Atlanta. Another was in the Buckhead section at the junction of Roswell Road and Peachtree Road, and the other on Edgewood Avenue adjacent to the Municipal Market.

Robert W. Woodruff contributed large sums to the welfare of man, largely by his own efforts creating places where the sick might go for proper attention; refuges where the weary can find a few minutes of sunshine and beauty and relaxation from the daily grind; colleges and schools with the necessary endowments so that those less fortunate might have the benefit of an education; organizations to help the generations behind him to be better citizens; community service centers in low income neighborhoods; churches to provide sanctuary for the friends and neighbors who gather to worship; many more gifts of immense impact to the "humble and nameless" who walk through life's span.

To these went literally many millions of dollars from his foundations and from his personal wealth. Their contribution to mankind could never be measured in terms of dollars. All were in good taste and from the heart.

As magnificent as these have been, they picture only a part of the Woodruff known to those who are close to him. For each magnanimous gift on record, there are thousands of smaller Woodruffisms about which few people know and which picture the true character of The Man. There are literally thousands, for he's spent his entire life doing things for other people. Innumerable times they themselves had no idea how or why they had been so blessed, though some might have been able to guess.

There was, for instance, a period of the great depression in the mid-1930's, when the city of Atlanta found itself in sad financial condition. There was no money for payrolls and the city had to cut salaries. Even worse, the lowered salaries had to be paid off in script.

The banks agreed to take this script, but they discounted it at ten percent, which meant a still further reduction in salaries for the employees. Christmas, 1936, was a mighty bleak prospect for many of these.

Woodruff passed down word that, if necessary, The Coca-Cola Company would redeem all of the script paid in the December payroll at its face value. The banks, perhaps a bit shame-faced, agreed to pay full value of the paper.

It is doubtful that even a handful of the thousands of municipal employees ever knew the reason why the script they were paid could be cashed in at full value instead of at a ten percent loss.

What has never been recorded is that, as an anonymous donor, Woodruff established scholarships in a number of southwest Georgia colleges, where boys and girls unable to otherwise afford it can get a higher education. There's a Woodruff catch to this. This scholarship assistance is available as long as the student maintains satisfactory grades. His idea is to help, but only where a person is trying to help himself.

He went a step further in his interest of higher education, especially for Negroes who several decades ago were denied many of the advantages they have today. He was a great admirer of Dr. George Washington Carver, who headed Tuskegee Institute in Alabama. For many years he served as a trustee of Tuskegee and provided funds for the construction of a facility that had as its primary function the preservation of food products.

265

Woodruff has had a broad interest in the Negro colleges in Atlanta and helped develop them into what now comprises the Atlanta University Center. Out of this and along with his personal support of Tuskegee, he took an active interest in the United Negro College Fund to raise money to help defray the operational costs of some forty Negro colleges in the southern and middle Atlantic states. Later he joined a few friends on a special committee of the United Negro College Fund set up to raise money for capital expansion. And it was indeed a special committee, with such men as John D. Rockefeller, Jr., Richard K. Mellon, Dr. Robert E. Wilson of Standard Oil of Indiana, Devereaux Josephs of the New York Life Insurance Company, Harvey Firestone and Thomas Morgan of the Sperry Corporation.

Many millions of dollars were contributed—vast sums more for the individual colleges than each would have been able to raise through its own efforts. Through this activity Negro education and improvement, where it was most badly needed in the country, made giant strides. This is considered a gesture of patriotism by those who know about it. It was more. It was one of Woodruff's many contributions to those in need.

While a deeply religious man who conducts his business and personal life along those principles laid down by the Ten Commandments, Woodruff has never been a regular church attendant. After all, he had his own preacher who wrote sermons especially for him. He is, however, very much concerned with those who do worship as a congregation. He built churches of several denominations in Baker County and regularly makes gifts to the churches of his domestic household staff and other employees.

He goes even further. When Lawrence Calhoun, a devoted employee for many years, died, he made possible a memorial to Calhoun at the Butler Street Methodist Church in Atlanta. The lower level of the building was converted into a gymnasium and recreational area. This has been used both by the members and their children and as a community center for that section of the city.

When James Roseberry, another faithful employee, passed away, Woodruff installed an electronic organ in the Liberty Baptist Church to which Roseberry belonged and since has made annual contributions for general maintenance of the church property.

When he lost Mattie Heard, Woodruff rebuilt the pulpit at her Wheat Street Baptist Church and had a marble lectern installed in her memory. He also had the interior of the church completely redecorated, with extensive repairs to the stained glass windows in the church and installed one such window also in Mattie's memory.

Those are but a few examples of his generosities and tributes in Atlanta. The records show other gifts in such places as Wilmington, Delaware; Cleveland, Ohio; New York City and Cody, Wyoming, where at one time or another he maintained residence.

Woodruff has his own way of accomplishing missions. He recognizes and uses the assists that come his way.

The cancer unit at the Woodruff Medical Center was well staffed and was saving lives of cancer patients who came to it in time. They lost a lot of lives of persons who waited too late. How could this number be decreased? The ideal way was to persuade every adult person to have a periodic examination.

A person who came as near doing this as anyone appeared in Arch Avary, an officer of the Trust Company of Georgia. Avary had gone through surgery for cancer and was now in excellent health. Being thankful that he was spared, he began to make speeches to civic clubs, in classrooms and churches, to meetings of all types, to anyone who would listen, urging them to have annual checkups for cancer.

Some of the bank officials who outranked Avary began to be concerned that he was devoting more time to crusading for cancer than he was to the banking business. Word of this drifted back to Woodruff, who is on the Trust Company board.

"Let him spend as much time talking about cancer as he wants to," Woodruff said.

Warren P. Sewell, owner of a factory that manufactured clothing, was one of those impressed by Avary's appeal and offered a free suit of clothes to anyone who would bring proof that he'd had an examination for cancer. He gave away hundreds of suits to people all over the South, for the crusader ranged a wide territory with his message.

Avary was able to report to Woodruff and to Sewell that hundreds of people who had been examined were afflicted with minor malignancies and possibly owed their lives to this campaign.

How can you put a value on good deeds done? Or list each its proper worth in the eyes of the Lord? The magnanimous contributions to humanity are likely to get the applause; the seemingly insignificant gestures may be the ones of which the stars in your crown are made.

Once, during a cold winter when the supply of coal was short, Woodruff, who knew his preacher heated his house with coal, had a ton delivered to him just before Christmas.

He sent a monthly check to his teacher of grammar school days, who had retired from teaching and was forced to live on her rather frugal means. With the first check went a letter which said, in part, that it was "in affection and grateful appreciation, which I feel are due you for any good fortune that has come to me in the business world."

Woodruff says that during his life he never co-signed or endorsed a note for anyone. It is well known, however, that a number of times when a bank planned to foreclose on a note, or when he learned that one of his friends had to sell Coca-Cola stock to pay off a note, Woodruff simply called the bank and said he would guarantee the loan. No other action was necessary. His word was as good as his signature.

Woodruff was ever thoughtful of other people. What might appear a seemingly insignificant gesture was often important to the persons involved. If one of his mayors needed to pull a finesse which meant something for the city of Atlanta, then the mayor and those who might help him were Woodruff's guests at luncheon or dinner. If Grantland Rice came to the plantation to shoot, there were always people with whom Rice had a common interest—Bobby Jones or Ty Cobb or Ralph McGill. When Woodruff went west to play golf with President Eisenhower, he might carry with him Richard Garlington or some other golfer friend whom he knew would enjoy playing with the President. If the head of some state department needed to get closer to the governor, or vice versa, Woodruff would have them hunt together for several days. He planned his guest lists carefully, always with the thought of helping someone or making the experience more enjoyable for that person.

Hundreds of his friends each year receive a single rose on his or her birthday. The card that accompanies this remembrance is unnecessary. It is the floral signature of only one man. Those gifts from him on their birthdays make a lot of people happy.

The Man, Robert Winship Woodruff, has lived expansively. He has created. He has shared. He has given hope and faith and love. What more could any man ask out of life? He has had his moments of reward, and yet in spite of all he has done was never completely satisfied. He sums up his life in a simple statement: "When I compare the things I've lost with the things I've gained, the things I've missed with what I might have attained, there is little room left for pride."

"When I compare the things I've lost with the things I've gained, and the things I've missed with what I might have attained, there is little room left for pride."

"Life is mostly froth and bubble. Two things stand like stone: Kindness in another's trouble. Courage in your own."

"It has never been my desire to have a yacht, a racehorse or a mistress—in that order."

"So far as our company is concerned, I constantly expect trouble. Maybe it's because we are constantly on the lookout for trouble that we have been able so far to avoid it."

"If you can get somebody to do something better than you can do it yourself, it's always a good idea."

"The future is always going to belong to the discontented."

"There is no limit to what a man can do or where he can go if he doesn't mind who gets the credit."

The high distinction of being adjudged one of

America's 50 Foremost Business Leaders

has been conferred upon

Robert W. Woodruff

as the result of a nationwide vote conducted by

Forbes Magazine of Business

among Industrial, Financial, Railway, Insurance, Utility, Mercantile, and other Business Leaders, including its own hundreds of thousands of executive readers.

In paying this tribute to the nation's most outstanding Men of Affairs, upon the occasion of its own Thirtieth Anniversary, Forbes urged that due consideration, by those making selections, be accorded pro bono publico services rendered, in addition to outstanding business --- company --- achievements.

Citation

His superb salesmanship and broad-gauge business principles have made his product known and in demand all over the world. Generous sharer with all handling it. His innate modesty and kindly understanding have won him many devoted friends. His benefactions in the field of medicine are further evidence of his wide human sympathy.

Attached hereto is the seal of the B.C.Forbes & Sons Publishing Company, Inc., Publishers of Forbes Magazine of Business who join most heartily in endorsing this Citation of Honor.

FOUNDER & PUBLISHER

Chapter 9
Ever The Boss

Everything, with the exception of eternity, must eventually come to an end, and no one has ever lived long enough to be sure about that. The giant redwood that has weathered centuries of storms and heat and cold must at last give up its tenacious life and become a part of the forest mold that helps to generate new life. There comes a time when the old stag, fierce in strength and endurance that kept his enemies at bay, goes down before an encircling pack of wolves.

So it is with any giant among men, whose physical strength and endurance and power of will have kept him a colossus of his kind. But as with the stag and the mighty redwood, those chapters before a final rendezvous with the ravages of time may be the most dramatic of them all.

Robert W. Woodruff says often that he has lived beyond his allotted years. History will record otherwise. At a time of life when other giants of his era were relaxed and enjoying their well-earned laurels, content to allow their creations to be carried on by those attempting to walk in their footsteps, Woodruff has chosen to remain on stage. His vast experience in business affairs, his judgment of human character and his deep perception, which enables him to see over the second hill and into the valley beyond, remains as much a part of him in his 93rd year as it did almost 60 years ago when he set in motion the machinery that made "Coca-Cola" the best-known trademark on earth.

Many men, perhaps to their regret, have misjudged Woodruff's declining physical activity, his seeming lack of concentration in a discussion of business details, his apparent inability to take prompt and decisive action in what they considered emergencies, as an indication of senile weakness. Some of those men who made plans based on personal ambition rather than the welfare of Mr. Woodruff's business were suddenly and rudely awakened to the realization that what they had considered inattention or sleepy-eyed acquiesence by the Boss was instead a sharp evaluation of both the details as well as the lack of details presented to him.

It was scarcely conceivable that any man past his 90th year could know all the facts, whether or not they were part of the report. But the Boss didn't rely on one report, or two or three. His sources of information were the financial and physical conditions from all segments of his world-wide empire. He studied such things as sales figures and chart curves and when these went the wrong way he dug out the reason like an old grizzly digging for a gopher.

In his late 80s, Woodruff had become somewhat concerned with the growth rate of his organization, and gave much thought both to conditions and individuals who might be responsible. He continued to maintain his office in The Coca-Cola Company building and kept his staff, most of whom had been with him many years. He continued through this period as a member of the Board of Directors and Chairman of the Finance Committee. Although he was not pleased that a few of his more ambitious employees in top management, who considered him a doddering old man on his last physical and mental legs were taking it upon themselves to make decisions with which he did not always agree, he kept his counsel. He also kept an eye on moving events and the work of younger men who had come up in the ranks. Many of these he invited to lunch in his office, where affairs of the Company were discussed. He was laying the groundwork for substantial years ahead for The Coca-Cola Company.

A few close to Woodruff suspected it, but even they had only a vague idea that after his 90th birthday the Boss would actively step back into the picture and make dramatic changes. Indirectly and very gently, as he had done almost 58 years before when he first assumed the presidency of The Coca-Cola Company, he set the wheels in motion to bring about the changes he considered necessary to turn the Company around and again put it on a firm basis with a substantial growth rate.

Quietly, he "allowed" some of his older friends who had served on The Coca-Cola Company's board of directors for many years to retire and he suggested that those vacancies be filled by younger men who had proven themselves in the world of commerce and who measured up to his standards. His wishes, as they had been since 1923, were followed. This was his first step in the period of transition. He could have moved faster and more harshly but this would have been out of character, so he stood in the background as the organization slowly and surely righted itself in such a way that there were no injured human values. But his concern for the problems that lay ahead was in no way reduced.

"The Company," he told me while smoking our pipes by the fireside, "is in a hell of a shape."

"How could that be?" I asked. "Your organization generally is sound and making a profit while other corporations are losing their shirts."

"To begin with," he said, "we owe a hundred million dollars. It's the first time we've ever borrowed money since I've been with the company. Part of our world market is losing ground and reports indicate that this is the result of poor management. The value of our stock is much too low and this is a reflection on what investors think of our future."

"But the Company's own financial statements show you are making a profit."

"Our annual rate of growth is declining," he said. "To keep in step with the expanding economy, it should be much higher. We've got some adjusting to do."

Mild words, but I had the impression that the Boss was as concerned about his organization as he had been in 1923 when the Company was millions of dollars in debt, the stock that had sold for $40 was down to $18 a share and the future looked bleak. Woodruff had stepped in then, expanded Coca-Cola from a local to a nationally known drink and then over a period of decades into a world-wide product.

In the late 1970s the Company's prospects, according to Woodruff, were as dim as they had been in many years. Morale among the employees was at a low ebb. The annual rate of growth was sliding down the scale. Other rival soft drink products were slowly obtaining a large share of the market.

Some of the more critical business analysts put this state of affairs squarely on the shoulders of Paul Austin, chairman of the board. Woodruff defended his chairman and said a combination of circumstances was responsible. He discussed this situation with Austin and the conclusion was that he should keep his position of Chairman until he was one year past normal retirement, which came at the end of February, 1981.

After this, there were a number of informal conversations between Woodruff, Austin and certain board members about who should step into the retiring chairman's shoes. The Boss spent long hours studying the records of the men under consideration. He invited them singly and in groups to his luncheon table, often with a board member or two present, and discussed with them a variety of subjects. Late at night he sat alone with his pipe by the fireside and ruminated over the qualifications of these men as they applied to the future of The Coca-Cola Company.

All of these discussions finally boiled down to a selection of three leaders to share the responsibility of what Mr. Woodruff termed "putting the Company back on its feet." These were Roberto C. Goizueta, as chairman and chief executive officer; Donald R. Keough, as president and chief executive officer; and John K. Collings, Jr., as chief financial officer.

Woodruff did not wait until Paul Austin retired to bring about these proposed changes. He wanted to take no chance that if anything happened to him, the new arrangement might not go through. In early June, approximately nine months before his retirement, Austin called a special meeting which was a surprise to everyone but Woodruff for the election of the officials who were to succeed him. Austin made the recommendations and the board members, all of whom in one way or another owed their positions as directors to Mr. Woodruff, voted in the new slate of officers, to take effect when Austin retired.

Past 90 years of age, after 57 of those with The Coca-Cola Company, Mr. Woodruff was still "The Boss."

Paul Austin had been largely responsible for bringing Roberto Goizueta up through the ranks. It was Woodruff who saw in him a perfect blend between the traditional and the modern. From a prominent Cuban family, Goizueta could have coasted along as the scion of a ready-made empire, working or taking his leisure as the notion struck him. But his ambitions leaned in another direction and he chose a course of his own.

Roberto took his pre-college training in a New England prep school and graduated from Yale as a chemical engineer. In the early 1950s, The Coca-Cola Company expanded its operation in Cuba by building in the city of Havana one of the most modern of all its operations. Everything, from syrup-making to the final product of bottled Coca-Cola, was under one roof. It was here in his homeland that Roberto Goizueta began his career with the Company in 1954, in the Technical Department of Cia. Embotelladora Coca-Cola S.A.

When this operation was seized and nationalized by the new government in 1961, Goizeta was transferred to Nassau as chemist for the Caribbean Area of The Coca-Cola Export Corporation and two years later was named staff assistant to the senior vice president for Latin America, for all techical operations that included citrus, coffee, tea and soft drink products.

From that point his steps in the Company were progressively longer. He was charming and forceful as well as practical, and seemed to possess that innate sense of grasping any situation and making exactly the right decisions and moves, much as Woodruff had done half a century before. These were qualities which brought him so impressively to the attention of the Boss when he was transferred to the Atlanta office in 1965. From his first assignment there with the Technical Research and Development Department, he rose rapidly through the upper ranks and in 1980, Roberto Goizueta was elected president and chief operating officer and a director of the Company. The next year he became chairman of the board and chief executive officer.

Along with his appointment to this position, Goizueta was blessed with two strong right arms in Donald R. Keough and John K. Collings, Jr., both recognized by the Boss as outstanding employees.

Donald Keough was one of the top men of Duncan Foods when that company was purchased by The Coca-Cola Company in 1964. He remained with that division; in 1967 was named vice-president and director of marketing and in 1971 was elected to its presidency. For his work in the food industry he received several distinguished awards. Before his election as President of The Coca-Cola Company, he was senior executive vice-president in charge of all domestic and foreign soft drink operations and the Company's wine division.

John K. Collings, Jr. was the third member of this original triumverate put together by Woodruff and his directors.

John Collings had joined the company in 1970 when Aqua-Chem, Inc., became a wholly-owned subsidiary of The Coca-Cola Company. He had been associated with Aqua-Chem since 1969 when he was elected president and chief operating officer, a position he held until 1971 when he became chief executive officer. He was elected Chairman of the Board and chief executive officer of Aqua-Chem, Inc. in 1972 and in 1976 he resumed the presidency. He was elected vice president of The Coca-Cola Company in 1978, and one year later was elected executive vice president, treasurer and chief financial officer.

Collings' untimely death at age 53, shortly after the new management team was in operation, was a sharp loss to The Coca-Cola Company and to Woodruff. But waiting in the wings were backup teams for such disasters. Sam Ayoub, president of Coca-Cola Far East/Australia, with as perfect a background for the job as John Collings, was assigned to step into the vacancy.

Ability recognizes no boundaries and Ayoub brought an additional international flavor into the Company. A native of Egypt, he began his business career as an auditor in the municipal government of Alexandria. After that he held banking positions in foreign exchange and international finance with the First National City Bank of New York, in Bombay, India and in Cairo, Egypt. From 1945 to 1955, he served as manager of the State Bank of Ethiopia.

In 1956, at the request of Emperor Haile Selassie, Ayoub organized Ethiopian Airlines in Eritrea and served as its manager until December 1958. The next year he joined the Coca-Cola Export Corporation in New York, in the Fiscal Division. From that date, over the next score of years, his far-sightedness and judgment elevated him through the various positions of assistant treasurer, treasurer, vice-president of the Export Corporation, vice-president and treasurer of The Coca-Cola Company, then senior vice-president and in 1980 executive vice-president, General Operations, with the added responsibility for Australia, the Far East and China.

Woodruff saw in these men a coordinated team that would enhance the image of his Company and improve it financially. His judgment, even in his 90th year, as subsequent events have proven, had never been more sound.

Woodruff was satisfied with his new Coca-Cola team: with it he had laid long-range plans and objectives and he had made the transition smoothly without leaving any discontent except for those who may have expected to profit in one way or another when he was gone.

The June 10, 1980 issue of *The Wall Street Journal* recognized and summed up Woodruff's powers as a patriarchal commander with front page headlines: " 'The Cigar,' " it stated, using a name by which he was affectionately known to a few of his contemporary associates, "Has Come Back."

They could have pointed out that he had never been away.

The *Journal* went on to say: "Mr. Woodruff, a legendary figure in American business, who retired as Coke's chief executive a quarter of a century ago, hasn't been publicly active since the days when he socialized with his close friends Dwight Eisenhower and golf great Bobby Jones. But lately he has grown angry over a number of occurrences at the Company and has abandoned his role as Coke's almost invisible patriarch. Suddenly "The Cigar," as he is known within the Company, reasserted himself into the thick of the Company's affairs.

"After presiding at Coca-Cola for 57 years, Mr. Woodruff's power is unquestioned. During his tenure as chief executive, he shaped the Company into an American institution and led it on a program of international expansion. He controls a huge block of stock and most directors, including Mr. Austin (the current board chairman) owe their positions to him. Company executives are used to accomodating his every wish.

"Arousing Mr. Woodruff's attention even more was what he perceived to be a serious erosion of the Company's finances that resulted in a $100 million debt offering May 28—Coke's first violation of a no-debt rule he laid down before the Depression. In recent months, stiffer soft drink competition and a weakening in consumer spending combined to slow the growth of Coke's earnings. Its capital position also has deteriorated because of cash outlays for the Company's new $120 million headquarters building, the $65 million purchase of Atlanta Coca-Cola Bottling and other expenditures."

The changes suggested by Woodruff and made by the board of directors began to show up almost immediately in the Company's financial reports. For its third quarter the next year, the auditors reported that its net income rose 42.8% compared to the same period the year before. Net income per share was up 14% for the full year. This was "despite the adverse impact of a strong dollar on its foreign operations."

It is interesting to note here that the corporate strategy of the new executive team called for long-range expansion into such consumer products as packaged foods, entertainment and leisure, and health and beauty aids. For ideas as well as support, the team called a strategy meeting of 50 division managers and corporate staffers from all corners of the Company's world empire. Goizueta carried a report of this enthusiastic meeting to his board, which approved his overall program of strategy.

To help solve the problem of where first to expand, Goizueta employed a national consulting firm. After almost a year of investigation, the consultants came up with a recommendation that the Company's best first step would be the acquisition of Columbia Pictures Industries, Inc. To the casual onlooker, this seemed rather illogical since beverages had been the Company's main business for so many years, but Columbia Pictures was a profitable organization and, as Goizueta pointed out, was not big enough to change the character of The Coca-Cola Company, and yet was large enough to have an impact on its image as a growth company.

Both companies went ahead with their negotiations and these were finalized pending approval by both boards of directors. The Coca-Cola Company directors had approved the broad strategy of expansion, but even before the details of this first purchase were presented to them, Goizueta made a special trip to Ichauway Plantation to explain to the 92-year-old Woodruff what had transpired, to give him all the facts and figures, and to get his approval.

There was never any question that this was considered Goizueta's most important and necessary move prior to any such major change.

It was only after his conference with the Boss that he began to contact the other directors.

The average man, at this stage of Woodruff's life, and probably long before, would have patted himself on the back and sat back to glory in his decisions which had brought new enthusiasm and accomplishments to his organization. Not the Boss. Although partially crippled by the stroke that had almost felled him some years before, he had other problems that needed his immediate attention. One of these was the situation at Ichauway Plantation, to which some of the news media mis-stated that he had retired. It was true that he spent much of the fall and winter hunting seasons there with group after group of friends who hunted with him over the years. Throughout the remainder of the year he visited his "farm" every month for a few days to enjoy the peacefulness, watch the crops through all periods from planting to harvest, and to celebrate with his employees and their families and his neighbors on such occasions as the annual 4th of July barbecue.

Woodruff has complete confidence in the ability of the people he likes. He has always said that the way to get the most done is to start a job and then turn it over to someone capable of finishing it. Through most of his life and with a vast majority of his associates it worked that way, but there were a few exceptions. Ichauway was one. His faith in those who worked for him there led him to believe implicitly the reports which were often tempered to keep him from being displeased or annoyed with conditions which might really exist. He sensed the growing unrest and dissatisfaction of his Ichauway employees. Everyone on the place revered the Boss and no one wanted to distress him by reporting unsavory news. When he visited, they wanted him to relax and enjoy the big house and the farm, as he always had.

Woodruff doesn't miss much. The plantation buildings that housed his personnel had gradually fallen into a state of disrepair. The small food patches for the wildlife which for many years had been planted throughout the forested acres away from the fields assigned to crops were neglected.

I got the impression that the manager wanted to make as good a showing as possible in his farm profit-loss column. He went on the basis that the people working for him should be content with whatever quarters were provided, whether or not they needed repairs. The planting and cultivation of quail food patches cost money, so he cut down drastically on the number of these plots. This showed up in the smaller number of quail coveys Woodruff's hunter guests were able to find in a day. In spite of that the shooting was still good, so no one complained.

The story is that at one time in his 90th year, Woodruff went through a short period of illness in his Atlanta home. While he was confined, the manager drove up from Ichauway to see him. After his visit, he came back to Ichauway and reportedly informed his crews: "Boys, you can relax. Mr. Woodruff will never make it down here for another season."

A few of the plantation personnel were surprised when the Boss showed up *before* the season. Most were pleased when they realized that he was not a doddering old man making his last tracks, but was very sharply aware that Ichauway was not running as smoothly as he liked.

As he had done since his military academy days, he went right to what he considered the source of the plantation problem. His manager had been with him for 25 years and his batting average over that period in dog training, quail production and general farm operation was high. But in the past two or three years his health had not been at its peak, and certain outside influences appeared to have influenced his management of the plantation.

Woodruff made an attempt to bring his farm back into good working order, by discussing all the details with his manager, of whom he was very fond, and outlined a procedure they should follow. The manager agreed with him about conditions and promised to remedy them to Woodruff's satisfaction. But because of his sickness and his personal problems, he dragged his feet for several months in the same rut. Always the Boss had been a considerate and forgiving man who had given him a free hand on the farm. So why hurry? He couldn't have been more amazed when at the end of the shooting season he thought Mr. Woodruff would never survive, the Boss retired him, put him on a substantial pension and replaced him with Bill Adkins, the assistant manager.

Adkins had the same effect as a new broom. Within the next year, the crops were more productive, the houses where the plantation personnel lived were rebuilt, feed patches were planted and the quail coveys increased. The *esprit de corps* was higher than it had been in many years.

Both The Coca-Cola Company and Ichauway Plantation that he had put together with the touch of a master were revived by his efforts.

The Boss lives on, solid as the Rock of Gibraltar.

Because of the stroke several years ago that left him with uncertain balance, he is no longer able to walk through the woods on a quail hunt, as he had done the first 80 years of his life. "It's rather difficult to shoot birds," he observed, "with a cane in one hand and a gun in the other."

But he hasn't given up hunting altogether. He continues to participate in the hunts by being on hand with his hunting teams for at least a part of each day. Usually in the afternoon he drives out and joins the hunt, either by riding on the hunting wagon or riding his horse, which the boys always have waiting for him at the scene. He rides for an hour or more, watching his shooters and commenting on the kills and misses. "Only trouble with riding a horse," he quipped, just before his 92nd birthday, "is that it takes two men to get me on and four to get me off."

Naturally he doesn't enjoy those hunting days as much as he did when he was one of the shooters, but he continues to derive a great deal of pleasure from them. This is especially true when he can ride the wagon or sit in the saddle and watch his guests who have bragged about their skill with a scattergun miss rather easy shots when a covey roars off the ground and flies straight away.

"Dammit," one of his friends commented, "I'm a pretty good shot until the Boss comes around. He does something to me. It must be because I try too hard."

One afternoon he was out as an observer when I hunted with Bob Strickland, chairman of the board of the Trust Company of Georia. We were on a part of the plantation near the main residence. It was seldom hunted and was simply loaded with quail coveys. The Boss called it his "chicken yard."

That afternoon Bob and I had an acute case of "Woodruffitis" that many of his shooters get when the Boss is around. It seemed as though the devil himself had put a jinx on us. The dogs performed beautifully. We hardly had time to get into the saddle before the pointers found another covey or were in singles again. Neither Bob nor I could buy a quail feather. The coveys flushed so close under our feet that we could have killed them with a fly swatter. They flew straight away and at such a leisurely pace it seemed that missing one with a pattern of No. 8 pellets appeared almost impossible for any shooter not standing on his head. We weren't standing on our heads, but we may as well have been shooting blanks. On every covey rise or single we unloaded four shots from our two double-barrels and every bird flew on.

The driver of our hunting wagon kept the Boss as close to the activity as safety allowed, close enough for us to hear him laugh every time we goofed so miserably. For us that only made matters worse. Strickland and I might as well have been discharging our shells into the ground or at the sky.

At one particular point the covey we had missed, plus two more that flushed nearby, pitched over a low hill and seemed to land just on the other side.

"The Boss can't see us there," I said to my companion, "so we will be under less of a handicap."

Birds were scattered all over that hillside. At almost every step one or two got up under our feet. I'm sure we unloaded a box of shells but the jinx had us hog-tied. Not a bird did we put in the bag.

About the time we got through shooting, Bobo, Mr. Woodruff's fine Labrador retriever, bounded over the hill and joyously began to scout the territory for dead and crippled birds. There were not ony of either, so Bob and I slunk back to the wagon, our tails between our legs.

"What'd you send Bo over there for?" one of the handlers asked.

"With so much shooting," the Boss replied with a straight face, "I figured that you must have at least one cripple down."

In his late 80s and 90s, even though he had become a legend in his time, Woodruff continued to grow in stature. He has in no way relegated himself physically or mentally to a wheelchair as many men of lesser caliber and with his wealth might have done. Naturally the strokes and advancing years have taken their toll; he walks with a cane and often has help by holding onto someone's arm for additional support, but he has remained active in many affairs. On certain occasions, as the wedding of a young friend, or when an older friend is given an outstanding award, he manages, sometimes by great effort, to be there, because he knows these friends are pleased by his appearance.

He has been honored with many awards in recent years by local, national and international organizations. One of the most prestigeous was the Humanitarian Award, given by Lions Clubs International. Only six other individuals ever received this for great services to mankind. One of the nominees for this award in 1981 was Pope John Paul II. With great glee, the boys at Ichauway Plantation announced to their fellows, "The Boss done beat out the Pope."

On April 28, 1981, when Woodruff celebrated his 58th anniversary with The Coca-Cola Company, the feelings of all his employees and friends were well summed up in a poem written for the occasion by June Tillery, one of his secretaries, and presented to Mr. Woodruff.

Some folks think that even at age 58
One should begin preparing for Heaven's gate
And certainly most of us agree
We're not much good workwise past 63

But the rare ones never seem to tire
They continue to amaze and to inspire
And the rarest of them all
Still walks thrugh our hallowed hall

Retirement for Robert Woodruff has not yet begun
He astounds us all at age 91!
We're grateful to be able to share
The wisdom of one so rare

His accomplishments are too many to enumerate
But we emphasize how deeply we appreciate
The 58 years he has enriched us all
No other man ever stood so tall!

Woodruff has left a lot of respect and admiration along the way. Not only among his employees, but with his friends as well. He never expected rewards or acclamations for what he did. His philosophy is best summed up in a letter he received from Glenn E. Neilson, an old Cody, Wyoming friend who was wealthy and had followed many of the examples set by the Boss in human relations. In the letter, Neilson wrote:

"Your insight into business, political affairs and philosophy of life influenced me many times and helped me to meet situations easier than I otherwise might have done.

"Once, when I was attempting to express appreciation for those many things, I made the statement, 'Bob, I don't know how I can ever repay you.'

"I have quoted your reply many times, which was this: 'Glenn, don't try to repay me. It is not possible in this life to always repay those who do things for you. Just remember the world is round; so if I have helped you, you help someone else and in that way, we will both make the world better.' "

The weight of many years makes some persons bitter and often cranky; some may deteriorate mentally; others grow gracious and considerate. The Boss is one of those who has grown more gentle and thoughtful with the passing years. His concern for others, which has been an integral part of his life from childhood, has seemed more intensified in the past few years. His public charities, always bestowed with a wisdom that meant the greatest benefit for the largest number of people, have grown in volume and reached into an increasing number of fields of medicine, education and in training programs for the underprivileged. Emory University, its School of Medicine, hospital and clinic, has been one of his favorite charities over many years. To a large extent he has been responsible for the growth and expansion of these institutions. His largest donation, after his 90th year, was a gift to Emory University of $105 million. This was said to be the largest such gift ever made to such an institution by any individual.

Woodruff has never lost an iota of his exquisite sense of humor. I have often heard him say that no man should take himself too seriously. His witty observations and repartees appear to have sharpened over the years. Almost everyone who knows him has a bright little story of his ready retorts.

One of my most memorable occurred during a honeymoon in New Orleans with my new wife. We were supposed to have a date with the Boss when we returned home but decided to remain in the Mardi Gras city longer than we had planned. So I wired Woodruff: "Boss. Think I'll stay here a few more days. It's wonderful down here."

Back by wire came his immediate answer: "Charlie. It's wonderful anywhere. Come on home."

In the last year Woodruff's eyesight has faded so that words in print or script are often difficult to decipher. Items in the newspaper, and those letters in which they know he is interested, are usually read to him by Joseph Jones, Mrs. Martha Ellis, his niece, or someone else close to him. Some of his terse comments to these are classic. Once Mrs. Ellis read a flowery note from a lady admirer and at the end asked, "It's from a Mrs. So-and-So. Do you know her?"

"Not by that name," Woodruff replied.

We were sitting around the gunroom table at the plantation and listened to another letter that Mrs. Ellis read from an acquaintance that Woodruff knew only casually. This gentleman proposed a great personal sacrifice on behalf of the Boss. In essence he wrote: "I do not know the state of your health, but the parts of a man's anatomy usually wear out, just as they do in all flesh as well as in all machinery. I just want you to know that if you ever need any organ of my body to replace any one of yours that no longer functions properly, you are welcome to mine, any time. This includes kidneys, liver, lungs, heart or whatever. All you've got to do is let me know."

When she had finished the letter, Martha Ellis laid it on the table and said, "Now isn't that the sweetest thing."

"I think he's a damn fool," Woodruff grunted, but his eyes said that he didn't really mean it, and was both grateful and complimented.

Joe Jones was reading an item to him about one of the honors bestowed on Woodruff. In the article a reporter called him a "tycoon."

The Boss looked up. "What kind of a 'coon is that?"

"You're supposed to be the wildlife expert," Joe said to me. "You tell him."

Woodruff had very recently completed his rehabilitation changes in The Coca-Cola Company and put his plantation back on a sound basis, so I said, "That's a big 'coon that walks late at night."

"That applies," Joe commented.

Calvin Bailey, Woodruff's personal valet and close confidant who is with him constantly, told me a story that is very expressive of the Boss's character. They went by to visit George Woodruff, the Boss's younger brother who was in the hospital.

"The doctors say you are well enough to get up and get out of here," the Boss said. "You'll get back on your feet quicker if you put on your clothes and move around."

"I don't feel well enough," George said. "I just can't do it."

"A Woodruff," the Boss stated, "can do anything he wants to do."

So George got up, dressed, went home for a day or two and then returned to his office.

A month or so later, the Boss was at Ichauway for a few days. He had arrived there tired from the pressure at his office. He had no guests and insisted on staying in his room with his robe on and having his meals served there, even though Cal Bailey urged him to get out and ride around the farm.

After about two days of this, Cal said, "Mr. Woodruff, you shouldn't spend all of your time cooped up in this room. You'll feel better if you'll sit for a while in the gun room and then take a ride."

"I don't feel like it," the Boss replied. "I can't do it."

"Mr. Woodruff," Cal said, "I heard you tell Mr. George that a Woodruff can do anything he makes up his mind to do."

The Boss sat for a few minutes before he answered. "Bring my clothes," he said, "and have a car brought around to the front yard."

Throughout his life Woodruff has remained a very religious man, but not in the usual pattern that might appeal to the average person as the way a layman is expected to live. Not since his boyhood days when Asa Candler, founder of The Coca-Cola Company, was his Sunday School teacher, has he been a regular church goer. His interest in and support of several religious institutions, and his influence in helping to get a number of inspirational periodicals started, is not commonly known. Nor is the fact that he built or rebuilt a few modest churches in communities which otherwise could not have afforded them. He had his own favorite city churches and pastors and donated liberally to them. But his fundamental consecration was much deeper than any of this.

Like Abou Ben Adhem, he was close to God because he loved his fellow man, and as he grows older, this relationship with the Almighty seems to intensify. He still makes no public display of this spiritual association, but those close to him are aware of it in many ways. Small things, but significant.

On the fireplace mantel in his bedroom stands a small plaque with these words: *Lord, help me to remember that nothing is going to happen to me today that You and I together can't handle.*

Sit in silence with him beside the fireside and the chances are good that he'll quote the 23rd Psalm or will softly sing, "Just a Closer Walk with Thee," one of his favorite hymns over many years.

He has never made a habit of saying grace before each meal, but on occasions he considers significant he has a few moments of devotion, with words from one of Robert Louis Stevenson's prayers, as he asks the blessing:

Give us grace and strength to forebear and to persevere—give us courage and gaiety and the quiet mind. Spare to us our friends, soften to us our enemies. Bless us, if it may be, in all our innocent endeavors. If it may not be, give us strength to encounter that which is to come, that we may be brave in peril, constant in tribulation, temperate in wrath, and in all changes of fortune, and down to the gates of death, loyal and loving to one another.

Woodruff looks forward to each birthday, which seems to arrive with pleasant regularity. Each is a milestone farther from his 70th, to which friends came from all over the world for a gala celebration. Now only a few friends gather around his table at Ichauway Plantation, to which he has retired for a large part of the shooting season.

Dr. James T. Laney, president of Emory University, was there on his 90th and gave this blessing that so impressed Mr. Woodruff he has asked Dr. Laney to give it again on each birthday since:

> *We thank Thee, Lord, for this glorious day*
> > *and for the very special event that we celebrate here—*
> > *the birthday of Mr. Woodruff.*
> *We acknowledge before Thee his towering presence*
> > *through the years and across the land;*
> *His unexcelled generosity, his commanding vision,*
> > *his unswerving loyalty;*
> *And praise Thee for the countless numbers*
> > *who have been blessed through him,*
> *Inspired by his courage, strengthened by his determination,*
> > *enabled by his support.*
> *Bless him, O Lord, in the coming years*
> > *and grant him deep satisfaction and fulfillment*
> > *and a full measure of Thy peace and serenity.*
> *Now give us festive hearts and true affection as we*
> > *celebrate together this special day about the table,*
> > *and keep each of us within the circle of Your tender care.*
> *Through Christ our Lord. Amen."*

This very well expresses the sentiment in the hearts of all who know the Boss.

Chapter 10
The Woodruff Business
and Personal Philosophy

If we were required to do the briefest possible summation of the philosophy entwined through all of Robert W. Woodruff's business and personal life, there is no way we could improve on the words of a leaflet he carries around in his pocket. He has read and re-read it until it is dog-eared and tattered.

It is believed the words are those of his friend Bernard F. Gimbel, the late chairman of Gimbel Brothers, Inc. So greatly was Woodruff impressed by its message that he had the pamphlet reprinted to pass out among the key men in his organization. One might say that over the years it has almost become the spirit of Coca-Cola.

What this message says might be considered a short sermon taken from the text of the words on an engraved plaque he keeps on top of his office desk: There is no limit to what a man can do or where he can go if he doesn't mind who gets the credit.

We see in the longer version of these words the very essence of those values which accounted for one of the most remarkable success stories ever told and the character of the remarkable man who has stood for two generations at its head.

These are the words that Woodruff carries with him and by which he has lived:

> Life is pretty much a selling job. Whether we succeed or fail is largely a matter of how well we motivate the human beings with whom we deal to buy us and that which we have to offer.
>
> Success or failure in this job is thus essentially a matter of human relationships. It is a matter of the kind of reaction to us by our family members, customers, employers, employees, and fellow workers and associates. If this reaction is favorable we are quite likely to succeed. If the reaction is unfavorable we are doomed.

The deadly sin in our relationship with people is that we take them for granted. We do not make an active and continuous effort to do and say the things that will make them like us, and believe in us, and trust us, and that will create in them the desire to work with us in the attainment of our desires and purposes.

Again and again we see both individuals and organizations perform only to a small degree of their potential success, or to fail entirely, simply because of their neglect of the human element in business and life. They take people and their reactions for granted. Yet it is these people and their responses that make or break them.

Let me illustrate this with a few figures and facts in business and personal situations.

Loss Caused By Our Indifference

A survey made by the *Retail Ledger* shows that out of each one hundred customers a retail business has today, it will lose eighty-one within the next ten years. It will lose fifteen the first year, thirteen the second year, and so on down to the tenth year when its total loss will have been eighty-one.

What is more astonishing, however, are the reasons for this loss. The survey showed that sixty-eight percent of these eighty-one customers quit because of discourteous or indifferent treatment and poor service. Another fourteen percent quit because grievances were not adjusted. Thus eighty-two percent of those quitting, or 66.42 persons, did so because of poor human relations. Only eighteen percent quit for all other causes combined.

These figures should make our good business hearts bleed.

These are people that we have spent a lot of money to get.

They are customers for whom we maintain a costly overhead.

They are customers for whom we make every effort to get the highest quality goods for the dollar they can afford to pay.

These we lose—eighty-one out of each one hundred—mostly for reasons that are avoidable, and chiefly because we take them for granted.

We might, for instance, well ask ourselves, did we keep in

contact with these customers with an occasional letter or word of appreciation?

Did we see to it that our letters were simple, and friendly, and attractive, and easy to read?

Did we keep the voices on our telephones friendly and smiling?

Did we keep our places of business pleasant and attractive for them, so they would enjoy their visits to our stores or offices?

Did we maintain an atmosphere of warmth and friendliness in our business places?

Did we make the customer feel that we were sincerely concerned about his problems and needs and not just interested in making money?

Did we train our sales people and service people to go forward and greet them with a smile as the customers entered our stores or came up to the counters to buy or get service?

Did we, above all things, keep high the morale of our employees and representatives so that their enthusiasm would be transmitted to the customer?

Did we put into practice our firm belief that good public relations must begin within our organization, and that public reaction to us is pretty much an enlargement or extension of the attitude and morale of our employees, and of their reaction to us and to their work?

Anyhow, in the past we have lost eighty-one out of each one hundred of these good customers each ten years mainly because we took them for granted. We lost them because we did not take into consideration that they could go around the corner to any other reputable store, or office, or bank, or insurance company and get about the same quality product for about the same dollar that they could in our place. We lost them because we forgot that the customer will go where he feels at home; where he feels he is wanted and appreciated, and where there is the warmth of friendliness and interest.

We Take People For Granted

About the same situation is true of our employees, whom, too, we take for granted. It is not surprising that a distinguished industrial psychologist said that the Eleventh Commandment should be "Thou shalt not take people for granted."

We hire these men and women—the most expensive equipment in all creation—and the most complicated and sensitive, and we permit them to perform at a small percentage of their potential, or to go to pot entirely—because we take them for granted.

We buy a machine for our business, and with it comes a book of directions or a factory mechanic to insure its proper installation and its highest performance. We have a capital outlay that we must protect, and from which we must get the maximum return in production. But for the human beings whom we bring in, we have no set of directions or trained mechanics; yet our capital outlay for them is a continuous one, month after month, and for years. It can easily, over a lifetime, run into several hundred thousand dollars for each of them.

And yet we make little effort to see what makes them tick, or how we could make them tick better.

Employees Need More Than Wages

We pay them a wage or commission and expect full performance; yet we know they are not economic slaves. We know that wages are only one of the many incentives that man needs to give himself completely to our team.

Man needs, too, to find expression for himself in his work. We know that he needs praise, and understanding, and a sense of belongingness, and a feeling of security and importance. But we don't take the time, nor make the effort to assure ourselves that he is given these necessary satisfactions.

We forget that he is a human being who has the same needs and hopes and dreams and aspirations that we have. We forget that he is moved deeply by the urge to protect his wife and children and to give to them the best things of life. We forget that for himself and for them he wants to grow and get ahead and accomplish and be recognized and be somebody.

We forget that he, even as we, has problems and difficulties and doubts and fears—

And so we just take him for granted. Eventually we lose him— even though he may remain on our payroll as dead timber.

Skill Alone Not Sufficient

We make the same mistake in our personal and job lives where again we take the important human element for granted. We make great effort to obtain job knowledge or to acquire skill, but we pay little attention to the personality traits and habits that determine reaction of others to us.

Job knowledge or skill, we must admit, is fundamental and essential; but it will not by itself make us successful. The fact is that it is only about a twenty-percent factor in our success or failure.

Extensive surveys of actual case histories have shown us that the eighty-percent factor determining success or failure is one of personality or of human relationship. It is our ability to get along with people that counts, even in the most technical of professions such as engineering.

Now if this is true in jobs in which we deal primarily with machines or other inanimate things, how much truer is it in such work as selling in which we deal entirely with human beings? Or how much more important still is it in the close personal relationship of one's social or home life? The factor involved in success in one's personal life is then nearly one hundred percent that of human relationships.

But what is human relationship? It is personality, which can be defined as the reaction of other people to us. Or, putting it in another way, personality is the sum total of our traits and habits which makes others respond to us as they do.

Good Personality Is A Matter Of Habits

Good personality or human relations is a matter of forming habits of thinking and talking and acting that make people like us and trust us and believe in us. It is a matter of cultivating the simple habits that make others like to deal with us and associate with us; simple habits such as friendliness, dependability, sincerity, cheerfulness, and honesty.

Good human relations is a matter of forming habits of understanding people, of being tolerant of others, of being considerate, of being willing and active in helping others and of sharing with them.

It is an attitude of being willing and anxious to help others to live more fully, to help them grow and enjoy and make the best of their lives.

The basic rule of good human relations is to think and talk and act in terms of the interest of the other person. It is to get one's thinking off one's self and one's own little world and of directing it to the other person. There are many habits that we can develop that are particularly effective in getting for us the friendship and loyalty and devotion and goodwill of others.

Adherence To Moral Law Fundamental

First among these, and this is a fundamental one to all good human relations, is the habit of abiding strictly by the Moral Law or the Ten Commandments in our relationships with people.

The Moral Law or the Commandments have to do essentially with not hurting others. We cannot hurt other people physically, emotionally, financially, or any other way if we wish our relationships with them to be good. Hurting them makes them afraid of us—it makes them feel unsafe and insecure—and this breeds bad reactions and poor relationships.

The following three personality habits are of particular importance to the business or professional man in his relations to his customers and clients.

These are friendliness, helpfulness, and dependability. These are, of course, important in all human situations.

Friendliness inspires trust, and people tend strongly to do business with those whom they trust. It gives them a sense of assurance and confidence that they are going to be fairly treated. It is true, too, that all people like a little human warmth and that they respond freely to it.

Most of us, of course, are friendly people, but unfortunately not too many of us show our friendliness on the outside. Others cannot see through us to see how friendly we are on the inside. For this reason, it is imperative that we show friendliness externally.

One of the most natural ways of doing this is through the smile, which is the key to the human heart. We must learn to smile, and to approach others with a smile, the employee, the customer, and the family member.

The second of these three personality traits is helpfulness. It is closely allied to friendliness because it is a natural way of expressing friendliness. Here the business or professional man has great advantages since he has almost unlimited opportunities to be helpful to his customers or clients.

Being helpful is developing the habit of going out of our way to do things for others. It is observing the needs of the other person, and then doing something about them. It is difficult for us to be helpful because we are so constantly involved with the things that concern us, ourselves. But it is a habit which pays tremendous dividends.

The third of these is dependability, which many students of human relations consider to be the most important of good personality traits. Dependability is coming through with one's performances and promises as expected. It is a matter of delivering the goods, of keeping one's promises, of being reliable in one's statements, of being truthful and honest in one's dealings. And this, we must admit, is extremely important to the customers and clients who must largely depend upon our knowledge and experiences in the purchases they make or the services they require.

Franklin's Famous Formula

In these three traits we have a resume of Benjamin Franklin's famous sales formula, and one that is invaluable to us. Franklin said,

"He who would achieve success must give freely of that which costs him nothing: friendliness, sincere interest, and good counsel." In other words: be friendly; concern yourself deeply with your customer's problems or needs; and give your very best to help him solve those problems or to fulfill his needs.

If we wish to develop our good human relations to a still higher degree, we will form other good personality habits. For instance, we will learn to give recognition to people. Giving recognition sincerely is one of the habits most effective in winning the friendship and cooperation of others. Let us look for the nice things about people, and then say something about these nice things to them. It could be something in their appearance, something they say, or have done. It could be about their families, or about the way in which they do their work.

Recognition Is An Essential Need

William James, the great American psychologist, says that the deepest yearning in the human heart is the desire to be important.

All of us want to count; we want others to think well of us. It is an essential human need. And, consequently, we can't help liking the person who sincerely recognizes the good things about us.

Another important habit is to talk about the things that interest others, not about those that are of interest to us alone. We are all to ourselves the center of the universe. Hence our world revolves around us. The wise businessman and employer will take himself out of that center and let his employees or his customers occupy it. He will talk about their interests. In fact, he will let them do the talking about their little world; their homes, their wives, their children, their jobs, and the fish they caught last summer. If we do not have time to talk to our customers, employees, friends, or family members about the little things that interest them, or that are near and dear to them, we do not have time to be successful.

How to Fail

Perhaps it would be more effective, in the brief time we have, to express negatively some of the traits and habits that enter into human relationships. And so I should like to give certain tested rules of how to *fail* in one's relationships with people. Here are a few of the more important ones.

1. Strut your superiority. Talk and act superior to others. Be arrogant if possible. People will quickly avoid you.
2. Don't praise or say nice things to others.
3. Criticize people and especially in front of others.
4. Don't pay any attention to your appearance; after all, it is a personal matter. Clothes don't make the man.
5. Don't be friendly with others. It lowers your status and breeds familiarity.
6. Don't smile at people. It's bad.
7. Take all the credit.
8. Talk about yourself. You are the one who counts.
9. Be indifferent to the interests and problems of others.
10. Don't help people get ahead or build up their self-esteem. Keep people down. Remember if we help others grow they will in turn elevate themselves above us.

Any one of the personality traits reflected in these ten rules can damage our human relationships immeasurably.

A Capsule Course

Returning to the positive things that we can do to better our human relations, I should like to call your attention to a "Capsule Course in Human Relations" which was published recently in *Forbes Magazine*. I believe all of us could profit from the practice of its five simple points.

1. Five most important words: I am proud of you.
2. Four most important words: What is your opinion?
3. Three most important words: If you please.
4. Two most important words: Thank you.
5. Least important word: I.

Good human relations is a matter of taking infinite pains in our dealings with people.

It is a matter of giving ourselves to others. Experience shows that the Great Law which applies to the giving of material things to others applies also to the giving of oneself. "Give and it shall be given unto you—good measure, pressed down, and shaken together, and running over, shall men give unto your bosom. For with the same measure that you mete withal, it shall be measured to you again." People will as a rule give themselves to us in full measure if we give ourselves to them.

And, finally, I should like to repeat the summation of all principles of good human relations as found in the Sermon On The Mount—"Therefore all things whatsoever ye would that men should do to you, do ye even so to them: for this is the law and the prophets."

Index

Other **Cherokee** Titles

THE BEST OF RALPH McGILL, by Michael Strickland *et al.* Memorable columns by the Pulitzer Prize-winning "Conscience of the South." $12.50

CHRONICLES OF "CHICORA WOOD," by Elizabeth Allston Pringle. A member of South Carolina's landed gentry recalls plantation life, Charleston society, and the Civil War and its aftermath. $10

"DR. BULLIE'S" NOTES. Reminiscences of Early Georgia and of Philadelphia and New Haven in the 1800s, by James Holmes. A born story-teller remembers his encounters with the great and the humble from the War of 1812 through the Civil War. $10

FROM RABUN GAP TO TYBEE LIGHT, by E.J. Kahn, Jr. A noted writer for *The New Yorker* presents a picture of contemporary Georgia against a background of its rich and colorful past. $5.95

GEORGIA: UNFINISHED STATE, by Hal Steed. A nostalgic tour which highlights the remaining pockets of Old South culture in an awakening giant. Illustrated. $10

GEORGIA'S SIGNERS AND THE DECLARATION OF INDEPENDENCE, by Harvey H. Jackson *et al.* The Georgians who affixed their signatures to the United States' most priceless document. $8.95

THE GLORY OF COVINGTON, by William B. Williford. Stories of the beautiful Greek Revival houses in an historic Georgia town, with profiles of their owners since 1828. $12

MOUNTAIN SINGER, by Raymond A. Cook. A distinguished educator who knew him personally presents the life of Byron Herbert Reece with a large selection of his hauntingly beautiful poetry. $12.50

MURDER IN ATLANTA!, by James S. Jenkins. Fascinating account of the Heinz and Refoulé cases and of other celebrated twentieth century murders. $8.95

POEMS OF DANIEL WHITEHEAD HICKY. A collection of gems from the pen of one whose poetry has been hailed by *The London Poetry Review* as "sensitive and delightful." $6.95

ST. SIMONS ENCHANTED ISLAND, by Barbara Hull. Delightful history of a popular resort. $7.95

THE OGLETHORPE LADIES, by Patricia K. Hill. While General James Oglethorpe was establishing the Colony of Georgia, two of his sisters were feverishly plotting to return the Stuart "Pretenders" to the thrones of England and Scotland. $7.95

THE WAR-TIME JOURNAL OF A GEORGIA GIRL, by Eliza Frances Andrews. A first-person account of a well-born young lady's frolics and fears as she travels across Georgia in 1864-'65. $12

UNCLE REMUS — HIS SONGS AND HIS SAYINGS, by Joel Chandler Harris. A collection of the most popular folk tales ever written by an American. $6.95

CHEROKEE PUBLISHING COMPANY
P.O. BOX 1081 ● COVINGTON, GEORGIA 30209

(On mail orders include $1 postage. Georgia residents add 3% State Sales Tax and, where applicable, 1% MARTA or local option tax.)